T0317037

MENACHEM MENDEL SCHNEERSON

Menachem Mendel Schneerson

Becoming the Messiah

EZRA GLINTER

Yale

UNIVERSITY

PRESS

New Haven and London

Yale University Press books may be purchased in quantity for educational,
business, or promotional use. For information, please e-mail sales.press@yale.edu
(U.S. office) or sales@yaleup.co.uk (U.K. office).

Set in Janson Oldstyle type by Integrated Publishing Solutions.
Printed in the United States of America.

Library of Congress Control Number: 2024932058
ISBN 978-0-300-22262-3 (hardcover : alk. paper)

A catalogue record for this book is available from the British Library.

This paper meets the requirements of ANSI/NISO Z39.48-1992
(Permanence of Paper).

10 9 8 7 6 5 4 3 2 1

Frontispiece: Menachem Mendel Schneerson in November 1928,
shortly before his wedding. (JEM, The Living Archive)

For the land shall be filled with the knowledge
of the Lord, as the waters cover the sea.

—Isaiah 11:9

CONTENTS

A NOTE ON STYLE AND USAGE

WRITING A BOOK about Hasidism inevitably requires Hebrew, Yiddish, and occasionally Aramaic words. I have tried not to overdo it, but they are sometimes unavoidable. Rather than ask readers to flip to a glossary, I include explanations within the text. The reader will no doubt become accustomed to Hasidic terms that are used frequently throughout the book.

I have attempted to follow standardized rules of transliteration for Hebrew and Yiddish, except for diacritics, which are omitted here. Where there is a widely accepted English spelling, I use it. The name of the central movement, for example, is spelled "Chabad" rather than "Habad," which is technically correct but less common. Which spellings have attained the status of convention is somewhat subjective; my hope is that my choices do not interfere with the reader's experience.

With people, I use their given names rather than their English equivalents. Thus I refer to Yosef Yitshak Schneersohn, rather than Joseph Isaac, and Chaya Mushka, rather than Moussia. Here, too, I have made exceptions for conventional spellings—notably, "Menachem" rather than "Menahem," when referring to the subject of this book.

With respect to places, I have used the historically appropriate names for the period under discussion. Thus I refer to the city of Nikolaev when it was part of the Russian Empire, but call it Mykolaiv in a contemporary context. I also use Yiddish place names when applicable. Occasionally I have supplemented historical names with their contemporary equivalents.

Prior to February 1918 the Russian Empire used the Julian rather than the Gregorian calendar—for the sake of ease and consistency, however, all dates are given according to the Gregorian (New Style) dating system.

Translations are my own except where indicated otherwise.

MENACHEM MENDEL SCHNEERSON

Prologue

FAITH IS AN ENIGMA. Between those who have it and those who don't lies a chasm of incomprehension. For those without religious belief, the faithful are superstitious purveyors of myths and fairy tales, intellectual cowards shielding themselves from the struggle for meaning and the bitterness of mortality. For the devout, nonbelievers are pathetically blind, oblivious to the miracles of creation and the Divine spirit that moves through the world. Each may object to this characterization, but neither will move closer to the other.

How, then, could I, a nonbeliever, understand someone like Menachem Mendel Schneerson? It is hard to imagine a person who embodied the mystery of faith more perfectly than he did. Here was a man who received a scientific education in the universities of Paris and Berlin, spoke at least six languages, read widely, and kept abreast of political and social developments his entire life. He was also an uncompromising fundamentalist who subscribed to creationism, denied the theory of evolution, and believed that the sun orbited the earth. A thoroughgoing traditionalist, Schneerson opposed liberal religion, eschewed interfaith dialogue, devalued secular education, and insisted on rigid gender roles. Yet he was fascinated by modern technology, enlarged the role of women in his community, and practically invented Jewish outreach. From his office in Brooklyn he oversaw the expansion of a small Hasidic group into a worldwide empire, though he barely left his neighborhood except to visit a cemetery in Queens.

Schneerson was a mystic steeped in the esoteric realms of Kabbalah and Hasidism. He was also an organizer who insisted that action was the most important religious value. His theology transformed the face of modern Judaism, but he dedicated immense amounts of time and effort to traditional Talmudic scholarship; most of his work is incomprehensible to anyone without a rabbinic education. Though he came from an anti-Zionist tradition, he was deeply invested in the State of Israel and sought to influence its cultural and political life. Unlike every other Jewish leader, he never even visited. With his black frock coat and thick Yiddish accent he embodied an old-world Judaism. Through vision and foresight, he became an outspoken champion of Jewish life in the new.

The most conspicuous aspect of Schneerson's life, and the one for which he is most famous, was his unceasing, unrepentant messianism. Such beliefs are a touchy subject. While the prospect of redemption has been a source of material hope and spiritual sustenance, it has also led to disaster. The history of the Jews is littered with false messiahs. Some of them were benign; others left destruction in their wake. Occasionally, messianic failure led to heresy and schism, as believers tried to rationalize their disappointment within new theological frameworks. Yet redemption remains a canonical belief. What it entails has never quite been agreed on, but the faithful believe that the Messiah is coming. Schneerson believed it more than most.

In a commentary on a poem by Judah Halevi, the German Jewish philosopher Franz Rosenzweig wrote: "The false Messiah is as old as the hope of the genuine one. He is the changing form of the enduring hope. Every Jewish generation is divided by him into those who have the strength of faith to be deceived, and those who have the strength of hope not to be deceived. Those having faith are better, those having hope are stronger."[1]

Schneerson, according to this definition, belonged to the category of "better." But it is hard not to view him also as "stronger." For him, redemption was not abstract—it was a practical reality. Others were content to let God send the Messiah according to His own inscrutable timetable; Schneerson thought he could make redemption happen. Did he know what his belief looked like from the outside? Advertising conviction when it becomes indistinguishable from delusion takes courage.

As for those on the outside—what do we see? Was Schneerson a raving end-times prophet leading his flock off a cliff? How can we make sense of the fact that such an intelligent man held beliefs that, to a nonbeliever, are absolute nonsense? It may not be possible.

And yet, I tried. I traveled to the cities of his youth, seeking inspiration from the homes in which he lived, the synagogues where he prayed, the streets that he walked. I spent hours watching his videotaped gatherings and listening to his recorded speeches, absorbing the power of his oratory. I spoke with the people who knew him, trying to comprehend the source of his charisma. Most importantly, I studied his teachings, immersing myself in the thought world of his faith to better understand his life on his terms.

This book is not a comprehensive explication of Schneerson's theology. It is not a history of the Chabad movement, nor a sociological study of its present incarnation. It is mostly a conventional biography, laying the narrative of Schneerson's life against its historical backdrop, drawing connections between the man and his times. But I have tried to show how deeply Schneerson's religious philosophy informed his activities, and how it shaped the group he led. Without it, understanding Schneerson or his movement is impossible.

In writing this book, I had to contend with Schneerson the saint—the man of rumor, miracle, and myth. This is the Schneerson many of his followers know best. Simon Dubnow, one of the first modern historians of Hasidism, wrote: "Our task is . . . to discover the actual truth—to the extent that is possible— about the mythic hero. Yet, while doing so, we cannot afford to overlook the legend, either . . . The historian thus has a dual mission to accomplish: to deal with both the history that became legend and the legend that made 'history.'"[2] In this book I have not neglected the mythic aspect of Schneerson's persona— the person his followers believed him to be in addition to the person he was. I have tried to separate those layers; to excavate, as much as possible, the actual person from under the accretions of exaggeration, fabrication, and controversy. Admittedly, telling where one begins and the other ends is sometimes difficult.

Above all, I took Schneerson seriously. This often meant being critical, which will irritate his followers. Yet many of them have gone too far in the other direction. In their devotion to him, and in their heartfelt desire to spread his message, they have turned him into Santa Claus. Their rebbe is unobjectionable, but also, hagiographic stories notwithstanding, unremarkable and uninteresting. The Schneerson I experienced was not flawless. His thinking could, at times, tend toward the superficial and tendentious. But he was a man of intelligence and insight who deserves serious consideration.

Schneerson is a polarizing figure. At one of those poles live the followers and fellow travelers who, if they don't regard him as the literal Messiah, think of him as a righteous leader and sage. At the other pole live his critics, who see him as a religious fanatic and deluded messianic pretender. It is not my intention to dictate which of these views is correct. Rather, I hope to present Schneerson's ideas and actions as they were. Whether readers view them with admiration or hostility will depend on their own values.

I am not so naïve, however, as to think that I am unbiased. Insofar as I have presented my own ideas, I hope that I have done so clearly and convincingly. But as Schneerson well knew, an argument does not always require overt statements; it can also be formed through selection and emphasis. Although this book is not in the first person, the material I have chosen to include or emphasize reflects my own judgment about what is important in understanding a fraught and complex subject.

Ultimately, I may not be able to understand Schneerson as well as someone who shares his worldview. Perhaps, unencumbered by hero worship, I can understand him better. Maybe my understanding is no better or worse than that of any biographer who takes the life of another human being and tries to reduce it to a collection of words. Or maybe Schneerson is correct. To truly understand, we must wait until the Messiah comes.

1

The Prodigy of Ekaterinoslav

NIKOLAEV IS A CITY built for ships. In 1789, when Prince
Grigory Potemkin seized the area that is now southern Ukraine
in the third year of the second Russo-Turkish War, he founded
a shipyard to repair battle cruisers wounded in the fight with
the Ottoman navy. The location was well chosen. Perched atop
a high peninsula, forty miles north of the Black Sea, the port over-
looks the Southern Bug river where it meets the quick-rushing
Ingul winding east. The summers are hot and the winters cold,
and all around lies the vast, grain-rich steppe, breadbasket of the
empire. Around 1820 the governor, Admiral Aleksey Greig, built
a marine astronomical observatory on Spassky Hill, and for nearly
one hundred years the port served as a base for the Black Sea
Fleet, Potemkin's own force. The new city of Nikolaev, which
sprang up around the shipyard, was named for Saint Nicholas,
patron saint of sailors.

Nikolaev never had the luster of Odessa, the busy cosmopolitan city to its southwest. Compared with Odessa's lively commerce from across the Black Sea and the Mediterranean, Nikolaev was a dour industrial cousin made for shipbuilding, transportation, and export. Outside the port it was a sleepy town, with leafy streets running south from the Ingul in a tidy grid. But it, too, benefited from the industry and agriculture sprouting up across Ukraine in the nineteenth century. In 1862 it became a commercial port, moving crops of wheat and sugar beets, and a decade later it was connected by rail to the rest of the Russian Empire. Cruisers for the imperial navy were built in its shipyards, and grain from the interior flowed through its docks. Like its livelier cousin to the south, it drew people from across the empire seeking work, if not necessarily fortune.

The first Jews came to Nikolaev almost as soon as it was founded, arriving from Polish Galicia and nearby agricultural colonies in Kherson. They worked as artisans, making shoes for sailors, and as merchants in the grain trade. Like Jews throughout Russia, they built religious schools and modern ones, including a vocational school of several hundred students. In 1813 the Old Synagogue—also known as the Shoemaker's Synagogue— was built just blocks from the river, and in 1885 the community completed construction on a majestic choral synagogue overlooking Great Sea Street. By the end of the century the Jewish population of the city had reached more than twenty thousand people, over a fifth of the population.[1]

For Jews, Nikolaev's military importance was both a blessing and a curse. In 1829 they were expelled from the city on the pretext of disloyalty to the empire, although the edict was delayed and eventually lifted. Even during the expulsion years exceptions were made for the wealthy and the useful. One of these was Sender Rafalovich, an industrialist and exporter who in 1854 brought in the city's first Hasidic rabbi, Avraham David Lavut, from the nearby Romanovka settlement. Lavut, a scholar known for his legal tract on the subject of divorce, took up the pulpit at the Old Synagogue and helped raise his grandchildren, who had been orphaned by the untimely death of his son-in-law. Lavut's family soon established itself. When Lavut died in 1890, he was succeeded by his oldest grandson, Meyer Shlomo Yanovsky, who had married the daughter of another local rabbi and fathered three daughters of his own. In 1900, Yanovsky's eldest child, Chana, a bright and charismatic young woman, married Levi Yitshak Schneerson, a promising scholar from the town of Pod-dobryanka and a direct descendent of the third leader, or rebbe, of the Chabad-Lubavitch Hasidic dynasty. The couple were soon blessed with children. Less than two years later, on Friday, April 18, 1902, the eleventh day of the Hebrew month of Nisan, Chana gave birth to a son. They named him Menachem Mendel, "he who comforts."

Hasidic tradition is full of legends about the early years of the righteous. Before the founder of Hasidism, the Ba'al Shem Tov, was born, the prophet Elijah visited his parents to tell them that they would have a son who would spread God's message to the world. Even as a boy, the future mystic was said to perform miracles. Two generations later, when the founder of the Chabad Hasidic movement, Shneur Zalman of Lyady, turned three years old, the Ba'al Shem Tov announced that "a great soul [has] descended on earth" who will "illuminate the world."[2] By the time Shneur Zalman was eight, he is said to have written a full Torah commentary based on the teachings of medieval sages. Before the sixth Lubavitcher rebbe, Yosef Yitshak Schneersohn, was born, his mother was visited in a dream by three men who told her she would have a son so long as she gave eighteen rubles to charity. After giving the money, she became pregnant with the future rebbe. According to another story, when Yosef Yitshak was eleven years old, he went to the grave of his ancestors to pray for his father's recovery from illness. Upon his return from the graveside, his father was cured.

This photograph, taken in a Nikolaev studio in late 1904 or early 1905, is the only known image of Schneerson as a child. (JEM, The Living Archive)

Menachem Mendel's birth was accompanied by similar omens. A few days before his parents' marriage Chana became ill, and it seemed that the wedding would be postponed. But when instructions arrived from the fifth rebbe, Shalom Dov Ber Schneersohn, to continue as planned, Chana miraculously recovered. When Menachem Mendel was born, Shalom Dov Ber sent his parents six telegrams instructing Chana to wash the infant's hands before feeding him and, when he awoke, to dress him in a yarmulke and tzitzit, an unheard-of practice for a child under the age of three. Soon after birth the newborn contracted typhus but recovered after the rebbe sent a get-well telegram. At the age of two Menachem Mendel was already asking the

9

four questions at the Passover seder, and when Chana took him for walks, people stopped to gaze at him in the street. He was a good-looking child. A picture taken in a local photo studio shortly before his third birthday shows him in an embroidered sailor suit and neckerchief, curly hair almost to his shoulders, staring into the camera with a child's solemnity.

The Schneersons led a tranquil life. After their wedding Chana and Levi Yitshak moved into a small house just a short walk from the Old Synagogue and Chana's parents' home near the river. According to custom and marriage agreement, the Yanovskys supported Levi Yitshak while he spent his days studying Talmud and Kabbalah. In 1904, Chana had a second son, Dov Ber, and in 1906 a third, Yisrael Aryeh Leib. But life in Nikolaev was not always easy for Jews, and revolution was in the air. In December 1904, after months of unrest among peasants, industrial laborers, and socialist revolutionaries, the workers at the Putilov railway and artillery plant in Saint Petersburg went on strike. During the following months thousands of factory hands, students, and railway workers left their posts; peasants across the empire seized land and tools. In January 1905 workers marched on the Winter Palace in Saint Petersburg to deliver a petition to the tsar; the army met them with gunfire. There were naval uprisings in the port cities of Sevastopol, Vladivostok, and Kronstadt and a mutiny on the battleship *Potemkin*. The unrest reached Nikolaev as well. "The whole of South Russia is agitated as never before," Lenin wrote that summer. "In Nikolaev and Sevastopol disturbances arose in the government arsenals . . . Nearly seven hundred peasants were killed in the last four days."[3] In October workers in Nikolaev proclaimed a general strike, along with workers in cities throughout the empire. Even Menachem Mendel was touched by the revolutionary spirit. According to his mother, the boy took to walking around the house yelling, "An end to the autocracy!"

until his grandfather told him to stop, afraid that the boy's shout-
ing would endanger the family.[4]

Even before the uprising, antisemitic violence had been increasing throughout Russia. When Tsar Alexander II was assas-
sinated by anarchists in 1881, attacks against Jews flared with a
ferocity not seen since the seventeenth century, when the Cos-
sack leader Bohdan Khmelnytsky led a rebellion through south-
central Ukraine, leaving dozens of brutalized towns in his wake.
In Nikolaev there was a pogrom in May 1881—among the worst
in the Russian Empire that year—and again in April 1899, when
the Jewish community suffered two days of looting and arson.
Now Nicholas II directed violence against Jews. The reaction-
ary press was given a free hand, as were the monarchist societies
known as the Black Hundreds. In October 1905, when the tsar
issued a manifesto accepting demands for civil rights, universal
suffrage for men, and parliamentary government, right-wing
nationalists carried out reprisal attacks against striking workers, socialists, and Jews. That month, with the cooperation of
local army and police forces, pogromists tore through Nikolaev
targeting Jewish businesses. Women and children took refuge
in the basement of a pharmacy near the Old Shul, a dank, low-
ceilinged space connected by tunnels to the city catacombs.
Mothers huddled on the dirty floor, desperately quieting their
children as a violent mob roamed above. And among them walked
an angelic-looking boy who quieted and comforted the other
children with a touch or a word, saving everyone, perhaps, from
pillage, rape, and murder.

The Schneersons might have stayed in Nikolaev if Levi
Yitshak hadn't needed a job. To improve his chances, he obtained
rabbinic ordinations from Hayim Soloveichik, a renowned Lith-
uanian Talmudist, and Eliyahu Hayim Meisel, the chief rabbi of
Lodz. But his efforts were unsuccessful until 1908, when three

rabbis of Ekaterinoslav, an industrial center 190 miles to the northeast, died in the space of six months. Even then, Levi Yitshak's appointment was hardly assured. Thirty years old, he was too young for his critics and too old-fashioned. As a Chabad Hasid he opposed Zionism and the Haskalah, the Jewish enlightenment movement, and unlike other rabbis his age, he couldn't speak Russian well. A century earlier his erudition and lineage might have been decisive, but by 1908 the Russian-speaking Jews of Ekaterinoslav were looking for a leader who could look, dress, and speak the part of a modern community representative. Nonetheless, with the help of the fifth Lubavitcher rebbe, Shalom Dov Ber, Levi Yitshak prevailed. To fill the open positions the community appointed Pinhas Gelman, a well-dressed, charismatic rabbi who wrote in Hebrew and gave sermons in Russian and, to satisfy the city's Hasidic residents, Levi Yitshak. Authority was split along geographical lines, with Gelman taking the older part of the city together with the surviving senior rabbi, Binyamin Zakheim, and Levi Yitshak presiding over the newer Jewish neighborhood uphill. In 1909, Levi Yitshak's family joined him in Ekaterinoslav, where Menachem Mendel would spend the rest of his youth.

Ekaterinoslav is too far inland to be a shipbuilding town like Nikolaev, but it, too, is defined by its river. In good weather mothers take their babies to stroll along the wide banks of the Dnieper, and old men sit on folding chairs with fishing lines at their feet, hoping for a bite from its blue-gray waters. Ekaterinoslav was also founded by Potemkin and was named after his patron, Catherine the Great, who inaugurated the city in 1787. It was supposed to be a third capital of the empire after Moscow and Saint Petersburg, but the town remained small until the mid-1880s, when coal and iron deposits were discovered to the east and a railway was built over the river, stretching from Moscow to Odessa. Like Nikolaev, Ekaterinoslav was in the Pale of Settlement, the part of the empire where Jews were permitted to live, and Jewish residents flocked to the city. Jews owned flour and sawmills and played a major role in the grain trade and the metallurgical industry. By the time the Schneersons arrived the city was modern and prosperous, with a thriving Jewish population nearly seventy thousand strong. It included religious and secular factions, a small Karaite community, and thriving Zionist groups, which were encouraged by Ekaterinoslav's own history of anti-Jewish violence. At the turn of the century there were seventeen synagogues and prayer houses—including a choral synagogue with a mixed choir of men and women—along with both traditional and modern schools.[5]

The Schneersons' first home was past the river and the center of town, on the first floor of a three-story brick building constructed in the eclectic style of the time. The apartment was across the hall from the home of Chana's first cousin Tsipora Shlonsky, her husband Tuvia, and their six children. Unlike the Schneersons, the Shlonskys were Zionists and socialists, and they hung portraits of both Maimonides and Mikhail Bakunin on the wall of their home. Although they were traditionally Jewish, they were not meticulous about *halakha*, Jewish law, and while going through a religious period in his adolescence, their oldest son, Avraham, who became a renowned Israeli poet, preferred to eat his meals in the Schneersons' scrupulously kosher kitchen. The families, despite their differences, were close; they visited each other's homes, celebrated holidays together, and shared books and conversation. Tuvia Shlonsky, an admirer of the Zionist writer Ahad Ha'am, would spend hours talking about religion and literature with Levi Yitshak and lent the rabbi copies of the Hebrew literary journal *Ha-Shiloah*. The children were especially intimate; in a 1977 interview, Verdina Shlonsky, who became a celebrated pianist and composer, recalled how they would climb in and out of the ground-floor windows instead of passing through the hallway. She described Chana as beautiful, well dressed, and sociable and Levi Yitshak as tall and handsome, with a beard like Theodor Herzl's. Her older cousin Mendel was a quiet, serious boy with sparkling eyes and an avid curiosity about everything, especially science.[6] In his bedroom, another acquaintance recalled, he covered the walls with astronomical maps.[7]

For much of his youth Menachem Mendel was instructed by his father or private tutors or was simply self-taught. But for four and a half years he attended a religious elementary school around the corner from his family's apartment, in a building that also housed a bookstore, wallpaper shop, bakery, and Jewish men's school. His teacher was Zalman Vilenkin, a childhood friend of Levi Yitshak's who was hired to teach by the Schneersons, Shlonskys, and a few other families. Nachum Goldschmidt, the son of a kosher slaughterer who also attended Vilenkin's school, recalled Menachem Mendel as a reserved and solemn student; his younger brother Yisrael Aryeh Leib, usually called Leibel, was mischievous and playful. The middle son, Dov Ber, or Berel, suffered from an undetermined malady—perhaps mental illness—and it is unclear if he attended school or for how long.

Life for the Schneersons was comfortable, marked by Levi Yitshak's rising stature in the community and the generous salary he drew as rabbi. They stayed close with their family in Nikolaev and returned periodically to visit. In 1911, Chana's sister Gitl married Levi Yitshak's younger brother Shmuel, who served as the city's government-appointed rabbi. At the wedding, as one of the Schneerson cousins recalled, Menachem Mendel looked "strikingly handsome" and Leibel, "very cute."[8] In the spring of 1913, the senior rabbi of Ekaterinoslav, Binyamin Zakheim, died, prompting another round of redistricting. Gelman moved to Zakheim's former area, and Levi Yitshak took over Gelman's, which was closer to the river and the center of town. The Schneersons moved to a more spacious apartment, which boasted a telephone and served as a center for communal activities. On Hasidic festivals Levi Yitshak held special gatherings there, while the children—led by Menachem Mendel, the oldest of the group—collected money from the adults to buy kasha.

Then, in the summer of 1914, disaster struck. For European Jewry the First World War was a watershed; afterward, nothing was the same. By the end of the war hundreds of thousands of Jews had been killed or displaced, and Jewish communities centuries old had been wiped out, never to be replaced. Poverty and disease ran rampant throughout Jewish-occupied areas, which repeatedly switched hands between competing powers. Even those who avoided migration could find themselves living in a different country as borders were redrawn. At first, the Jews of Ekaterinoslav were the lucky ones. Their city was far from the front lines and was only indirectly affected by the war. In March 1915 the Schneerson family celebrated Menachem Mendel's bar mitzvah in their home with singing and dancing that went well into the night. According to Chana Schneerson, the house was packed with people from various factions of the city's Jewish community, and Menachem Mendel gave two bar mitzvah speeches, one based on Talmudic learning and one based on Hasidic mysticism.

While Ekaterinoslav was spared the worst horrors of the war, other parts of the empire were less fortunate. Although hundreds of thousands of Jews enlisted in the tsarist army, government and military leaders were suspicious of their allegiance, and Jewish communities were often charged with disloyalty. As German forces advanced into Russia in the spring and summer of 1915, more than half a million Jews were expelled from territories near the front. Even Jews who were not expelled were often forced to flee the fighting that engulfed their homes, moving to urban centers like Warsaw and Vilna. Ekaterinoslav saw an influx of refugees suddenly dependent on international relief organizations and the local community. The Schneersons' home became a buzz of activity, and Chana and the boys took to sleeping at a neighbor's quieter, courtyard-facing apartment. "During those stormy days, the rabbi's residence gave off the impression of a beehive," recalled one of the refugees, Aharon Friedenthal, in his 1961 memoir. "Jews were continuously streaming in and out. Some were searching for help and support, for bread and clothing for their families, while others came looking for medicine and help for sick and exhausted refugees. Still others sought legal assistance for arrested family members—fathers, brothers, uncles."[9]

Amid the chaos Menachem Mendel was busy studying. Around 1915, Levi Yitshak hired one of the refugees, a scholar from Lithuania named Isser Nissan Dribin, to tutor his son for a year, and at the age of seventeen Menachem Mendel began a correspondence with Rabbi Yosef Rosen, otherwise known as the Rogatchover Gaon, a scholar from Latvia renowned for having one of the most brilliant Talmudical minds in Europe. Schneerson, throughout his life, would remark on the Rogatchover's unique method of Talmud analysis, which he took as an inspiration for his own style. But for the most part he studied independently, under the supervision of his father. There is little evidence that he attended the non-Hasidic yeshiva in Ekaterinoslav, and he was never sent to a Lubavitcher institution in another city. Perhaps solitary study suited his personality. Perhaps his parents felt he would do better under their watchful eye than away from home, especially in the middle of a war. He was, by all accounts, shy, studious, and well liked, but with few close friends outside his family. His acquaintances from the period remembered him as the "young rabbi," a pale and slim young man who could often be found studying standing up in his bedroom.

Menachem Mendel was, nonetheless, interested in pursuing a secular education. As a child he had been interested in science, mathematics, and astronomy, and he and Leibel made a hobby of studying languages like English and Italian from dictionaries. To advance further he had to pass the high school matriculation exams, so on his father's advice, he approached a man named Israel Eidelsohn to help him prepare. Eidelsohn would later be sent to Siberia by the Soviet authorities and eventually, after emigrating to Palestine and changing his last name to Bar-Yehuda, become a minister in the Israeli government. But at that time he was a Zionist youth leader and gymnasium teacher, and he agreed to be Menachem Mendel's tutor. According to Chana's testimony, Menachem Mendel took and passed the test in 1919, although his diploma, if it ever existed, was lost. But his interest in the sciences remained; along with the Hasidic attachments of his family and upbringing it would guide his decisions over the next two decades. As he was about to discover, his life, and his world, were about to change forever.

2

────◆◈◆────

All Is God

AROUND 1752 the mystic, teacher, and faith healer Rabbi Israel ben Eli'ezer wrote a letter to his brother-in-law, Rabbi Avraham Gershon of Kitev, describing an "ascent of the soul" he had experienced on the Jewish New Year of 1746. In heaven he had seen the living and the dead "rushing back and forth to ascend from world to world." In the lower realm of paradise "the wicked were repenting and their sins were forgiven," causing "great joy among them." Rabbi Israel went further until he entered the sanctuary of the Messiah. There he asked, "When will the Master come?" The Messiah replied, "By this you shall know: It will be a time when your teachings have become publicized and revealed to the world, and your wellsprings have spread outward . . . then all the evil accretions will be destroyed, and it will be a time of grace and salvation."[1]

By the time he wrote the letter Rabbi Israel was already renowned as the Ba'al Shem Tov, or Master of the Good Name, and was leading a circle of mystics in the Podolian town of Mezhbizh. The letter he wrote never reached his brother-in-law, who was living in the Land of Israel, and wasn't published until 1781, twenty-one years after his death. But the Ba'al Shem Tov's vision was only a beginning. Over the coming centuries the Hasidic movement he started would have a transformative effect on Jewish history and religion. In time, his teachings would reach nearly every place that Jews lived.[2]

Little is known about the Ba'al Shem Tov—also known as the Besht, based on the acronym of his title.[3] He was born around 1700 and raised in Okopy, a small town on the Dniester River. Around age fifteen he left for eastern Galicia, where he became a schoolteacher and married Hannah, the sister of the Brody rabbi, Avraham Gershon. According to hagiographic accounts, the rabbi was displeased by the match and sent the couple to the Carpathian Mountains, where Israel earned his living digging clay from the hills. "The mystic's thoughts were lost in the upper spheres, while all around him loomed the majestic Carpathians," imagined Simon Dubnow. "Here, amid the silence of nature, the recluse heard the voice of God."[4] Eventually the couple moved to Tluste, where, in the mid-1730s, Israel decided to reveal himself to the world. Like other *ba'alei shem*, or "masters of the name," who roamed the Polish towns and countryside in the eighteenth century, the Besht was a faith healer who performed miraculous cures through manipulations of Divine names. But there was something to his vision aside from medical wonderworking. Unlike other ba'alei shem, who were forced to lead itinerant lives, in 1840 the Besht was invited to settle in the prosperous commercial center of Mezhbizh. There he served for twenty years as a community-supported kabbalist and healer and led a circle of pietists with whom he shared his esoteric faith.

Like other mystics before him, the Besht wrote little. His teachings began to spread only after his death through disciples like Ya'akov Yosef of Polnoye, the main theoretician of early Hasidism, and the Maggid, or preacher, Dov Ber, who gathered his own group of followers in the new center of Mezritsh. After Dov Ber's death in 1772, those students dispersed throughout Eastern Europe, bringing their master's teachings wherever they went. While they settled mostly in the regions of Podolia and Volhynia, one of the Maggid's youngest disciples, Shneur Zalman, went to the town of Lyozna, in what is now Belarus. His school of Hasidism, which stressed an intellectual approach to spiritual growth, became known as Chabad, an acronym for *hokhma* (wisdom), *bina* (understanding), and *da'at* (knowledge), stages of illumination corresponding to the first three Divine emanations, or *sefirot*, of early kabbalistic theosophy. The combination of Shneur Zalman's scholarship, theological sophistication, and organizational ability was successful in spreading the Chabad approach; by the early nineteenth century his movement had become the predominant form of Hasidism in White Russia, with outposts in dozens of cities and towns.

While each of the Maggid's disciples interpreted his teachings in his own way, it was Shneur Zalman who systematically developed his teacher's theology. Drawing on a selection of biblical, rabbinic, and kabbalistic passages that became virtual slogans for the movement, Hasidic leaders taught a doctrine of radical Divine immanence. "His glory fills the world," Isaiah prophesied; or, citing the medieval *Tikkunei Zohar*, "There is no place devoid of Him."[5] According to Hasidism, the world is nothing but a manifestation of the Divine, which gives it existence at every moment. God is not the world, as pantheism would have it. But the world *is* God.

If the world is dependent on God for its existence, God, too, is dependent on the world. Although Divinity is infinite and indivisible, it is incapable of self-revelation. So long as God remains alone, there is nothing to which He can be revealed. Yet

This image ostensibly shows the first Chabad leader, Shneur Zalman of
Lyady, even though it was painted by Boris Schatz in 1878, sixty-six years
after Shneur Zalman's death. (Boris Schatz / Wikimedia Commons)

full and unmediated revelation precludes the presence of anything else, which would be unable to maintain its existence in
the face of overpowering Divine brilliance. The purpose of the
world, therefore, is to reveal Divinity through the veil of creation. Paradoxically, the only way God can be revealed is by
being concealed; by obscuring the Divine light, creation allows
it to shine. Following the Kabbalah, from which it drew many
of its concepts and terms, Hasidism placed the Jewish people at
the center of this purpose. It is the human task, through the performance of the commandments and enactment of the Divine
will, to reveal God's presence in the world.

Such concepts of Divine immanence were not original to
Hasidism, nor to Judaism. "You were more inward than my most
inward part and higher than the highest element within me,"
wrote Augustine in his *Confessions*.[6] "We ought not to understand
God and the creature as two things distinct from one another,

but as one and the same," argued the ninth-century Irish theologian John Scottus Eriugena. "For both the creature, by subsisting, is in God; and God, by manifesting himself, in a marvelous and ineffable manner creates himself in the creature."[7] Earlier Jewish sages like Saadia Gaon of the tenth century, the medieval German Jewish pietists known as the Hasidei Ashkenaz, and the sixteenth-century kabbalist Moses Cordovero advocated similar views. For the Hasidic masters, however, these ideas took on new life and breathed a new spirit.

In earlier kabbalistic teachings, God was primarily imagined as a transcendent being, outside creation. The mystic quest was therefore a journey outward, fraught with peril. One of the few Talmudic accounts of mystical experience emphasized the elite nature of such pursuits: "Four entered the orchard . . . Ben Azai looked and died . . . Ben Zoma looked and was injured . . . Aher cut down the [heavenly] plants . . . Rabbi Akiva departed in peace."[8] The apocalyptic Hekhalot literature described this journey as a descent through the heavenly palaces to the Divine throne, a description modeled on the visions of Ezekiel in the Bible. In medieval and early modern Kabbalah, the quest was refigured as an ascent through the sefirot, culminating in the infinite, unknowable *En Sof,* or "Without End." Mystical enlightenment, with its rigors and dangers, was not for everyone.

The Hasidic conception entailed a fundamental shift. Unlike the old mysticism, Hasidism taught that Divinity was present throughout creation and that any distance from God was perceptual, not real. Through the study of the Torah, fulfillment of its commandments, and especially prayer, any person could commune with God, in whose presence they were already living. Whereas traditional kabbalists performed ascetic practices to purify the soul in preparation for its ascent, Hasidim tempered this attitude with the awareness that the world itself was holy. Basing themselves on the verse "In all your ways you should know Him," they preached a doctrine of "worship in corporeality"; for the righteous every act, however mundane, was religiously significant.[9] Thus, wrote Martin Buber, the teachings of Hasidism "can be summoned up in a single sentence: God can be beheld in each thing and reached through each pure deed."[10] Anyone might pierce the veil and apprehend Divinity. All they had to do was get out of the way.

For Shneur Zalman, this immanent view of the Divine was only half of a larger paradox.[11] The kabbalistic tradition had long drawn a contrast between the "lower unity" and the "higher unity," the human perspective and the Godly. From the human perspective the world seems to exist even if, through prayer and contemplation, its conditional nature is perceived. From the Divine perspective, nothing has substantial existence other than God. "For just as He was solitary, one and unique, before the six days of creation, so is He now after the creation," wrote Shneur Zalman. "And this is because everything is as nothing and naught, literally, compared to His being and essence."[12] According to a shopworn metaphor, the relationship between God and the world is like that between the sun and its rays; we might perceive them as separate, but from the sun's perspective, it's all just sun.

Even according to such acosmic formulations, the world must have some purpose. The Chabad masters therefore argued that just as anything in creation implies its opposite, so does God; to be truly complete, the Divine must include both its opposite as well as itself. The infinite, to be truly encompassing, must have the capacity to be finite. Thus the world was created, not for its own sake, but to be reassimilated within its Divine source. Here, too, humanity is necessary. In the process of creation God is said to have taken nothing—that is, the Divine "no-thing"—and turned it into something, the world. The task of human beings is to return the "something" of creation back to the "nothing" of God by joining their minds with the Divine though a process known in Hasidic terminology as *devekut* (cleaving) and, in the more common Chabad locution, *bittul*, or self-annihilation. As Shneur Zalman taught, "For this is the purpose of the creation of the worlds from nothingness to being, in order to transform the aspect of being into the aspect of nothingness."[13] If people draw the Divine into the world with speech and action, it is in contemplation and prayer, through the medium of consciousness, that they restore self and world to their origin.

In such teachings Shneur Zalman presented the relationship between God and the world as an ongoing dialectic between being and nothingness, Divine influx and withdrawal, God's ontological truth and humanity's epistemological reality. In "drawing down" the Divine presence, on the one hand, and "self-nullification," on the other, humans assist and imitate the Divine, which is both immanent and transcendent, "filling all worlds" and "surrounding all worlds," who creates for the purpose of both revelation and reabsorption. Just as the heavenly creatures in the vision of Ezekiel are described as "running back and forth," so God and the world oscillate between one pole and another.[14] Only within the essence of Divinity, at a level "above reason and knowledge," are these paradoxes resolved.

For the Ba'al Shem Tov and his circle, and for the Maggid of Mezritsh and his disciples, the demanding tasks of devekut and bittul may have been immediately relevant. But as Hasidism proliferated in the later decades of the eighteenth century it became necessary to make the Hasidic ethos meaningful to wider groups of people, not all of whom were capable of such accomplishments. The solution to this problem, as it emerged in the first generations of the movement, was the doctrine of the *tsaddik*, or rebbe: the supremely righteous man through whom all others could attain their elevation. This idea may have been Hasidism's most important innovation and enabled its transformation into a mass phenomenon.

The tsaddik, it was believed, was not just a person who became righteous through diligence and hard work; rather, he was a unique soul originating from the highest levels of the Godhead who included within himself all the souls of his followers. This doctrine, first expounded by Ya'akov Yosef of Polnoye, used abundant metaphors to emphasize the unique stature of the tsaddik. "Tsaddikim are spirit and form, and the masses of people are physical matter . . . As long as they cling to the tsaddikim, who provide form for the matter, there can be life for the body because of the soul."[15] In more radical formulations the tsaddik was described in nearly Divine terms. According to Elimelekh of Lizhensk, another early Hasidic leader, the tsaddik has "custodianship over all the benefits and all the means that can affect the life of a Jew" and "the tsaddik has the power to do anything, including the power to bring the Messiah."[16] Through faith in the tsaddik and obedience to him, believers were certain to benefit from their leader's stature, both spiritually and materially. However, just as the people were required to cling to the tsaddik, the tsaddik was obliged to serve the people. Unlike earlier mystics, whose spiritual accomplishments were ends in themselves, the heights attained by the tsaddik were meaningful only insofar as they contributed to the good of the community. Even if the tsaddik had to sacrifice some of his potential for that purpose, the loss was worthwhile. In essence, tsaddikim manifested in themselves the paradoxical teachings of Hasidism regarding God—as simultaneously occupying the spiritual and the material realms, the heavenly and the earthly, the human and the Divine.

The tsaddik thus took on supreme importance in Hasidism, and visits to the tsaddik's court became an essential part of Hasidic life. They were opportunities for his followers, the Hasidim, to meet personally with the tsaddik and to receive his guidance and blessing, which was endowed with miraculous powers. If Hasidim had the means, they would offer the tsaddik a donation called a *pidyon hanefesh*, a "redemption of the soul." Aside from metaphysical conceptions, Hasidim could partake in the rousing atmosphere of the tsaddik's court, which included song, dance, prayer, and communal meals, where the rebbe would propound his teachings. Stories about the miraculous deeds of tsaddikim proliferated orally and as a genre of Hasidic literature; telling them became a religious ritual in its own right.

Compared to other Hasidic leaders, Shneur Zalman had a concept of the tsaddik that was relatively modest. He didn't consider himself a miracle worker but a teacher and spiritual guide who could help others begin the religious undertaking that was otherwise the domain of a select few. In this he was unusually successful, and with the rapid growth of the movement in the 1780s and 1790s, he could no longer attend to the needs of his multiplying flock. In 1793 he instituted a set of regulations governing how often and under what circumstances Hasidim were allowed to visit him, with new adherents generally favored over older ones. More consequentially, in 1796 he published his magnum opus, *Likkutei Amarim* (Collected Sayings), popularly known after its first word, *tanya* (it is taught); the book was meant to substitute for personal instruction from Shneur Zalman himself.

In conception *Tanya* was different from any previous Hasidic work. Until then, Hasidic ideas had been presented using the familiar forms of biblical preaching and homiletics; in the coming decades there would be collections of Hasidic stories and ethical instruction, but few systematic explications of Hasidic beliefs. *Tanya* presented Hasidism directly. In the book Shneur Zalman elucidated Hasidic theology within a psychological and ethical framework, using kabbalistic concepts and language. While other Hasidic branches emphasized spiritual growth through ecstatic prayer and attachment to the tsaddik, Shneur Zalman taught that the main route to enlightenment was intellectual contemplation of Divinity using kabbalistic and Hasidic sources, including his own works. Through such contemplation an individual's spirit would be aroused to fear and love the Creator, and the believer could proceed through the stages of mystical awakening and self-nullification.

In addition to emphasizing the necessity of contemplation, Shneur Zalman stressed the importance of normative religious observance. Drawing on the Zoharic dictum that "the Torah and God are one," Shneur Zalman taught that when a person performs the commandments or studies words of Torah, the Divine will and wisdom become manifest in his body and thoughts. "The limbs of the body of the person that are fulfilling the commandment . . . become a vehicle of the Divine will . . . And similarly the mouth and tongue speaking words of Torah and the brain thinking words of Torah."[17] Unlike earlier kabbalists, who believed in the necessity of proper intent, Shneur Zalman taught that the spiritual effect of the commandments was accomplished regardless. With such teachings Shneur Zalman made the Hasidic ethos accessible to those of limited intellectual or spiritual capabilities, and the Chabad movement less objectionable to its critics than it might have been.

Shneur Zalman's innovations did not go unopposed, even within the Hasidic camp. Some of the fiercest criticism came from one of his older contemporaries, Avraham of Kalisk, who had immigrated to Palestine in 1777. In letters distributed to the Hasidic community, Avraham accused Shneur Zalman of departing from the way of his teachers by spreading mystical secrets to a wide public. Although Hasidism was committed to "spreading the wellsprings" of the Ba'al Shem Tov, not all tsaddikim believed that this meant teaching Kabbalah to all comers. For the more conservative Hasidic leaders, there was a difference between those who might participate in the Hasidic fraternity and benefit from its joyful communal life and those who were fit to receive esoteric wisdom, even in a tame form.

The strongest opposition to Shneur Zalman, and to Hasidism as a whole, came from the Mitnaggdim, or "opponents"— rabbinical scholars and community leaders who maintained a stronghold in the same areas of White Russia and Lithuania where Chabad was putting down roots. In 1772, the year of the Maggid's death, an anti-Hasidic tract was published in the city of Brody, accompanied by decrees of excommunication that had been issued by other communities in the area. Some of the accusations leveled against Hasidim in this and subsequent polemics were true: they did establish separate prayer houses, make changes to the liturgy and the method of ritual slaughter, and adopt special modes of dress. They were also charged with neglecting Torah study and suspected of Sabbateanism, "merrymaking and partying," and "a great deal of pipe smoking."[18]

Further bans and excommunications were issued in the early 1780s in reaction to the first publications by Ya'akov Yosef of Polnoye and, later in the century, in response to the publication of *Tanya*. When the Mitnaggdic leadership of Vilna outlawed Hasidic synagogues in late 1797, the Hasidic community turned for help to the Russian government, which responded by curtailing the Jewish leadership's civil and judicial autonomy. In retaliation, the Mitnaggdim denounced Shneur Zalman to the tsarist authorities, and he was arrested in October 1798 on suspicion of conspiring with both Napoleon and the Ottoman Empire (an accusation supposedly substantiated by his role in collecting funds to support the Hasidic community in Palestine) and of forming a subversive new sect somehow connected with Freemasonry. After being imprisoned and interrogated for fifty-three days, Shneur Zalman was released on November 27, the nineteenth day of the Hebrew month of Kislev, which thereafter became a holiday for Chabad Hasidim. Less than two years later, he was again arrested on suspicion of leading a new and heretical sect and was again released, in April 1800. For Chabad Hasidism the recognition of their leader's innocence seemed Divinely ordained and was taken as vindication of their movement and its beliefs against their antagonists.

* * *

The Mitnaggdim's opposition was rooted in a fear of Hasidism's separationist tendencies, its disruption of the social order, and the elevation of its tsaddikim over traditional authorities. But the dispute was also connected to one of the most fundamental theological questions in Judaism. In the mid-sixteenth century the kabbalist Isaac Luria Ashkenazi, later known as the Holy Ari, proposed a solution to one of the most vexing problems for any monotheistic faith. If God is infinite and indivisible, as Judaism contends, how can a world exist that is finite, divisible, and not God? Kabbalistic cosmology had previously proceeded along straightforward emanationist lines: the unknowable En Sof had, in the initial stage of creation, emanated ten expressions, or sefirot—collectively the "mystical organism" often depicted as concentric circles, a tree, or even a human body.[19] The sefirot then became the vehicles by which God interacted with the world. The medieval *Book of the Zohar* used these as a new means of exegesis, a way to draw a web of connections between biblical words, characters, images, and colors and the Divine qualities to which they were said to correspond. But this left Luria's question unanswered. Even if it was possible to countenance a tenfold Godhead that was simultaneously indivisible, where did that leave the world itself? The existence of a non-Divine world meant that God is everything except the world and is thus limited by that which He is not. For Luria this problem was solved—or at least labeled—by the doctrine of *tsimtsum*, a process of withdrawal or contraction enacted by God as the first step of creation, which subsequently allowed the world to exist.

Unsurprisingly, tsimtsum—a doctrine as impenetrable as the question that prompted it—hardly laid the matter to rest. If God was able to contract Himself and create a world in the void, was He really infinite? Seemingly, tsimtsum was only a name for the problem, not a solution to it. For Hasidic thinkers, with their extreme emphasis on Divine immanence, the proposition of a transcendent Divinity removed from creation was doubly unacceptable. They therefore rejected a literal understanding of tsimtsum and replaced it with a metaphorical one. The "contraction" of Divinity didn't separate God from the world but instead concealed the Divine behind the veil of creation in order for God to be revealed. As Shneur Zalman put it, "The matter of withdrawal and emanation does not apply at all to Divinity, but rather that of concealment and manifestation."[20] With this conception the unity of God remained intact, even if the ontological status of the world became an unfathomable mystery. While Hasidic thinkers could not escape the dilemma that tsimtsum represented, they could shift the question back to the world and away from God, who was once again whole.

The Hasidic movement was not the first to advocate this idea, but the opposition its proponents faced was especially fierce. For their opponents, the identification of the world with God suggested a pantheistic, or even pagan, worldview. The problem of evil was more troublesome in the Hasidic conception, since it was less disturbing to ascribe it to an independent worldly reality than to a Divine origin, as Hasidism did. (In response, Shneur Zalman asserted that evil consisted in just such an assertion of independence from God, however illusory.) Most of all, the Hasidic interpretation cast into doubt the many distinctions contained in the Torah between the holy and the profane, between righteousness and sin. If God is everywhere equally, what is the difference between the Holy of Holies and a barn? Why should some foods, or clothes, or sexual acts be prohibited if everything is really God? Seemingly, the insistence of the Torah on a myriad such distinctions was proof that the world did exist independently and that the doctrine of tsimtsum should be taken literally. For such reasons the Vilna Gaon, a preeminent kabbalist, Talmudist, and leader of the Mitnaggdim, was said to oppose the Hasidic interpretation of tsimtsum, although controversy persists regarding his true position. Even those who agreed with the Hasidic interpretation—and continued to accept the Torah's demands as part of the larger Divine purpose—found the popular emphasis on absolute immanence disturbing. But the Hasidic point of view contained its own theological opportunities, which generations of thinkers were eager to exploit.

In keeping with the twofold purpose of creation proposed by Shneur Zalman—revelation of the Divine within the world and the reabsorption of the world within the Divine—it followed that each stage of creation, which in the kabbalistic cosmology proceeds through three higher worlds before reaching our own material realm, serves its part toward those ends. But the ultimate purpose of creation, Shneur Zalman taught, is not the higher worlds, which are merely links in the chain, but our own lowest world, which seems furthest from God. Yet it is precisely its distance that makes it suitable for the Divine plan. After all, the only way for God to be revealed is for God to be concealed, and it is behind the thickest veil that the strongest light can shine. Similarly, the Divine achieves its greatest perfection by reincorporating its opposite in its strongest manifestation. Although the higher worlds are privy to various aspects of revelation, only in the lowest world is the Divine essence itself revealed. As the rabbinic *Midrash Tanhuma* states, in one of the teachings cited most often by Chabad thinkers, "When the Holy One Blessed Be He created the world, he desired to have a dwelling in the lower worlds just as there is in the higher ones."[21] Ultimately the process of creation and fulfillment of the Divine purpose is neatly circular; as the *Book of Creation*, one of the earliest kabbalistic texts, says of the sefirot, "Their end is in their beginning, and their beginning is in their end."[22] The lowest world is the one God wants to make a home for his highest essence.

This train of thought had the advantage not only of reconciling the problem of tsimtsum with the doctrine of Divine immanence but of offering a historical, and potentially messianic, resonance. The reason this world has the greatest revelatory potential is because it contains the lowest and darkest places. Throughout Jewish history, the sages taught, the greatest revelations had happened at times of Divine concealment. Prior to the biblical exodus from Egypt, the Jews had descended through forty-nine levels of impurity, coming only one step away from annihilation. During the time of Purim, when God hid His face from the Jewish people, the Jews merited a second revelation akin to the giving of the Torah at Sinai. "Wherever things are most hidden, there you will find the essential perfection," wrote Aharon ha-Levi of Staroselye, one of Shneur Zalman's main disciples.[23] Similarly, Hasidim believed, the teachings of the Ba'al Shem Tov had emerged specifically at a moment of darkness for the Jewish people. According to a midrash, God said to the Jewish people, "When you have sunk to the lowest level, at that time I will redeem you."[24] Chabad Hasidism, in its own history, had experienced moments of vindication at times of persecution, as with Shneur Zalman's arrest and subsequent release. Over the following centuries Chabad and its leaders would experience further tribulations, including arrests, imprisonments, schisms, and exile. But in the greatest darkness, they believed, the brightest light could shine.

By the third decade of the twentieth century, the world was growing dark indeed.

3

In the Court of Lubavitch

IF THE FIRST WORLD WAR affected the Schneersons only indirectly, its aftermath was devastating. In March 1917 the workers of Petrograd (formerly Saint Petersburg), frustrated by economic grievances and the mass fatalities of war, went on strike. Their revolt shut down the city's industrial production and attracted sympathizers among intellectuals, white-collar workers, and the military. With the army unable to suppress the protests, Nicholas II abdicated, leaving power in the hands of the Duma (parliament), which created a provisional government together with regional workers' councils, or soviets. This delicate arrangement did not last. When the provisional government decided to continue the European war, the Bolshevik party launched another revolution in October and succeeded in putting power solely in the hands of the soviets. In March 1918, the new government ended the Russian war effort with the signing of the Treaty of Brest-Litovsk and ceded Russian claims to Ukraine,

Finland, and the empire's Polish and Baltic territories, where puppet governments were installed by the Central Powers.

For Jews, this was a disastrous turn of events. The provisional government had promised to abolish antisemitic legal restrictions and create a self-governing Russian Jewish Congress, but it was now a nonentity. Although the Central Powers had made similar pledges to win Jewish support during the war, they now had no reason to follow through. National minorities such as Ukrainians and Poles saw the Jews as sympathetic to the Bolshevik regime, while food shortages and the Jews' historical participation in the grain trade led to popular resentment. No sooner did the Bolsheviks seize power than civil war, accompanied by pogroms, broke out across the former empire.

Ekaterinoslav, located in the heart of what had been Russian-ruled Ukraine, was at the center of these conflicts. Following the February Revolution, it became part of a short-lived Ukrainian People's Republic; after the annulment of the Treaty of Brest-Litovsk by the armistice of November 11, 1918, it was reoccupied by the Bolsheviks. Over the next year it continued to switch hands between competing forces, including the German and the Austro-Hungarian armies, which allied with Ukrainian Hetman Pavlo Skoropadskyi; the anarchist Black Army of Nestor Makhno, which maintained an autonomous government in southern Ukraine between 1918 and 1920; and the anti-Bolshevik Volunteer Army led by Russian Lieutenant General Anton Denikin. Nearly every occupation involved violence against Jews, especially under Denikin and the Ukrainian paramilitary leader Nykyfor Hryhoriv. The terror came to an end only when the Soviet Red Army once again captured the city at the end of 1919, this time for good.

Though the Bolshevik consolidation of power brought stability and relief from violence, it heralded new troubles. A crop failure in the Volga region led to famine, which was compounded by the Soviet government's appropriation of Ukrainian grain to feed the Russian population and to sell abroad. In 1921 and 1922 typhus and cholera swept Ekaterinoslav, killing more than five thousand Jews. According to Chana Schneerson, her son Menachem Mendel became ill while trying to treat others. Most concerning to Levi Yitshak and his family was the new regime's antipathy to organized religion and institutional Jewish life.

By the first decades of the twentieth century the old ene-mies of Hasidism had been replaced by new ones; instead of the Mitnaggdic rabbinical establishment, there were Zionism and socialism, both of which drew Hasidic youth away from tradi-tion. Not even a rabbi's family was immune. As a teenager, the Schneersons' youngest son, Leibel, fell under the influence of local Zionist leaders like Israel Eidelsohn and Emmanuel Bru-stein, who was the city's government-appointed rabbi. In protest, Chana Schneerson refused to speak anything but Yiddish and ordered that all works of secular literature be removed from the house. As one acquaintance recalled, "The only secular publi-cation thereafter allowed in the Schneerson home was *Pravda*. However, due to the Shlonsky influence this restriction did not last long."[1] Leibel later turned from Zionism to Trotskyism and published several articles about Marxism under the name Bidoy Petrob. The Schneersons' middle child, Berel, was also caught up in the political eddies and may have been arrested at one point because of his activities.

None of these influences was as devastating as Soviet Com-munism. At the outset the new regime promised full legal and social emancipation for Jews and supported Jewish culture in a secularized form. But it viewed Judaism, like all religion, with hostility. And while it continued for a time to support individ-ual religious freedom, it suppressed organized expressions of belief. In its first years, the new government closed synagogues, outlawed religious schools, dismissed rabbis and religious teach-ers from their posts, conducted show trials of clergy, enforced a six-day workweek, and introduced antireligious instruction in state schools. Zionist activity was forbidden in the city, leading to the arrest of some one thousand people in September 1922. Two years later the local branch of the Joint Distribution Committee, which had assisted refugees during the war, was closed, and its head of operations arrested. For Levi Yitshak these developments were deeply disturbing, especially following the death in 1921 of Pinhas Gelman, which left him as the city's only rabbi. Still, he was not alone in his troubles. Chabad had historically been based in areas now controlled by the Soviet Union, and all its adherents were affected by the new regime.

Like most Hasidic movements, Chabad developed in dynastic fashion, with leadership passing from father to son or another male heir. Succession had sometimes been turbulent. In 1801, Shneur Zalman, following his second imprisonment in Saint Petersburg, moved from Lyozna to Lyady, a small town on the Mereya River. Ten years later he was uprooted again when he fled Napoleon's advance into Russia. The journey proved too much for the aging rebbe, and in December 1812 he died at age sixty-seven in a village near Kursk.

After Shneur Zalman's death the movement was at a loss. How could it replace a founder of such monumental stature? The problem was exacerbated by a contest over leadership between Shneur Zalman's primary disciple, Aharon ha-Levi Horowitz, and his eldest son, Dov Ber. While Aharon ha-Levi taught an ecstatic method of prayer and Divine service consistent with the tendencies of Hasidism as a whole, Dov Ber advocated a more restrained path, focusing on the higher mysteries of spiritual self-annihilation, or bittul. The movement was divided in two, with Aharon ha-Levi moving to Staroselye, in the Mohilev province of Belarus, and Dov Ber relocating the dynasty to Lubavitch, a small Russian town known for its flax trade. Although Aharon ha-Levi drew many of Shneur Zalman's followers to his camp, his son Hayim Refa'el failed to continue the new dynasty, leaving Dov Ber's line to inherit the movement.

Chabad had yet to undergo its most serious schism. In 1827, Dov Ber died and was succeeded by his nephew and son-in-law, Menahem Mendel Schneersohn, who was a legal authority known as the Tsemah Tsedek (Sprout of Righteousness) after the title of his collected responsa. Like his grandfather Shneur Zalman, the Tsemah Tsedek was an accomplished scholar and a capable administrator; the movement flourished under his leadership. That unity was short-lived. When the Tsemah Tsedek died in 1866, the movement split, with four of his seven sons setting up courts in different towns—a common occurrence among tsaddikim with multiple heirs—and his youngest son, Shmuel, becoming heir to the Lubavitch court. Aside from one child who died young, only the Tsemah Tsedek's oldest son, a businessman named Barukh Shalom, declined to take a leadership role.

Following the death of Shmuel Schneersohn in 1882, the court of the Lubavitcher rebbe passed to his second son, Shalom Dov Ber, whose tenure coincided with a newly challenging era for Chabad. In the middle of the nineteenth century the Jewish enlightenment movement, or Haskalah, began making inroads in the traditional life of Eastern European Jewry; by the century's end political Zionism and secular socialism were gathering strength. In response to these threats, Shalom Dov Ber worked to expand his movement's influence. A prolific letter writer, he made use of technological advances in postal and telegraphic communications, and he traveled widely, meeting with Orthodox leaders throughout Eastern Europe and Germany. Shalom Dov Ber also developed Chabad theology through his Hasidic discourses, which were renowned for their philosophical sophistication and earned him a reputation as the "Maimonides of Hasidism" among his followers.

Shalom Dov Ber's most important innovation was the first

Lubavitcher yeshiva, Tomkhei Temimim (Supporters of the Complete Ones), established in 1897. In the yeshiva students read not only the Talmud but also Hasidic literature, whose study was institutionalized for the first time. This innovation was a response to the Jewish enlightenment, which had been capturing intellectually minded Jewish youth, and to the educational methods of elite non-Hasidic yeshivas, which Shalom Dov Ber believed were a "gateway to secularism."[2] The students of Tomkhei Temimim would safeguard the Hasidic way of life and serve as a military-style corps in the battle against assimilation and enlightenment. In a fiery sermon given on the holiday of Simhat Torah, 1900, Shalom Dov Ber proclaimed them to be like soldiers fighting the wars of King David, warriors "who can—and will—rescue the people of Israel from the enemies of God."[3] Following graduation, many of them were sent to serve as rabbis, teachers, and ritual slaughterers in remote Jewish communities, strengthening Orthodox practice and expanding Chabad's sphere of influence. Although Chabad had operated similar networks under previous rebbes, Shalom Dov Ber broadened its reach to include non-Hasidic and even non-Ashkenazic populations, including the ancient Jewish community of Georgia. Like his grandfather the Tsemah Tsedek, Shalom Dov Ber's tenure was characterized by its long duration and by the reconsolidation of the movement. Although other Chabad factions persisted for several more decades after he became rebbe, the Lubavitch branch, and the name of the town, became synonymous with the movement as a whole.

When Shalom Dov Ber became rebbe, his only son, Yosef Yitshak, was just thirteen years old, but Yosef Yitshak quickly took a leading role in his father's court. For almost thirty years he served as his father's chief administrator, helping to run the yeshiva and the network of emissaries. When Shalom Dov Ber died in 1920, after moving the community from Lubavitch to Rostov during the First World War, Yosef Yitshak was prepared for leadership. While previous Chabad rebbes had distinguished themselves with their executive skill and theological sophistication, Yosef Yitshak succeeded primarily through his abilities as an administrator, fundraiser, and champion of the movement. Like his father, he was a handsome man, with a red beard, blue eyes, and seemingly boundless energy. He, too, was a prolific letter writer, and he traveled widely in Europe and overseas. His writings and talks often concerned the history and folklore of the movement, preserving its traditions for future generations. Through his rhetoric and example he attracted the loyalty of thousands of Hasidim and inspired them to uphold the Hasidic cause even at great personal cost.

As the anti-religious militancy of the Soviet Union became apparent, most Orthodox leaders in the country emigrated at the first opportunity. Yosef Yitshak took the opposite position.[4] As he told his followers, staying in the country and fighting for religious observance was a sacred duty. In 1917, three years before he became rebbe, he founded Agudat HaTemimim, an association of graduates from the Lubavitcher yeshiva, and during the first years of Soviet rule, he mobilized this vanguard to strengthen religious communities buckling under the strain of government oppression. In 1922, at a secret meeting in Moscow, he helped create a Committee of Rabbis to coordinate these efforts through a central office and to serve as a counterweight to state forces undermining religious life. While religious schools were outlawed, home instruction was permitted, a loophole Yosef Yitshak and his followers exploited on a broad scale. With financial help from the U.S.-based Joint Distribution Committee, the new organization supported a network of clandestine yeshivas and established a rabbinical institute in Nevel to train a new generation of rabbis and ritual slaughterers. In a widely distributed letter from the summer of 1925, Yosef Yitshak wrote: "We must understand that we did not come to this land by chance, and it was not by chance that we encountered the bitterness of exile, darkness, hindrances, and hardship. It is the will of the Creator, Blessed Be He . . . that we illuminate the darkness of this land with the light of Torah and worship."[5]

Unsurprisingly, Yosef Yitshak's activities brought him under the scrutiny of Soviet authorities. Still, he was not dissuaded. After being expelled from Rostov by the political police, he sought a position where he could have the most influence, and in 1924 he relocated the court to the cosmopolitan center of Leningrad.

It is unknown when the possibility of Schneerson's marriage to Yosef Yitshak's middle daughter, Chaya Mushka, was first raised, or who raised it. According to Chabad tradition, the match was suggested by Shalom Dov Ber, although the details of this story are unclear. But the prospect of a match with the rebbe's daughter was a serious matter and attested to the esteem in which Yosef Yitshak held Levi Yitshak and his family. The issue was particularly consequential because Yosef Yitshak had three daughters but no sons; the next rebbe would likely be one of his sons-in-law or one of their children. His eldest daughter, Chana, was married to Shmaryahu Gourary, a businessman and a scion of one of the wealthiest Hasidic families in Russia, but the other two were still unwed.

By the 1920s, marriage by parental fiat was largely a thing of the past, and as a child of Lubavitch "royalty," Chaya Mushka was well acquainted with modern culture. Born in 1901 in the town of Babinovitch, she was educated in both Jewish and secular subjects, and her mother, Nehama Dina, was well read in both Jewish and Russian literature. Schneerson needed to become acquainted not only with his potential father-in-law but also with his potential bride. In October 1922, during the holiday of Sukkot, he made his first trip to Yosef Yitshak's court, where he made a favorable impression. Early the next summer he joined the family in the resort town of Kislovodsk, where he met Chaya Mushka for the first time before traveling back with

Schneerson's relationship with Yosef Yitshak Schneersohn,
his father-in-law and the rabbi who preceded him as head of Chabad,
was a defining element of his leadership. (JEM, The Living Archive)

Yosef Yitshak to Rostov. "I studied the 'laws of Mendel,' may he
be well, for several hours each day," Yosef Yitshak wrote back to
Chaya Mushka, reporting his impression of the young man. "It
was very pleasant . . . He would like to hike the mountains again—
really, the walk to the mountain. I can say that I know him a
little already."[6]

Over the next few years Schneerson shuttled back and forth
between Ekaterinoslav—renamed Dnepropetrovsk in 1926—and

Yosef Yitshak's court in Rostov, then Leningrad. Occasionally he accompanied his brother Berel to see doctors in Kharkov, and on at least one occasion he visited the Lubavitcher yeshiva in Kremenchug. In August 1924 he received rabbinical ordination from his uncle Shmuel Schneerson and briefly served as the rabbi of a small synagogue in Ekaterinoslav, although he did not seem interested in a rabbinical career. During his trips to Leningrad he pursued his passion for astronomy, making several visits to the Pulkovo Observatory just outside the city. According to a story told by a friend of the family, in the winter of 1925 he predicted that an eclipse would take place; when it failed to occur, he "wasn't his usual self" until he read in a scientific magazine that the eclipse did happen, but not where he expected it.[7]

Around 1926 or early 1927, just as Stalin was solidifying his hold over the Soviet Union, Schneerson moved to Leningrad on a more permanent basis, possibly to take classes in engineering at Leningrad State University. Schneerson's younger brother Leibel also moved to the city around this time and frequented Yosef Yitshak's circle while taking classes in physics. Schneerson likely stayed with his brother, local Hasidim, or possibly Yosef Yitshak before moving in with the Chabad Hasid Shmuel Nimoytin on Nevsky Prospect, just blocks from Yosef Yitshak's home and the center of the court. Nimoytin's son Refael, with whom he shared a room, remembered him constantly reading or writing and at one point teaching himself to write English shorthand. "He was constantly busy," Nimoytin recalled in a 1991 interview. "He would almost always arrive to the room last, and would leave first in the morning. He was reserved, barely speaking to anyone."[8]

Around this time Schneerson's engagement to Chaya Mushka was finalized. In early 1926 his mother paid a visit to Leningrad, possibly to negotiate the terms of the match. Although there is little indication of how Chaya Mushka felt about her future husband, her father was growing fond of him. He appointed

Schneerson his "minister of education" and assigned him tasks like writing and transcribing correspondence. The strangest assignment that Schneerson undertook was working with a Russian professor, popular mystery writer, medical school dropout, and occultist named Alexander Vasilyevich Barchenko, who operated a laboratory for the investigation of paranormal phenomena on the top floor of the Soviet cryptography office. When Barchenko approached Yosef Yitshak in 1925 looking for information on the kabbalistic meaning of the Star of David, Yosef Yitshak assigned the job to Schneerson, who spent three months corresponding with the professor, visiting him in Moscow, and preparing a manuscript on the subject.

While Schneerson was establishing himself in Yosef Yitshak's inner circle, the future of Chabad was looking grim. Even after leaving Rostov, Yosef Yitshak was monitored by agents of the Soviet secret police (OGPU) and by the Yevsektsiya, the Jewish section of the Communist Party. He did little to allay their suspicions. At a Purim celebration in the spring of 1927, having drunk by his own admission "possibly more than usual," he announced to a full room that "whoever hands his child over to a Yevsektsiya school will not live out the year."[9] Eliyahu Chaim Althaus, one of Yosef Yitshak's followers and a confidant of the household, wrote of the evening with worry. "After Purim, our spirits were crushed. We felt it was only a matter of time before something terrible would happen."[10] It was, in fact, only a matter of months.

The arrest, imprisonment, and vindication of Chabad's leaders played a defining role in the self-conception of the movement. The persecution of Shneur Zalman was a pivotal moment in Chabad's development, and subsequent trials were similarly memorialized. According to Chabad tradition, every rebbe was imprisoned at some point before being freed. This historical motif was not just about danger overcome but about the triumph of Hasidism over its opponents. Thus, the arrest, imprisonment, interrogation, exile, and release of Yosef Yitshak was seen as an example of Divine providence, and the date of his freedom was enshrined in the cycle of Chabad holidays. Those who lived through the events of that summer must have found them terrifying.

On the night of June 14, Yosef Yitshak was at home receiving visitors for private consultations. Shortly after midnight, when he sat down for dinner, two OGPU agents burst through the door, accompanied by members of the Yevsektsiya. Their arrival could not have been a surprise. In 1924 he took the precaution of giving Chaya Mushka power of attorney over his financial affairs, an indication of her worldly competence and the necessity of a backup plan should he be seized. That night, according to Chabad accounts, Yosef Yitshak was unfazed. He drank his coffee and recited the Grace After Meals before retreating to his office.

Fortuitously, Chaya Mushka was not at home that night but out with her fiancé. When the couple came back, the OGPU agents were still in the house. Before entering, she and Schneerson sensed that something was wrong. Chaya Mushka went inside, appearing at the window a few minutes later with a prearranged signal. Schneerson quickly left to wake Althaus and, together with Althaus's son, relayed the news to Chaim Lieberman, Yosef Yitshak's secretary. Lieberman began burning incriminating documents relating to the movement's underground schools and finances; when the OGPU agents arrived, the fire was still going. During interrogation, Lieberman said that the men outside were drunks who had gotten lost, and neither Schneerson nor Althaus was arrested.

Meanwhile, Yosef Yitshak was taken to the prison on Shpalernaya Street, next to the local headquarters of the OGPU. As he wrote later, he believed that he would have been executed, but he took a wrong turn down a hallway and got lost, and the execution authorization expired. Throughout his imprisonment and interrogation his main concerns were for his family, disciples, and library, which included rare Hasidic manuscripts and a five-thousand-volume collection he had purchased in 1925 from Samuel Wiener, librarian of the Jewish Division of the Asiatic Museum in Leningrad. "I was deeply agitated and my entire body trembled," he wrote. "G-d forbid, was it possible that the sacred Chasidic manuscripts and writings were also taken?"[11] Meanwhile Schneerson was busy smuggling the manuscripts to other Hasidim, from whom they would later be retrieved.

More pressing than the fate of the library was that of Yosef Yitshak himself. Four days after his arrest a meeting was held at the home of the rabbi of Leningrad, David Tevel Katzenellenbogen. In attendance were Schneerson, Shmaryahu Gourary, Althaus, and other Jewish community representatives. Their strategy was to enlist the help of anyone who might convince the government to release Yosef Yitshak or at least to deal mercifully with him. Among the people they recruited were the rabbis Meir Hildesheimer and Leo Baeck in Germany, Rabbi Abraham Isaac Kook in Palestine and, at the instigation of Supreme Court Justice Louis Brandeis and American Reform Rabbi Stephen Wise, U.S. Senators Robert Wagner and William Borah, the latter of whom was chair of the Senate Foreign Relations Committee. Yekaterina Peshkova, a Russian human rights activist and the first wife of the author Maxim Gorky, was particularly helpful.

The effort was successful, albeit in stages. At first Yosef Yitshak was found guilty of "acts of sabotage against the revolution" and "teaching religion to minors," for which he was sentenced to ten years of labor in Siberia. Thanks to the intercession on his behalf, on June 30, sixteen days after his arrest, Yosef Yitshak was informed that he would be released from prison and sentenced to three years of exile in Kostroma, a city on the Volga

River, deep in the interior of the country. He was forbidden to leave the area, was required to present himself weekly at the local police station, and had to inform the authorities of any change of residence. On July 3 he left prison, returned home for six hours, and departed for Kostroma on an 8 p.m. train. Chaya Mushka, Shmaryahu Gourary, and Eliyahu Chaim Althaus accompanied him into exile.

Yosef Yitshak's stay in Kostroma was even shorter than his time in prison. Nine days after he arrived, on July 12—which fell that year on the Hebrew date of 12 Tammuz, his birthday—he reported at the local OGPU office and was told that his sentence was annulled and that he was free to go. Chaya Mushka telephoned home, informing her sister that they would be back in Leningrad for the Sabbath but not to publicize the fact. Still, word spread quickly, and a small gathering was held that night at the rebbe's residence. Thenceforth the day of Yosef Yitshak's release would be celebrated as a Lubavitcher holiday—a miracle "which we saw with our own eyes," as Schneerson often proclaimed.[12]

After being released, Yosef Yitshak kept a low profile, spending the summer in the town of Malakhovka, near Moscow. But he was in danger of rearrest so long as he stayed in the Soviet Union. Once again, foreign leaders came to his aid, including Mordekhai Dubin, head of the Orthodox Agudath Israel party in Latvia and a member of the Latvian parliament. On September 28, at a meeting at the foreign ministry in Moscow, the Soviet government relented, and Yosef Yitshak was allowed to leave the country for Riga. This time he would be accompanied by his family and entourage, as well as his library.

As far as Schneerson was concerned, if Yosef Yitshak was going to emigrate, he would too. Although Yosef Yitshak was the authorities' primary target, there is some indication that Schneerson was also under scrutiny. At some point in 1926 or 1927 he may have spent time in the town of Luga, outside Leningrad, with the purpose of lying low. He occasionally wrote letters using pseudonyms to avoid the attention that the name Schneerson would bring. And although Yosef Yitshak was still encouraging his followers to stay in the Soviet Union, Schneerson was his prospective son-in-law and a de facto member of his household. According to Chana Schneerson, when Yosef Yitshak was questioned as to why it was necessary to bring her son along, he replied, "Such a son-in-law just can't be found elsewhere!"[13]

Before leaving the Soviet Union, Yosef Yitshak traveled back to Rostov with Chaya Mushka to pray at his father's grave, while Schneerson returned home to spend one last Sukkot holiday with his parents. According to his mother's recollection, he put up a cheerful front, despite the impending separation. "It was as if his intention was to wipe from everyone's heart that this might be his final *Simhat Torah* dance at home, under the same roof as his family," she said. "Every time I saw my son's face I saw how painful it was for him that he was leaving us. His face, though, was also telling me, 'Mother, don't worry!'"[14]

Although Schneerson would meet Yosef Yitshak in Riga, they were not traveling together. On October 20, Yosef Yitshak departed from Leningrad with his family, entourage, and library, which together took up four full train cars. That same day Schneerson, accompanied by his mother, left Dnepropetrovsk for Leningrad. After spending the Sabbath in Kursk, they went to Leningrad, arriving on October 23, two days before Schneerson's scheduled departure for Riga. His Soviet passport, which he would use for the next five years, showed an intense young man with large dark eyes and a small beard, wearing a newsboy cap and a heavy wool suit and tie. Before leaving, Schneerson received a telegram from his father:

> May G-d grant you a good trip. May He guard your goings
> and comings now and forever. May you always be blessed in

all things, and go in the good path all of your days. All the best, and only the best! May you be successful all your life.

These are my soulful blessings from the depths of the heart.

Your father, who loves you with an eternal love.

Levik.[15]

Schneerson would never see his father again.

4

University Days

On October 21, 1927, Yosef Yitshak and his family arrived in Riga, where they settled in a suite of two apartments at 10 Pulkveža Brieža, a handsome stone building east of the Daugava River. In Latvia, Yosef Yitshak found a Jewish community different from the one he had left in Russia. By 1927 the country was home to around a hundred thousand Jews, including a small Chabad community. But unlike the Soviet Union, or the Russian Empire before it, Latvia was a liberal democracy, and—to Yosef Yitshak's benefit—Jewish parties were represented in its government. Latvian Orthodoxy resembled its acculturated German counterpart, and the school system practiced a philosophy of "Torah with the way of the land," combining religious and secular studies. Even Lubavitchers tended to embrace contemporary dress, to trim or shave their beards, and to participate in politics. During his six-year stay in Latvia, Yosef Yitshak protested these tendencies, arguing that while compromise might be necessary for some, traditional Hasidic ways were far preferable. Whatever his reservations, the stay in Latvia provided a welcome respite from the years of harassment in the Soviet Union.

No sooner did Yosef Yitshak get settled than he went back to work. He continued to lead the Committee of Rabbis and established a new organization to raise funds for Soviet Jewry. His efforts didn't help. At one time he had told his followers that the Soviet government was not opposed to personal religious observance in principle and that its legal and political systems could be relied on. "The religious Jew is a full citizen of the USSR, and is entirely permitted according to its laws to teach his children Torah and observe all the commandments," he had insisted.[1] The true enemy, he believed, was the Yevsektsiya, which he blamed for persecuting him and his followers. Still, he argued, that persecution was no different from the oppression of previous generations. This view turned out to be a tragic mistake. In the winter of 1928–29 the rabbinic training institute in Nevel was discovered and shut down, along with the two largest branches of Chabad's yeshiva network. A year later the government launched a campaign against religious functionaries, which led to the arrests of Chabad activists. Under pressure from the regime, the Joint Distribution Committee stopped supporting religious work, and without a reliable source of funds the Committee of Rabbis became defunct. Although Yosef Yitshak continued his efforts, there was little he could do.

All this made Schneerson's decision to leave the Soviet Union especially fortuitous. But unlike in Russia and Soviet Ukraine, where he had been occupied by family ties and personal interests, in Latvia his role was unclear. For a couple of months he served as one of Yosef Yitshak's secretaries, writing letters and attending meetings. He was eager to pursue his own path, however, and at the end of December he moved to Berlin.

* * *

Schneerson wasn't the only young Jew with his eye on the German capital. Berlin in the 1920s and early 1930s was a magnet for Eastern Europeans trying to broaden their horizons. Among Schneerson's peers were Joseph B. Soloveitchik, later a dean at Yeshiva University and a pillar of American Modern Orthodoxy; Abraham Joshua Heschel, who became an influential professor of Jewish ethics and mysticism at the Jewish Theological Seminary; and Yitzchak Hutner, a prominent postwar yeshiva head, who spent four months studying philosophy before returning to Warsaw. Germany was familiar to Chabad rebbes, who visited the country to fundraise, meet with Jewish leaders, and receive medical treatment. And Berlin was fairly close to Yosef Yitshak's court, allowing Schneerson to return for Jewish holidays.

For Germany's native Jewish population, the previous decade had been a time of social and professional opportunity. After the First World War, Jews were granted full rights as citizens, and the country's Jewish community grew to around half a million people. By the late 1920s, both antisemitism and Jewish nationalism were on the rise. While apostasy and intermarriage had increased at the end of the nineteenth century, they were now rare. Rather than trying to disappear into German society, most middle-class Jews saw themselves as Germans of the Jewish faith; expressions of Jewish identity included schools, youth groups, Zionist organizations, and some fifty Jewish periodicals.

The country's Jewish population was leavened by an influx of Eastern European immigrants, or *Ostjuden*, who came in large numbers following the First World War. They brought their own cultural enterprises, and for a few years Berlin became the center of Hebrew literary activity. For native-born Jews these foreigners were a source of curiosity and irritation. Some, like Martin Buber, romanticized them as an authentic relic of the past, and Buber's books were influential among Jewish youth. Others saw them as a visible target for antisemitism, and some

Jewish organizations joined their non-Jewish counterparts in trying to limit immigration. For assimilated German Jews, Ostjuden like Schneerson might be welcomed as co-religionists but could also be feared as unwelcome reminders of Jewish difference.

Schneerson remained mostly aloof from the institutional Jewish community. Upon arriving in the city he found a room in the home of Michael Wilensky, an academic who had once studied at the Lubavitcher yeshiva and was now preparing a medieval book on biblical grammar for its first printing. Schneerson's own task was to figure out how to register at Friedrich Wilhelm University without academic credentials. To that end he paid a visit to the Hildesheimer Rabbinical Seminary, the foremost scholarly institution of German Jewish Orthodoxy, which he hoped would provide him with a letter of reference. According to a story related by one of the students, the rector of the seminary, Yechiel Yaakov Weinberg, agreed to Schneerson's request pending a test on a subject of Schneerson's choosing. Schneerson chose one of Weinberg's own works, a fifty-seven-page legal treatise on the exhumation and reinterment of the dead, and was tested on it the next day. According to Chabad lore, Weinberg then granted him rabbinical ordination, although a record of this has never been found. Schneerson did receive a letter from the seminary's chairman of instructors, Yosef Wohlgemut, attesting that he had been accepted as a visiting student and that "his previous knowledge of Talmudic fields, as well as the level of his general education, indicates that he is exceptional."[2] Although he never formally studied at the seminary, he would attend lectures there and discuss scholarly subjects with Weinberg. In March, Schneerson returned to Riga for Passover, staying for seven weeks before returning to Berlin in late April to register for classes.

Throughout his youth Schneerson had been interested in the sciences, and they were the focus of his studies in Berlin. Although he remained a "visiting student" and did not receive academic credit, he was able to audit classes and prepare for the engineering education he would later pursue. In his first semester he took courses in analytical geometry, experimental and theoretical physics, mechanics of deformable bodies, introduction to higher mathematics, and introduction to philosophy. It was a good time to be studying science in Germany; among Schneerson's professors were Walter Nernst, who won the Nobel Prize in Chemistry in 1920, and Erwin Schrödinger, the physicist famous for his "uncertainty" equation, who would go on to win the Nobel Prize in Physics in 1933. At the same time, Schneerson continued his private religious studies and his correspondence with the Rogatchover Gaon, Yosef Yitshak, and his father, who shared kabbalistic insights and encouraged his son to send his own in return. He also wrote letters on everyday matters to his future mother-in-law, Nehama Dina Schneersohn. In a letter that summer he remarked on the weather, which was rainy and hot; on a glass writing desk he had purchased but needed to ship over the border; and on the habits of Berlin locals. "When the sun sets, all the doors open," he wrote. "One who walks down the street encounters families sitting in front of every home. They gaze at the moon, quite pleased with the world— and especially with themselves, their wives and children."[3] Just over a week later he noted the upcoming fast of the Ninth of Av and wondered humorously how German Jews would be able to go without wishing one another "good day," a practice forbidden at a time of mourning. At the end of July he returned to Riga and stayed through the fall festivals. In October, his long-delayed wedding was scheduled for the following month. He was twenty-six years old.

It had been almost six years since Schneerson and Chaya Mushka first met, and two or three since their presumed engagement, an unusually long time in Hasidic circles. The delay was likely due to the difficulties endured by Yosef Yitshak in the Soviet Union and, later, the futile hope that Schneerson's parents would be allowed to attend the wedding. Financial considerations also played a role. In August, Yosef Yitshak's secretary, Yechezkel Feigin, wrote confidentially to Rabbi Israel Jacobson, a Chabad activist in the United States, saying: "Money is short and the Rebbe is very pained by this . . . Eventually, whether a month earlier or a month later, the wedding will have to take place. But with what?"[4] Although they could have held a modest wedding in Riga, the marriage of Yosef Yitshak's middle daughter was not just a family celebration but an opportunity for the rebbe to demonstrate his relevance as a Hasidic leader, even in exile. To do that, he needed funds.

Whatever the constraints, by the fall of 1928 a date was set for November 27, the fourteenth of the Hebrew month of Kislev. With money provided by Chabad communities in the United States and elsewhere, Yosef Yitshak decided to hold the wedding in Warsaw, the most vibrant Jewish center in Europe and now home to the flagship Chabad yeshiva. Schneerson, who disliked being paraded around, found the to-do unsettling, but he had little choice in the matter. A contemporaneous account, written by a Hasid named Shmuel Zalmanov and included by Schneerson in his diary, noted that during the wedding reception the groom was seated at the head of the table "against his will."[5] But Schneerson was marrying the daughter of the Lubavitcher rebbe, and he had to accept all that this implied. How Chaya Mushka felt about her upcoming marriage is harder to gauge. In a letter to a friend she noted only, "I am not yet exactly a bride, because we have not celebrated the engagement, but it seems that I will get married this winter."[6] In a subsequent letter she remarked that because she and her groom had the same last name, "I will still remain a Schneerson . . . I admit that I am very pleased with this."[7]

In early November, Schneerson had just begun his second semester, taking courses in higher mathematics, experimental physics, and natural philosophy, when he left Berlin for Riga. The engagement contract was signed, and he was called to the

Torah on the Sabbath before the wedding, an event followed by a reception in the apartment of Yosef Yitshak's mother, Shterna Sarah. Before leaving for Warsaw, Schneerson received several letters from his father in which Levi Yitshak elaborated on the kabbalistic significance of the day, offered his son instruction in the rituals of the wedding, and told him to buy Chaya Mushka a gift on his and Chana's behalf. "Don't worry that we, your father and mother, will not be with you at the physical place of your wedding," he wrote. "We are together with you in our hearts and souls, which no physical space can possibly divide at all . . . may your parents—your father and mother, who are literally connected to you with their souls, behold all this."[8]

That Sunday, Schneerson and the bride's entire family departed for Warsaw by train, except for Chaya Mushka and her mother, who had left two weeks earlier to prepare. After being greeted by a large crowd at the train station, Schneerson was sent with Eliyahu Chaim Althaus to his hotel. "Let me pause for a moment to praise the Warsaw taxi drivers," Althaus wrote in a letter to his family. "They're fickle antisemites, but in one area they are quite predictable and stable: their love of money. Not waiting for us to reach him, one driver scared off the pursuing [crowd] . . . the door slammed behind us and we were saved from the throng."[9] That evening a "groom's feast" was held at 8 p.m. at the yeshiva hall; it lasted until two in the morning.

On Tuesday, the day of the wedding, the weather in Warsaw was rainy and cold. According to custom, Schneerson spent the day fasting, praying, and studying *Reshit Hokhma* (The Beginning of Wisdom), a pietistic work by the sixteenth-century kabbalist Eliyahu de Vidas. Both bride and groom were photographed—Chaya Mushka in heavy makeup and an elaborate white dress, Schneerson in a frock coat and *gartl* (prayer belt), gazing out the window. By mid-afternoon the sun came out, and at 6 p.m. Althaus, Shmaryahu Gourary, and Yosef Yitshak's uncle, Moshe Horensztajn, took the groom to the yeshiva by car. The

Schneerson became one of the most photographed rabbis of his time,
but only a few images exist of his wife, Chaya Mushka. This picture, taken
just before their wedding, is one of them. (JEM, The Living Archive)

Yiddish newspaper *The Moment*, which sent a reporter to the
wedding, described Schneerson as "a young man of average
height with a refined and intelligent appearance. He is dressed
in a black hat, a silk caftan, a stiff white collar with a black tie."
At 6:30, Chaya Mushka arrived with her mother in "a fancy car,
completely covered with roses," and proceeded to a bridal throne
in the women's hall, "decorated with roses and fancy arc lights."[10]
Following the recitation of a Hasidic discourse by Yosef Yitshak, he and Schneerson secluded themselves in a side room,

where Schneerson was dressed in a *kitl*, the ceremonial white robe, and Yosef Yitshak gave him his blessing.

According to Chabad tradition, the marriage ceremony was held outdoors, in the 6,000-square-foot yeshiva courtyard, which had been illuminated for the occasion with electric lamps. The event was attended by several thousand people, including the chairmen of the rabbinical councils of Poland and Warsaw, representatives of the Joint Distribution Committee, and Rabbi Tsvi Yehezkel Michelsohn of the Warsaw Rabbinate, who issued the marriage certificate. Yosef Yitshak officiated. "Suddenly I heard the first blessing being recited," Althaus wrote. "His voice thundered like the rapids: deep, solemn, and trembling . . . Tears flowed like water from every face, and everyone's hearts melted."[11]

After the ceremony the wedding celebration began at Weisman's wedding hall on Panska Street, which was set up for 250 invited guests, along with yeshiva students, who lined the walls. By the time Schneerson and Chaya Mushka arrived, he had changed into a brown suit, brown shoes, and white dinner gloves—a style he shared with others present. "The crowd of guests is completely different from those seen at other rebbes' weddings," the reporter from *The Moment* noted. "One sees no fur or black round velvet hats. Most are Jews clothed in European dress and only a small number are dressed in high silk caps." Following a buffet dinner, the celebration—accompanied by the "orchestra of H. Mittman"—lasted until the early hours. The only thing to mar the festivities were pickpockets, who stole a number of valuables, including the marriage contract, which had to be rewritten the same night. Even that could not ruin the mood. "We Hasidim were overjoyed to witness with our own eyes a blessed generation of offspring from our holy rebbes—and now, after 150 years, a seventh generation," Althaus wrote. "Despite the double darkness that covers the world in which we live, during these times of the footsteps of the Messiah, the small light that we have is bright and pure. It illuminates the darkness and nothing can prevent us from seeing its glow. Fortunate is the eye that beheld all this!"[12]

The next decade of Schneerson's life would, in later years, contribute much to the mystery that surrounds him. Although he turned into a religious leader of unusual fervor and effectiveness, throughout the 1930s he was a university student in Berlin and Paris, hardly the traditional background of a Hasidic rebbe. His decisions must have seemed problematic at the time. Germany was the birthplace the Jewish enlightenment, the Reform movement, and *Wissenschaft das Judentums*, the academic study of Judaism, all of which were anathema to traditional Orthodoxy. Its Jewish population was highly assimilated, and even its Orthodox segment was far from the traditionalist model championed by Yosef Yitshak. From that perspective, Paris, home to the bohemian and artistic circles for which it was justly famous, was arguably worse. While some Hasidim have asserted that Yosef Yitshak encouraged—or even instructed—Schneerson to go to Western Europe, there is no evidence for these claims. (Yosef Yitshak did support his daughter and son-in-law financially and paid Schneerson's university tuition.) According to other accounts, Yosef Yitshak was infuriated by his son-in-law's decisions, leading to "screaming sessions" behind closed doors.[13] Why, then, did Schneerson leave Yosef Yitshak's orbit and go to Berlin?

The question has puzzled outside observers as well as Chabad Hasidim, who have tried to provide explanations consistent with their conception of Schneerson as a holy man. It has been suggested that Schneerson was pursuing a mystical mission in Berlin, elevating the "sparks of holiness" from the "shells of impurity" to bring the messianic age closer. Others, in a more pragmatic, albeit anachronistic, vein, have claimed that Schneerson's years in Western Europe provided him with the skills he later used to develop his outreach operation in America. Schneerson neither wrote about his decisions at the time nor discussed them later, leaving a mystery that may never be solved.

But Schneerson may have had reasons for going to Berlin that even his father-in-law could appreciate. He was happiest when left alone to pursue his studies, and in Riga he would have been subject to the constant pressure of his father-in-law's court. Even in Warsaw he would have attracted attention as the son-in-law of the Lubavitcher rebbe. Living in Berlin, a bustling metropolis where Hasidic Jews were rare, allowed him to keep a low profile. Throughout those years he dressed in modern European style, favoring gray, double-breasted suits, and wore his beard short. According to his nephew, Barry Gourary, he covered his head with a beret. Ironically, the big city was not a place to raise his profile but where he could escape into obscurity. In an unusually revealing letter to Yosef Yitshak from the spring of 1930, Schneerson confessed: "There are people for whom the central, overwhelming focus of their lives is in the world of thought, the world of ideas, and their main activities . . . are focused inward . . . While I do not consider it to be a particular virtue, it seems to me that . . . I am such a person."[14] If anything, Yosef Yitshak's frustrations stemmed from Schneerson's unwillingness to display his qualities publicly. "Hiding from people doesn't lead to anything," he wrote to Chaya Mushka in 1933. "It causes me tremendous aggravation."[15]

Still, there were clear bonds of affection between the two men. In 1928, Schneerson began keeping a journal in which he recorded his father-in-law's habits, customs, and teachings. The document, written in Schneerson's small, precise handwriting on fifty loose-leaf sheets of paper, is almost entirely devoid of personal details, but it is filled with Chabad history and lore. Although the major influence on his religious and intellectual development had been his father, and to some extent the Rogatchover Gaon, the weight of influence was shifting toward his father-in-law. The esteem went both ways. Yosef Yitshak sent fatherly letters to his daughter and son-in-law, inquiring about their lives and chiding them for not writing more often. Both at Schneerson's wedding and on later occasions, Yosef Yitshak praised his son-in-law's scholarship, saying that this shy young man was a master of both the Babylonian and the Jerusalem Talmuds, the major Talmudic commentaries, and all of Hasidic literature. In letters he referred to Schneerson as a "genius" or even "the true genius."[16] Schneerson's writings from the period are a testament to this scholarship; aside from his journal they included essays on halakhic and Talmudic subjects, reflections on Hasidic thought and spirituality, almost three hundred pages of indices to Hasidic works, a catalog of unpublished Hasidic texts, and a manuscript of footnotes to Shneur Zalman's *Tanya*.

Yosef Yitshak may have even understood Schneerson's interest in science. Unlike some of his peers in Berlin, who were pursuing degrees in philosophy, Schneerson was following the prosaic path of an engineer. Although secular studies were frowned upon by Hasidism, there was never an objection to learning a trade. And despite Chabad's antipathy toward secular wisdom, its leaders made exceptions, especially for themselves. Schneerson's namesake, the Tsemah Tsedek, had dabbled in geometry, and Yosef Yitshak's library included an assortment of secular books, some of which he probably read himself. Shneur Zalman—who likely studied some scientific and philosophical subjects—wrote that one who engages in secular learning "is included among those who waste their time in profane matters," but it was permissible if "he employs [this wisdom] . . . in the service of God and his Torah."[17]

In Schneerson's case, not only was he learning a trade, but he was drawing spiritual value from his education. In an entry in his notebook under the title "Physics," likely written in the late 1920s, he reflects on Pascal's Law, which states that when pressure is applied to a confined and incompressible fluid, the change of pressure is transmitted uniformly throughout the fluid. The Torah, Schneerson wrote, is compared in the Talmud to seven liquids, and "it is in this physical, confined environment [of the world] that the laws of the Torah take hold." Thus, he continued, when pressure is increased due to observance of the commandments, "the confined environment and pressure causes increasing height in the barometer, in this case meaning a rise in the level of the soul."[18] In the following entry, "Arithmetic," he compares the geometry of a circle to the degrees of Divine emanation, with the center of the circle representing the Divine source, as well as the Sabbath among the days of the week. While such statements might be read as acknowledging the insight to be gained from secular learning, they are equally an assertion that the laws of mathematics, geometry, and physics are encompassed by the Torah's teachings.

This idea, perhaps, gave his life in Western Europe its greatest ideological significance. In traditional Judaism's confrontation with modernity, different groups took up positions along a spectrum of accommodation and rejection. German Jewish Orthodoxy, with its embrace of secular studies and certain laxities in observance, took the path of accommodation. Hasidic groups in Hungary went the opposite route, adopting the maxim "All innovation is forbidden." Some groups, like the Agudath Israel, a pan-Orthodox political party, occupied a middle position, embracing modern organizational techniques while rejecting perceived changes to ideology or observance. For Schneerson, the crisis of modernity couldn't be solved at any of these points. Voluntary ghettoization was not feasible in the long term and would alienate Jewish youth. According to the policies laid down by Chabad leaders, accommodation was not acceptable either. Moreover, Judaism was meant to encompass every time and place, and putting it in opposition to modernity would place a restriction on the Torah itself. Instead, he concluded, the solution must lie elsewhere.

In a journal entry written around 1933, Schneerson reflected that after the sin of Adam and Eve, serving God only in a place of holiness was no longer possible. Rather, a person had to "do his service below, to go down to the place of the husks in order to purify them, for that is why man was exiled from the Garden of Eden."[19] Almost two decades later, in a 1952 talk given on the anniversary of Yosef Yitshak's release from exile, Schneerson spoke about his father-in-law's decision to live in Leningrad rather than a small town. In this he resembled his biblical namesake Joseph, who, unlike his pastoral forefathers, became a viceroy in Egypt. And yet, Schneerson said, Joseph maintained his purity "because Joseph *was above the world completely*, and therefore the matters of the world did not distract him from the service of God." So, too, Schneerson taught, it was necessary for his followers to live in the world and be immune to its temptations, to be a part of society and remain unaffected by its ethos, to embrace its opportunities while granting nothing in return. "And this power [Yosef Yitshak] bequeathed to *us*," he continued. "In every place where we are found . . . not only are we not influenced at all . . . but the opposite: we are engaged with the dissemination of Torah."[20] Modernity was not at odds with Judaism, he believed, but could be encompassed within it.

Perhaps this attitude is what so endeared Schneerson to Yosef Yitshak in the first place. In the 1920s, while visiting Yosef Yitshak and courting Chaya Mushka, he was paying visits to the Pulkovo Observatory and attending classes at Leningrad University. While corresponding with the Rogatchover Gaon, he was trying to predict an eclipse. And unlike his brother Leibel, who was torn between the competing ideologies of Hasidism, Zionism, and socialism, he never saw any conflict or contradiction among his interests. For him, this did not imply a project of synthesis or reconciliation between Jewish and secular scholarship, or between the Hasidic and modern worlds. Rather, engagement with science and secular learning demonstrated to

Schneerson the all-encompassing scope of Judaism. For Yosef Yitshak, a traditional leader at a time when tradition was being swept away, this brazen self-confidence must have been powerfully attractive. For Schneerson, his university years may have seemed like a necessary test of this hypothesis, with himself as the test subject. And where better to perform the experiment than Berlin?

Upon returning to Germany in early 1929, Schneerson and Chaya Mushka settled into an apartment not far from Berlin's old Jewish Quarter. It was also close to the neoclassical edifices of Friedrich Wilhelm University, where Schneerson returned to his classes and Chaya Mushka began studying German at the Institute for Foreign Students. Along with his university studies, Schneerson attended lectures at the Hildesheimer seminary, saw friends like Soloveitchik, and read the newspapers. He prayed at a small Hasidic synagogue called Anshei Polin and spent some of his time acquiring rare books and making copies of the city's library catalogs for Yosef Yitshak. Both he and Chaya Mushka enjoyed reading, and one acquaintance recalled him sitting backwards in a swivel chair, discussing Russian literature for hours.

In the summer of 1929, Yosef Yitshak left Riga for a year-long fundraising trip to Palestine and the United States, accompanied by his older son-in-law, Shmaryahu Gourary. While Yosef Yitshak was gone, his wife, Nehama Dina; Gourary's wife, Chana; and their son, Shalom Dov Ber, went to stay near the Schneersons in Berlin. Later in life Shalom Dov Ber—by then known as Barry—described how he and Schneerson walked around town snapping photos with a Leica camera that Yosef Yitshak had bought his grandson as a gift and how Schneerson took him to the zoo. Around the same time, Schneerson was reunited with his younger brother Leibel, who had escaped from the Soviet Union under a false identity. When he arrived in

Berlin, he was suffering from typhus and lived with the Schneer-sons until he recovered. The next year he enrolled at the uni-versity and took courses in mathematics. As Barry Gourary re-called, "[Schneerson] and his brother were two opposites in appearance. While [Schneerson] walked around Berlin in a beret and a well-tailored suit, his brother wore a pair of slacks with his shirt out. While my uncle's hair was short, Leibel's was long and wild. However, it was clear that they cared for each other."[21] In Berlin, Leibel became engaged to Regina Milgram, a Lodz native who worked as a laboratory technician at the Hufeland Hospital. In 1933 the couple returned to her parents' home in Danzig before emigrating to Palestine, where they eventually married in Tel Aviv.

Schneerson, despite his cultured exterior, was privately, and to some extent secretly, pursuing a regimen of pietistic practices. According to one report, he obtained a key to the community mikveh, or ritual bath, and immersed himself each afternoon—an unheard-of habit for German Jewry, whose mikvehs were reserved for women. He fasted regularly, which worried his fa-ther. "You are not a Sampson in strength," Levi Yitshak cautioned him in 1929.[22] In a letter from 1935, Levi Yitshak wrote, "My beloved son, I hereby warn you not to undertake additional stringencies in matters of eating and drinking . . . endeavor to look after your health."[23] During Jewish holidays Schneerson was noticed for his apparent fervor and devotion. While in Riga for the Jewish New Year in 1929, Althaus observed that he broke out in tears and "extended his personal prayers for more than two and a half hours."[24] In late 1932 or early 1933 he began putting on four pairs of tefillin every day, each constructed according to the opinion of a different medieval authority. While outwardly he seemed to be a normal university student, if still religiously observant, inwardly he was exploring hidden spiritual terrain.

For four years, life in Berlin was filled with pleasant, quiet routines: classes at the university, lectures at the Hildesheimer seminary, personal scholarly projects, errands for Yosef Yitshak, social occasions with his brother and friends, and occasional trips to Riga. But Germany was becoming a precarious place for Jews. Highbrow antisemitism had become widely acceptable during the period of the Weimar Republic, and Jews were often blamed for the country's defeat in World War I. In 1929, following the international stock market crash, the National Socialist German Workers' Party (NSDAP)—otherwise known as the Nazi Party—promoted a referendum that sought to renounce the Treaty of Versailles and stop payment of war reparations. Although the effort was unsuccessful, it gave the Nazis legitimacy and was followed by electoral gains in 1930 and 1932, when the NSDAP became the largest party in the Reichstag. In early 1933, after failing to form a majority government, President Paul von Hindenberg appointed Adolf Hitler chancellor; a month later an arson attack on the Reichstag and the Reichstag Fire Decree led to the suspension of civil liberties and mass arrests of Communist politicians and party members. In March the Reichstag adopted the Enabling Act, allowing Hitler to pass laws without parliamentary approval, and in July Hitler proclaimed the NSDAP to be the only legitimate political party in Germany. When Hindenberg died in August 1934, Hitler combined the offices of president and chancellor, making him dictator over Germany.

The Nazis soon turned political success into violence. Following the party's 1930 parliamentary gains the paramilitary *Sturmabteilung*, known as the Brownshirts, smashed the windows of Jewish storefronts in Potsdamer Platz; its greater victories two years later were celebrated by torch-lit marches through the streets. In March 1932 the Dachau concentration camp was opened for political prisoners, and over the coming months the Nazis would instigate book burnings, boycotts of Jewish businesses, the repeal of Jewish emancipation, and the purging of Jews and Communists from the civil service. The Schneersons didn't wait to find out what the future held. In the spring of 1932 they left Berlin, and aside from a few brief visits, did not return. For the next seven years they would live and study in Paris, where Schneerson would finally achieve his goal of becoming an engineer.

Paris, despite its reputation as the bohemian capital of Europe, was a reasonable place for the Schneersons to go. The city had received periodic influxes of Jewish refugees since the 1880s and, by the 1930s, had a population of around 150,000 Jews, many of them Yiddish-speaking immigrants. Like Berlin, Lubavitcher rebbes had visited the city, and it was home to several of Schneerson's relatives, including Edmea Schneersohn, a first cousin of Yosef Yitshak's, who studied at the Sorbonne, and Isaac Schneersohn, a distant cousin, who had been a crown rabbi and liberal politician in Russia and was now a successful industrialist. In 1935 they were joined by Schneour Zalman Schneersohn, a first cousin of Levi Yitshak's, who would play a major role in the city's Orthodox community.

While most of the city's Jews were clustered in Le Marais, a small neighborhood of winding streets on the right bank of the Seine River, the Schneersons chose to live in the Left Bank district of Montparnasse. After a brief stay at 78 Rue Blomet, in the 15th Arrondissement, they moved into a small studio apartment at the Hotel Max, a six-story apartment building at 9 Rue de Boulard, just around the corner from the Montparnasse Cemetery. The building was located between the two campuses of the École spéciale des travaux publics, du bâtiment et de l'industrie (Special School for Public Works in Building and Industry), or ESTP, the engineering school Schneerson would attend. Although by 1933 the neighborhood was no longer the creative mecca it had been in the 1920s, it was still home to an international assortment of writers and artists. Their neighbors at the Hotel Max included a Hungarian journalist, two Russian painters, a boxer from Martinique, immigrants from China and Italy, and a French waiter. The neighborhood also included Gertrude Stein, who held her salon a few blocks north at 27 Rue de Fleurus; André Gide, who lived on the nearby Rue Vavin; the photographer Philippe Halsman, who had a studio on the other side of the cemetery; and the American writer Henry Miller, who lived a few blocks south. The area was also home to Chaya Mushka's sister Sheyna and her husband, Mendel Horensztajn, who would study engineering with Schneerson at ESTP. The couple began dating in 1929 and were married in the spring of 1932 in Landvarova (today Letvaris, Lithuania), a small town near Vilna. Unlike Schneerson, Horensztajn was not particularly religious, and Yosef Yitshak encouraged his older son-in-law to befriend the younger and draw him to a more religious lifestyle.

In Paris, Schneerson again faced obstacles to his academic career, including his lack of traditional credentials and his poor command of French. But he gained admission to ESTP on a trial basis and was accepted the next year by the school's mechanical and electrical engineering division. Once again, his plans had to wait. During the 1934–35 school year Schneerson did not return to ESTP, instead spending much of his time looking after Yosef Yitshak, who had been diagnosed with multiple sclerosis. In 1933, Yosef Yitshak moved from Riga to Warsaw and was making visits to doctors and health resorts in Marienbad and Vienna, often accompanied by Schneerson. In the summer of 1935, Yosef Yitshak moved again, this time to Otwock, a resort town fifteen miles southeast of the Polish capital.

Upon returning to Paris in the fall, Schneerson resumed his education, and for the next two years he pursued an engineering degree in earnest. But there was a difference between casually auditing undergraduate courses in physics and philosophy, as he had done in Berlin, and fully participating in the high-level engineering program offered by ESTP. In his first semester his grades put him near the bottom of the class, and he was warned that he would have to "improve in industrial design, particularly in mechanics, if he does not want to repeat the first year's courses."[25] He was impeded by the need to absent himself for the Sabbath on Friday afternoons; during the 1935–36 and 1936–37 school years he managed to accumulate 186 absences. After being briefly suspended for his unexplained disappearances, he received special permission to leave early on Fridays, provided he continued to pass his exams. In his second semester his grades improved, and he ranked twelfth out of a class of thirty-five.

Despite the demands of his engineering program, the Schneersons lived in Paris much as they had in Berlin. He corresponded with Yosef Yitshak and with his father, particularly on matters relating to Kabbalah and the Jerusalem Talmud. He spent some time doing jobs for Yosef Yitshak, such as editing his talks, preparing an anthology of his letters, handling some of his financial transactions, and attending to him personally when he came for extended visits in 1936 and 1938. Chaya Mushka continued her studies, taking French classes at the Alliance française. She and her husband likely enjoyed the city's museums and libraries, including the Sainte-Geneviève Library near the ESTP main campus. Schneerson studied privately at home with friends, gave occasional classes at Parisian synagogues, and prayed at the Chabad synagogue in Le Marais, a fifty-minute walk from home. In 1935 the city's ultra-Orthodox community asked him to become their rabbi, an offer Yosef Yitshak urged him to consider. "I don't have the words to express what joy this development has brought me, and how happy I would be if you would accept," he wrote. "It would bring me many measures of good health and would gladden my broken heart."[26] Schneerson declined the position and continued his efforts to become an engineer.

In the summer of 1937, the ESTP board of examiners concluded that "Mr. Mendel Schneerson should be awarded the degree of Mechanical and Electrical Engineer, after he has completed the statutory three-month internship."[27] Eight months later he received his diploma, and the couple moved from their small studio apartment to a larger home at 7 Villa Robert Lindet, in the 15th Arrondissement. The move was complicated by Schneerson's inability to find a job. Chaya Mushka wrote to her in-laws, "It was extremely difficult to decide because there are no jobs and it does not seem that any are coming soon . . . Mendel insisted that we had to decide one way or the other as there was no point thinking about it again and again."[28] Possibly to maintain his student status, Schneerson registered in the faculty of sciences at the Sorbonne. Although there is no evidence that he attended classes or received academic credit, his enrollment records for the following two years have survived.

While Schneerson looked for work, the couple began the process of applying for French citizenship. Until 1933 they traveled on Soviet passports; when those expired, they had obtained Nansen passports, issued by the League of Nations, which allowed them to travel but left them stateless. They had applied for Latvian citizenship, but their application was denied. (Yosef Yitshak's application and those of other family members were successful.) Now they were trying again. "We are doing all we can to be granted permanent residency," Chaya Mushka wrote to her in-laws in 1938. "Without it, life is extremely difficult."[29] In the course of Schneerson's deposition at the prefecture of police, he testified that although he didn't have an independent income, he was receiving about forty thousand francs a year from his wife's family, which he used to cover rent, tuition, and support for his parents in the form of food and clothing. He mentioned his brother Berel, who he said was an accountant living with his parents, although Berel was by that time likely living in an institution. In the deposition, as in other documents he was using, Schneerson claimed that he had been born in 1895, making him seven years older than he was. When asked about his activities during the First World War, he said that he had been released from military service "due to his quality as a student" but had served as an assistant to an engineer involved in war production. He also claimed to have been apprenticed to an engineer in Ekaterinoslav from 1920 to 1922 and to have studied at the Ekaterinoslav Polytechnic from 1923 to 1925 and in Leningrad from 1926 to 1927. While some of these claims were true (Schneerson maintained throughout his life that he had studied in a university in Russia), others were likely fabricated to improve the couple's chances of gaining citizenship. His case was strengthened by the fact that he and Chaya Mushka had become fluent in French and, as the interviewer noted, were "well assimilated" to French life.[30] As Schneerson rightfully claimed, he had no hope of returning to his native Ukraine.

Still, it was not a good time for Eastern European Jews to become French citizens. An influx of Jewish refugees from Germany had prompted a conservative backlash, and grants of citizenship or residency were difficult to obtain. In June 1939 their petition was denied, making any future in France extremely uncertain. In a letter to his parents Schneerson wrote that he had "various schemes regarding a position, or a partnership in my field," but that "some of them have already passed away, as they are no more than dreams."[31] For now their residency relied on Schneerson's student status, but how long could that last? If they had to leave Paris, where would they go?

Meanwhile, the situation in Europe was growing worse. In 1938 the Nazis carried out the Kristallnacht pogrom, and in January 1939, Hitler declared that war would mean the annihilation of Jews in Europe. In March, Germany occupied Czechoslovakia; in August it signed the Molotov-Ribbentrop nonaggression pact with the Soviet Union; and in September it launched the war against Poland, directly threatening Yosef Yitshak and his family. Then, in May 1940, Germany invaded France.

5

————◆◆◆————

A Home in America

WHEN THE WAR BROKE OUT, Yosef Yitshak was at home in Otwock. Although the German army took more than a week to reach Warsaw, the town was under aerial bombardment almost immediately. In the first days of the invasion a bomb hit a nearby orphanage, killing ten children. Another hit Yosef Yitshak's home, although no one was injured. Shmaryahu Gourary described the mood that Friday night: "The police issued an order prohibiting a fire or any other sort of light in the city; total darkness was to prevail . . . The chandeliers hung unlit, shivering in the eerie atmosphere."[1] With Yosef Yitshak's blessing, six American yeshiva students fled to Riga, and Yosef Yitshak wrote to Mordekhai Dubin, asking for help. On September 4, with the situation growing more dangerous in Otwock, Yosef Yitshak left for Warsaw in a car provided by the Latvian consulate. He took his family, a small group of students, and a collection of Chabad manuscripts, leaving the rest of his library and personal belongings behind.

In Warsaw he moved in with a family of Chabad Hasidim and awaited further developments. On September 8 the German army reached the city, and the next week—the start of the Jewish High Holy Days—put the Polish capital under siege. As the city was being bombed, Yosef Yitshak and his family moved from building to building and cellar to cellar, eventually taking shelter at the home of the Chabad publisher and philanthropist Zalman Shmotkin. By September 24 the city was under attack by more than a thousand German aircraft; the next day, "Black Monday," it was struck with hundreds of tons of explosives and incendiary bombs. Four days later, the Polish capital fell.

An ocean away in America, Yosef Yitshak's followers were mounting a rescue effort.[2] With the help of Sam Kramer, an Orthodox attorney and the son of Lubavitcher immigrants, the Chabad activist Israel Jacobson hired Max Rhoade, a politically connected lawyer, to secure American visas for Yosef Yitshak and his family. Yosef Yitshak's followers also reached out to Attorney General Benjamin Cohen and Supreme Court Justice Louis Brandeis, whom Yosef Yitshak had met during his fundraising trip of 1929. The Lubavitchers' efforts in America were successful. On October 2, Cohen wrote to Robert T. Pell, a senior official in the State Department, asking for help. The next day Pell contacted Helmuth Wohlthat, a German and a member of the Nazi Party who specialized in international industry and economics, to see if he would be willing to save "one of the leading Jewish scholars in the world."[3] Wohlthat was strategically chosen. He had studied at Columbia University in the early 1930s and had forged a relationship with Pell after the Evian conference on Jewish refugees in 1938. Seeing an opportunity to curry goodwill with the United States, Wohlthat secretly contacted Admiral Wilhelm Canaris, the head of German military intelligence, the Abwehr. Canaris, a skeptical Nazi who disapproved of SS atrocities and thought the invasion of Poland a mistake, enlisted Major Ernst Bloch, a distinguished veteran of

World War I and one of his most trusted officers. Bloch was a *mischling*, a German of part-Jewish ancestry, who had been declared of "German blood" by Hitler in 1939. Along with three other soldiers, two of whom were also mischlinge, Bloch was instructed to find Yosef Yitshak and bring him to safety.

Locating Yosef Yitshak was another matter. Bloch and his colleagues had to maneuver through the ruins of Warsaw without arousing the suspicions of the SS to find a rabbi who did not know of their mission and did not want to be found. Jews in the city were naturally unwilling to divulge the location of a Hasidic leader to a Nazi officer. Eventually, the information came from the Americans. Brandeis was informed of Yosef Yitshak's address by the Chabad lawyer Arthur Rabinowitz and relayed it, via Cohen and Pell, to the U.S. chargé d'affaires in Germany. At the end of November, Bloch found Yosef Yitshak's apartment and, after some confusion, convinced the residents he was there to help. Once he had obtained fuel coupons, train tickets, and military clearances for SS checkpoints, Bloch loaded Yosef Yitshak and his family onto a truck and headed for the train station. There the family received first-class tickets and boarded a train filled with Nazi officials and soldiers. On December 15 the group reached Berlin, where they stayed overnight at the Jewish Federation before boarding another train for Riga, accompanied by representatives of the Latvian embassy. On December 17, Yosef Yitshak crossed into Latvia.

In Riga, Yosef Yitshak and his family were able to recover from their ordeal. There were health issues to contend with; at the end of January Yosef Yitshak fell and broke his right hand, which required a cast for three weeks. His mother, now eighty years old, needed emergency surgery for an abdominal hernia. But with a Soviet invasion looming, they couldn't stay long. Money was a problem; despite the generosity of Yosef Yitshak's followers and a stash smuggled in by his daughter Chana under her clothes, funds were low. Finally, in early February, they received their American visas. A month later they took an eighteen-seat airplane to Stockholm and then a train to Gothenburg, where they boarded the SS *Drottningholm* for the transatlantic voyage. After two weeks at sea, on a cold and rainy day in March, Yosef Yitshak arrived in New York harbor. A crowd of hundreds had gathered at the pier, including a committee of twenty-five rabbis, a state senator, and a representative of Mayor Fiorello La Guardia. As Yosef Yitshak descended the gangway into the New World, rain falling on his fur hat, his frock coat fluttering in the breeze, he looked like an old steamer himself: battered, buffeted by wind and sea, but still stubbornly afloat. At long last, he had reached his final port.

While Yosef Yitshak was stepping foot on American soil, Schneerson and Chaya Mushka were in France, trying to get visas. The Immigration Act of 1924, which restricted immigration to an annual quota of 154,000 people, included an exemption for clergy that Chabad was able to exploit. In letters to American officials, the lawyer Max Rhoade had argued that Yosef Yitshak was a "sort of pope" and that his situation was similar "to what might happen if war conditions in Italy compelled . . . the Vatican to seek temporary refuge in the United States."[4] On this basis, Chabad's lawyers had proposed that the entire group be admitted as a single religious "hierarchy," rather than as individuals. Schneerson and Chaya Mushka would have been included in this hierarchy if not for his independent streak. In November 1939, while Bloch was looking for Yosef Yitshak in Warsaw, they filed an application for ordinary quota visas at the American consulate in Paris, with Schneerson's profession listed as "engineer." That June, their visas, which had been approved based on their membership in Yosef Yitshak's hierarchy, were revoked because of the conflicting application. By then the Germans had invaded Belgium and Holland, and on June 5 they began operation *Fall Rot* (Case Red), outflanking the Maginot Line and advancing south toward Paris. Fearing imminent occupation, the couple packed their bags and joined an exodus of Jews fleeing the city. Around June 11 they boarded a train for Vichy, days before the German invasion.

For two months the Schneersons remained in Vichy along with a swelling Jewish refugee population. In August they fled the city, now home to the collaborationist French government, and went to Nice, where they remained for the next several months. That fall they received word that their non-quota visa applications had again been denied, since there was no proof that Schneerson was actually clergy. As a last-ditch effort they transferred their application to the consulate in Marseille, where the U.S.-based Hebrew Immigrant Aid Society had successfully facilitated the emigration of several thousand French Jews.

Like Nice, Marseille was home to a community of Jewish refugees trying to get out of Europe. Zalman Schachter (later Schachter-Shalomi), a Polish-born, Vienna-raised rabbi who later founded the Jewish Renewal movement, was then sixteen years old and had come to the city with his family after being released from a French internment camp. In the synagogue he noticed an unusual man. Unlike most Hasidim, who wore black, he wore a gray suit and fedora. But unlike non-Hasidim, who were clean-shaven, he had a beard. After hearing him speak French, Schachter concluded that he must be Moroccan.

As Schachter told his student Netanel Miles-Yépez more than sixty years later, that year, on the holiday of Tu BiShvat, he and a group of students gathered for a lecture by one of the local rabbis. To his surprise, the lecturer turned out to be "the Moroccan," or, as he later learned, Schneerson. "He spoke about raising the sparks of holiness buried in the shells of our ignorance as a prelude to the coming of the Messiah and lamented, as we all did, that the Messiah had not yet come," Schachter recalled. "Not one of us was unaffected—we were all children of the Holocaust years, not knowing what our fate would be, and dreaming of redemption." As Schneerson finished his talk "he started to cough, which was a cover for the fact that he had begun to cry."[5] By then Schneerson may have known that five days earlier, on February 7, the State Department had authorized the consulate at Marseille to grant ordinary quota visas to him and Chaya Mushka. Now they just had to get out.

By the spring of 1941 the only practical route from southern France to the United States was through Lisbon, and with the influx of refugees into Portugal, the couple once again had to wait. Finally, in late May, the Schneersons received Portuguese entry visas, and in early June they left Marseille. Getting tickets for a transatlantic ship was another problem. Once again, help came from America. On June 11, Mordechai Bistritzky, a Boyaner Hasid, met with Yosef Yitshak in New York. Bistritzky's parents-in-law, Lubavitcher Hasidim named Levi and Ruchama Lagovier, had tickets for the ship *Serpa Pinto*, which was leaving Lisbon the next day. But the Lagoviers were still in Spain, unable to get Portuguese visas. Learning that Yosef Yitshak's daughter and son-in-law had the opposite problem, Bistritzky offered to transfer the Lagoviers' tickets to their name. The next day the Schneersons boarded the *Serpa Pinto;* less than two weeks later, on June 23, 1941, they arrived in New York. The Lagoviers, having lost their chance to escape from Europe, died in Auschwitz the following year.

Before 1940, Chabad was a marginal force in America. Like other Hasidic leaders, Yosef Yitshak had discouraged his followers from emigrating, fearing assimilation and the loss of religious ties. Such fears were well founded. Between the pogroms of 1881 and the mid-1920s, more than two million Eastern European Jews emigrated to the United States. But until the postwar arrival of Hasidic Holocaust survivors, the country was barren ground for Hasidic life. Even those who maintained their religion at home rarely exhibited it in public. Few men wore yarmulkes—let alone beards and sidelocks—and the practice of ritual purity among women was almost nonexistent. Those Jews who clung to their traditions could expect their children to discard them at the earliest opportunity. As the saying went, "America is different."

To this Yosef Yitshak replied, "America is not different."[6] In fact, it was America's difference—its democracy, its freedoms—that would provide fruitful opportunities for his son-in-law's efforts, but Yosef Yitshak's priority was to reestablish the community and the institutions he had left behind. Over the previous decades Lubavitcher immigrants had founded synagogues loyal to their particular liturgy and traditions; by the eve of the war they had around two hundred such synagogues throughout the country and claimed 150,000 affiliated members. Although historians dispute these numbers, estimating the Chabad-affiliated population of the United States as 40,000 or fewer, these synagogues made a decisive contribution to Chabad Hasidism in America. In 1924 they formed an organization called Agudat Hasidim Anshei Chabad (Union of Hasidim People of Chabad), and in 1940 they formed Agudas Chasidei Chabad (Union of Chabad Hasidim). (The two organizations coexisted until 1952, when the former was officially disbanded.) These groups, and their affiliated synagogues, provided Yosef Yitshak with options. He entertained proposals to settle in New Jersey and Chicago, but after his experiences in the Jewish hinterlands of Rostov and Riga, he decided that Lubavitch would have a greater impact if it was based in the country's most vibrant Jewish community, in New York.

Upon arriving in the city, Yosef Yitshak and his family settled in the Greystone Hotel on West 91st Street, while a hastily assembled building committee looked for a suitable residence and headquarters. After some searching, they landed on a 14,500-

Chabad's headquarters at 770 Eastern Parkway, Brooklyn, became a symbol
of the movement with its own theological significance. (Nick Russell)

square-foot three-story red brick mansion in the Crown Heights
neighborhood of Brooklyn. Until 1938 the house had been occupied by an abortionist, Dr. S. Robert Kahn, and it had been
repossessed by the bank after he was arrested for the death of
one of his patients. (Kahn was acquitted of manslaughter but was
convicted of tax evasion and sentenced to two-and-a-half years
in jail.) The doctor had decorated the property with Italian tile
and oak doors and outfitted it with wheelchair ramps and an
elevator, an important consideration for the ailing rebbe. The
committee raised $5,000 as a down payment toward the $30,000
purchase price, and Yosef Yitshak committed to a monthly rent
of $200; his older son-in-law, Shmaryahu Gourary, agreed to
pay $70. In addition to apartments for Yosef Yitshak and his chil-
dren, the building would house a synagogue, a yeshiva, a library,
and administrative offices. On August 16, 1940, the building at
770 Eastern Parkway officially changed hands, and Yosef Yitshak moved in just before the start of the High Holy Days.

When Yosef Yitshak chose Crown Heights as his new base of operations, the area was a well-to-do residential section of Brooklyn with a large and diverse Jewish community. The main thoroughfare was Eastern Parkway, a tree-lined boulevard designed by Frederick Law Olmstead in the 1870s that ran from Prospect Park in the west to the immigrant neighborhood of Brownsville in the east. Handsome prewar apartment buildings overlooked the parkway, while spacious single-family homes occupied the cozy streets to its south. The new Lubavitch center, facing Eastern Parkway at the corner of Kingston Avenue, was located right in the middle of this bustling scene. The population of the neighborhood was upwardly mobile, and many of Yosef Yitshak's followers, who could not afford to live in Crown Heights, would walk in on Sabbaths and holidays from the adjoining neighborhoods of Brownsville or Flatbush. When the Schneersons arrived, they joined the rest of the family in 770, staying in a small room that would later become Schneerson's office. The space was cramped, and they soon moved to a more spacious apartment on New York Avenue, a few blocks away.

Even though Yosef Yitshak and his family had found a comfortable refuge in Brooklyn, millions of Jews were still in mortal danger. In Europe, Yosef Yitshak tried to save dozens of Lubavitchers in Poland, Latvia, and France, but with little success. He had gotten visas for eleven families in Riga, but they were unable to travel and could not escape. After arriving in America, he began raising money and petitioning American authorities to save Lubavitcher students and managed to help thirty young men escape from Vilna to Kobe, Japan, and then to Shanghai, where most of them spent the war. His efforts were limited by his unwillingness to work with non-Orthodox and non-Jewish religious figures, as well as by his opposition to public demonstrations and protests. But Yosef Yitshak's main strategy had nothing to do with raising money or political activism. The only solution to Nazism, he believed, was messianic redemption, which would be brought about by repentance. His slogan throughout the war years was "repentance immediately, redemption immediately."

Theodicy, or the effort to "justify God's ways to men," has always posed a special challenge to Hasidism, which asserts that all of creation is nothing but a manifestation of God.[7] Evil, therefore, does not have an independent existence, and everything, including the most horrifying suffering, is of Divine origin. The Jewish exile, Yosef Yitshak contended, was not an accident of history but a Divinely ordained process intended to spur the Jewish people to repentance. The suffering of European Jewry under the Nazis, a calamity unprecedented even in the tragedy-strewn history of the Jews, was an extreme but necessary measure toward that end. Although the Nazis were responsible for their crimes—and, Yosef Yitshak contended, their barbarity was a form of unwitting panic at the prospect of impending redemption—the catastrophe could be relieved only by appealing to God. The current tribulations were the "birth pangs of the Messiah" and presented the Jewish people with a final choice: repent or die.

Shortly after arriving in the United States, Yosef Yitshak founded Machne Israel (Camp of Israel) and placed Schneerson at its head. The mission of the organization was to inspire a religious revival among American Jews and provide safe harbor from the violence of the pre-messianic era. It promoted the observance of kashrut (dietary laws), the Sabbath, family purity, and the wearing of tefillin; formed groups to say Psalms and visit the sick; conducted Torah classes for working men; encouraged its members to learn the Mishna by heart; and created a division for Jewish farmers. It also published a monthly journal called *Hakeri'ah VeHaKedusha* (Reading and Holiness) that aired Yosef Yitshak's eschatological views. Between May 1941 and September 1942, he released four proclamations, as well as several follow-up statements, some of which were placed in secular Jewish news-papers like the Yiddish *Morgn zhournal* (Morning Journal) and the Chicago *Jewish Daily Courier*.[8] "'Immediate redemption!' is not a fantasy," he wrote in his second proclamation. "It is not just a pious hope, not now. It is the call of the time. Redemption is behind our backs. It comes with quick footsteps. Fortresses will fall like splinters. Nations and lands will be overturned over-night. The whole earth will be shaken apart . . . Now, in our generation, God's word through His prophets will be fulfilled!"[9] In September 1942 he announced that the coming Jewish year of 5703 would be the last before redemption.

In the meantime, he argued, the Jewish people needed to busy themselves with repentance, not only to hasten the arrival of the Messiah but also to escape the terror that preceded it. Putting their hope in earthly measures, including the Allied war effort, only represented an "exile within exile"—a blindness from which his organization, Machne Israel, would rescue them. Without such an intervention the Holocaust would spread to American shores, and those unworthy of redemption would be killed. Ultimately, Yosef Yitshak believed, Jews would turn back to God, and the war would end with Divine victory, the destruc-tion of all oppressors, and the commencement of the messianic age. "Believe, and you will thank us and live to attain salvation and consolation!" he wrote. "Believe and follow our call, and you will, with God's help, avoid all the birth pangs of redemp-tion! . . . You will not have to wait long for the whole world to know that this is true!"[10] Tragically, for the Jews being murdered in Europe, redemption was not forthcoming.

It is unclear whether Schneerson shared Yosef Yitshak's views, although as the head of Machne Israel, Schneerson was associated with them. In later years he developed a form of Ho-locaust theodicy that was far more ambivalent than Yosef Yit-shak's fire-and-brimstone rhetoric. While Yosef Yitshak didn't blame individual victims for their fates, he considered the catastrophe a collective punishment for the nation's sins—a position Schneerson did not endorse. When Elazar Menachem Man Shach, one of the preeminent rabbinic figures in Israel, warned that the sins of secular Jews were likely to cause a second Holocaust, Schneerson protested vehemently. "We have no explanation whatsoever for the Shoah [Holocaust] . . . and certainly the explanation is not punishment for sin," he declared. "The destruction of six million Jews with such great cruelty . . . *Satan himself* could not calculate the sins of that generation to justify, God forbid, such a harsh punishment. Justifying the Shoah in this [way] . . . desecrates the honor of the martyrs who were killed in the sanctification of God's name."[11]

Schneerson didn't see this lack of explanation as an impediment to faith. In a 1965 letter to the writer and Holocaust survivor Elie Wiesel, he pointed out that even asking the question implied an underlying belief in a higher justice. In a 1984 letter he elaborated: "To your question . . . 'Why did God permit the Holocaust?' the only answer we can give is: 'Only God knows.' However, the fact that there is no answer to this question is, in itself, proof that one is not required to know the answer, nor understand it, in order to fulfill one's purpose in life."[12] To the extent that Schneerson did find causes for the Holocaust, he blamed it on the secularization of society, a concern that had repercussions throughout his leadership. As he wrote to Wiesel, "It turned out that it was no contradiction for someone to be a philosopher or a poet with fine manners, who participated in high society and a salon in Berlin, and then go to Treblinka and do all the things that were done there . . . The history of Nazism clearly demonstrates that we cannot rely on the human instinct for justice and integrity."[13] The best response to the Holocaust was to increase religious observance among the Jewish people and religious faith among people generally, which was the only way to ensure moral behavior.

Although Schneerson refrained from embracing his father-in-law's militant theodicy, he was profoundly affected by Yosef Yitshak's apocalyptic messianism. In his letters from the 1940s he would sign off with the slogan "repentance immediately, redemption immediately," and in later years he insisted that Yosef Yitshak's call was not just a message for its time but applied throughout the decades of his own leadership. While Schneerson didn't blame the Jewish people for their suffering, the Holocaust still contributed to the unfolding messianic saga. Yosef Yitshak declared the catastrophe the "birth pangs of the Messiah," the tribulations necessary before redemption could occur. Although the Messiah hadn't arrived, Schneerson believed that his father-in-law was correct; the Holocaust was the "birth pangs," and now the Messiah could arrive at any time. Although the destruction seemed to end in messianic disappointment, it also set the stage for renewed messianic expectation.

As the war wound down, so did Yosef Yitshak's messianism. In 1945, *Hakeri'ah VeHaKedushah* stopped publishing, and the slogan "repentance immediately, redemption immediately" dropped from use. The Holocaust had happened, and the call to repentance had failed to prevent it. So, too, any rescue efforts that once showed promise were now irrelevant. Countless Lubavitchers had died in concentration camps or Soviet gulags or were stranded behind the Iron Curtain. The only thing left was to gather the survivors and rebuild.

Like the rest of the Lubavitcher community, Schneerson suffered grievous losses. In 1939 his father was arrested by Soviet authorities and sentenced to five years of exile in the village of Shieli, Kazakhstan. As Chana Schneerson wrote in her memoir, the conditions there were abominable. In Shieli the exiles suffered from starvation, disease, insects, hostile locals, unpitying officials, and endless mud. After the term of exile was over, the couple was able to move to the city of Alma-Ata (now Almaty), but by that time Levi Yitshak's fragile health was in precipitous decline. On August 9, 1944, he died in Alma-Ata at the age of sixty-six.

While Levi Yitshak and Chana were in exile, the German army occupied Dnepropetrovsk. Most of the Jewish population was evacuated during the Soviet retreat, but the Jews left behind were nearly all murdered, including the Schneersons' second son, Berel. In Nikolaev, the Schneersons' remaining family members were either murdered by the Germans or, like Levi Yitshak, died after being sent into Soviet exile. Mendel Horensztajn, who had studied engineering with Schneerson in Paris, returned to Otwock with his wife, Sheyna, to care for his ill father. Although Chabad lawyers managed to acquire American visas for the couple, they were unable to get Polish exit visas and were murdered at Treblinka in the fall of 1942. Schneerson's brother Leibel survived the war in Palestine and had a daughter, Dalia, in 1944. In 1950 he moved with his family to England, where he enrolled at the University of Liverpool to pursue a doctorate in physics. Two years later he died of a heart attack, at age forty-six.

Although Schneerson rarely mentioned his losses, they likely weighed on him heavily. He had always been close to his family even when, as with Leibel, they strayed from Orthodoxy. There was, however, one piece of good news. His mother, Chana, who spent the war with Levi Yitshak in Kazakhstan, had gone to Moscow and then escaped from the country using a forged passport. In 1947, after traveling through Poland and a displaced persons camp in Pocking, Germany, she made her way to Paris. Schneerson, who had received his American citizenship the year before and was free to travel abroad, lost no time in packing his bags for France. It was an emotional reunion. At a gathering organized by local Hasidim, Schneerson spoke tearfully, citing the patriarch Jacob and his son Joseph, each of whom had been separated from his parents for twenty-two years. He stayed in Paris for three months while arranging for his mother's emigration to the United States. Chana Schneerson, having lost most of her family, including her husband and middle child, spent the remaining seventeen years of her life living near her eldest son and taking pleasure in his accomplishments.

It took some time for Schneerson to achieve the stature that would later seem inevitable. At first, he was unknown to most Hasidim. Although Yosef Yitshak stressed his younger son-in-law's scholarly bona fides, Schneerson had rarely demonstrated them. He spent the 1930s living in Berlin and Paris, attending a university, and becoming an engineer. With his gray suit and fedora, he didn't dress like a typical Hasid. To many of the old-time Hasidim from Europe, he seemed a bit too modern. But over the following decade Schneerson entered more deeply into Chabad society and became an understated star in Yosef Yitshak's court.

Shortly after arriving in the United States, he began leading *farbrengens*, communal gatherings, on the Sabbath afternoon preceding each new Jewish month. In those early years, around twenty-five or thirty people typically attended the Sabbath morning service, about fifteen of whom would stay to hear Schneerson speak. He also began delivering a weekly Mishna lesson after morning prayers and classes during the intermediate days of Sukkot and Passover. Before long he was attracting a following among younger Hasidim, especially the yeshiva students in 770.

At the same time, Schneerson tried to maintain his independence. Still hoping to practice his profession, he found a position as an electrical engineer at the Brooklyn Navy Yard, where he worked until about 3:30 p.m. every day. But Yosef Yitshak was adamant about enlisting his younger son-in-law into his own activities, and when the engineering job came to an end with the war effort, Schneerson acquiesced. Although he did not relish administrative work, perhaps he understood that these tasks were more important than anything he might accomplish as an engineer, especially in light of Yosef Yitshak's messianic fervor.

While still en route to the United States, Yosef Yitshak had made plans for his American organizations, which he modeled after those in Latvia. These included Machne Israel, Merkos L'Inyonei Chinuch (The Center for Education), which focused on educational programs outside of the Chabad school system, and a publishing house called Karney Hod Torah (Rays of the Torah's Glory), or Kehot. While his older son-in-law, Gourary, was busy running and fundraising for the budding Lubavitcher yeshiva network, Yosef Yitshak drafted his younger son-in-law to run these three organizations. Fortunately, these initiatives appealed to Schneerson's interests and required that he report only to Yosef Yitshak himself.

Schneerson was particularly devoted to the publishing house, where he was able to do what he liked best: editing and annotating manuscripts. In the 1940s he edited and published several books and hundreds of shorter pamphlets, including many of Yosef Yitshak's discourses and talks. In 1943 he wrote his own first book, *Hayom Yom* (Today Is), a wisdom calendar and guide to Chabad customs based on the teachings of Yosef Yitshak. The work had personal touches—for example, a lesson on how to celebrate birthdays was inserted on 11 Nisan, the date of Schneerson's own birth. Other works from the 1940s included a Passover Haggadah based on the teachings of Chabad rebbes and a short biography of the fourth Lubavitcher rebbe, Shmuel Schneersohn. The greatest demonstrations of Schneerson's scholarship were his letters, some of which formed the basis of an "ask the rabbi" column in the newsletter *Kovets Lubavitch* (Lubavitch Digest). He answered not only basic questions about Judaism but also sophisticated inquiries from Chabad scholars. Among the topics he addressed were the difference between individual and communal repentance; the reasons for learning the Mishna by heart; all Jews' merit to a place in the afterlife; the question of whether the currency mentioned in rabbinic sources was subject to inflation; and the difference between the resurrection of the dead and the world-to-come. Other projects were less scholarly but still important. For years he edited a children's magazine called *Talks and Tales;* according to one story, he told the designer that a comic strip character should look like Dick Tracy, resulting in a Tracy-esque version of Dodgers shortstop Pee Wee Reese named "Pee Wee Myers."

Although Chabad had suffered grievously in the first decades of the century, it was rebuilding. America, despite its spiritual drawbacks, provided a sense of stability the movement had lacked since fleeing its home village of Lubavitch during the First World War. But the rebbe, now almost seventy and in poor health, was no longer the vigorous leader he once was. Then, on January 28, 1950, the tenth day of the Hebrew month of Shvat, in the early hours of a Sabbath morning, Yosef Yitshak died.

6

Becoming the Rebbe

Yosef Yitshak had suffered from multiple sclerosis, and by the late 1940s he had experienced both a stroke and a heart attack. At the end of his life he could no longer stand or speak clearly, and he rarely appeared in public. Still, his death was a shock. It wasn't just that Yosef Yitshak had promised the Messiah's arrival in his lifetime; contemplating a living rebbe's death was always inappropriate. Nonetheless, the question of succession arose immediately. The situation was complicated by the absence of a will or any instructions regarding a successor. Without explicit directions from Yosef Yitshak, the question rested with his family and the community of Hasidim.

The two apparent candidates to become the next rebbe were Yosef Yitshak's sons-in-law, Schneerson and Shmaryahu Gourary. Barry Gourary, Yosef Yitshak's grandson and only male descendant, may also have been an option, although he had drifted from the Lubavitch community. In America he attended Brooklyn's Yeshiva Torah Vodaath, and in 1943 he began taking classes at Brooklyn College. By 1945 he had left the yeshiva and was going to the university full-time, studying physics. Although he still lived with his parents in 770 and helped care for his grandfather, he hoped to become a scientist, not the leader of a small Hasidic group. When Yosef Yitshak died, he was twenty-six years old and pursuing a doctorate at Columbia University. "I was not interested," he told the anthropologist Jerome Mintz in the early 1990s. "I'm more of a private person, a researcher, not a public person. So it didn't fit my goals."[1]

Eight days after Yosef Yitshak's death, Schneerson, Shmaryahu Gourary, and Nehama Dina Schneersohn, his sons-in-law and his widow, issued a joint letter seeking to inspire unity and a renewed sense of purpose. "In this hour of bereavement and grief, a tremendous responsibility falls upon our shoulders and yours: to safeguard, with G-d's help, the gigantic spiritual heritage which our late Rebbe left us all . . . Such was his central wish and aim in his lifetime; such, and even more so, surely is his desire in Eternal Life."[2] For a while, some Hasidim believed that the brothers-in-law would share the leadership, with Gourary maintaining administrative control and Schneerson occupying the role of scholar and spiritual mentor. But members of the community soon began aligning behind one or the other. After the Holocaust and repression in the Soviet Union, most Hasidim felt that Chabad could survive only if it had an effective and inspiring leader. Making that choice would be a fateful decision.[3]

Superficially, Gourary had the advantage. He had studied in Tomkhei Temimim, the central Chabad yeshiva, and had administered the movement's institutions for decades, much as Yosef Yitshak had done for his father. In New York he lived with Yosef Yitshak in 770, and his wife, Chana, was in charge of her father's care. Schneerson and Chaya Mushka were close to fifty years old and, barring a miracle of biblical proportions, were unlikely to have children. Gourary had a son, and even if Barry was unsuited to the position, he might have offspring who could continue the line. Although Gourary was perceived as an administrator more than a spiritual figure, he had a reputation for his encyclopedic knowledge of Chabad discourses, of which he had committed hundreds to memory.

Yet the matter was far from decided. Despite Schneerson's unconventional background, he had earned a reputation in America for scholarship, piety, and devotion to his father-in-law. Although he played a smaller institutional role than Gourary did, his leadership of the three organizations assigned to him by Yosef Yitshak gave him a platform from which to achieve visible successes in the areas of education, publishing, and outreach. He was a direct descendant of the Schneerson line through his great-great-great grandfather, the Tsemah Tsedek. Even his secular knowledge may have been an asset. While ordinary Hasidim were discouraged from pursuing a university education, a rebbe with both traditional piety and worldly skills could be advantageous, and the combination added to his mystique. All this earned Schneerson the backing of influential figures such as Israel Jacobson, who had been instrumental in rescuing Yosef Yitshak from Poland, and Chaim Mordechai Aizik Hodakov, one of Yosef Yitshak's chief secretaries.

Schneerson had also become a magnetic figure to the yeshiva students in 770, whose study hall was located near his office. One of these was Yoel Kahn, who arrived from Tel Aviv shortly after Yosef Yitshak's death. In later years Kahn became the principal transcriber of Schneerson's lectures and a senior scholar in the movement; even as a young man, he was a perceptive observer of the goings-on in Lubavitch. Schneerson's talks, he wrote to his father, offered a mesmerizing and mystical experience; Schneerson himself was "a spiritual person who is above nature."[4] As a speaker, Kahn wrote, Schneerson was "a very inward person, seemingly a cold person. He sits calmly and speaks quietly, and then suddenly bursts into tears. Then he carries on speaking, always quietly."[5] A month later he wrote, "In my opinion, the Hasidim in the Holy Land simply do not recognize what he is, he is a different sort of person entirely."[6] While he confessed that he didn't know whether Schneerson had the metaphysical qualities of a tsaddik, he seemed to be something "beyond human."[7] Yehuda Krinsky, a yeshiva student who would go on to become one of the institutional leaders of Chabad, said that although there was controversy among the adults, "among my group, there was no question . . . Us kids, we regarded him as the rebbe."[8]

It is impossible to know when Schneerson first considered the possibility of leadership. Unlike Gourary, he had not planned his life around the prospect. Even after Yosef Yitshak's death he continued to insist that his father-in-law was in charge, making the question of succession moot. In a letter that May he wrote, "This matter is not my responsibility . . . As for what will be with the Hasidim, that is for the rebbe to worry about. It is *his* responsibility."[9] Such statements had precedents in Jewish tradition. The Talmud declared that the righteous are considered alive even in death and that the patriarch Jacob never died because he lives through his descendants. According to the *Zohar*, "A tsaddik who has died is found in all the worlds more than in his lifetime."[10] As Shneur Zalman of Lyady explained, since a tsaddik's life is predominantly spiritual, it can express itself more strongly after death, when the impediment of the body is removed. In this vein, the fourth rebbe, Shmuel Schneersohn, reportedly said of his father that he "did not die, and whoever wants to make any requests [of him] can still do so."[11] Yosef Yitshak also claimed to communicate with his deceased father in dreams. Yet none of them insisted on the continued presence of their predecessors as adamantly as Schneerson did. Even after he became rebbe he continued to refer to his father-in-law as the current leader of Chabad, as if Yosef Yitshak had never died.

If Schneerson was stubborn, he was not obtuse. While he

was refusing to consider the possibility of leadership, Hasidim around the world were hatching schemes to make him accept it. In February a group in England circulated a letter supporting Schneerson; a group in Israel joined them in March. As the months passed, Hasidim in New York, Israel, England, and elsewhere continued to approach Schneerson in person and in writing, pledging their loyalty. In the summer of 1950, the Israelis issued another letter swearing fealty to Schneerson, which led the Israeli newspaper *Hamodia* to run an article headlined, "The Genius Rabbi Menachem Schneerson Crowned as Rebbe of Lubavitch."[12] In response, Schneerson continued to deny interest in the position, claiming that he simply wasn't suited for it. According to an apocryphal story, he threatened to run away to Mexico if the Hasidim didn't stop their demands.

It is difficult to say what calculations went into such statements. Some of his objections seemed genuine. He had long been averse to communal responsibilities and took them on only at the insistence of Yosef Yitshak. In a 1949 letter to Yaakov Landau, a Chabad Hasid whom he knew in Leningrad and who was now the chief rabbi of B'nei Brak, he wrote that "now, just as when we met, I take no pleasure in communal work."[13] Becoming rebbe would entail endless obligations, leaving little time for a private life or pursuits. Moreover, being a rebbe implied a new metaphysical status: he would be not just a teacher or a spiritual guide but a conduit to the Divine. While Schneerson was confident in his abilities, being a tsaddik wasn't a role he had envisioned. In response to an early entreaty, he is reported to have said, "What are you thinking? That Mendel Schneerson is a rebbe?"[14]

As sincere as these disavowals may have been, they were also consistent with Chabad traditions of leadership. When Shneur Zalman's contemporaries became tsaddikim after the death of the Maggid of Mezritsh, Shneur Zalman first became a follower of Menahem Mendel of Vitebsk. According to Hasidic lore, he agreed to become a leader only after being assured by his wife that people followed him primarily because he had studied with the Maggid. Shalom Dov Ber, the fifth rebbe, did not take up the position until ten years after his father's death, although the reasons for that are not clear. Yosef Yitshak was also said to have shown an initial hesitation to becoming rebbe. As Plato wrote in *The Republic*, a fit leader accepts authority "with reluctance or under pressure"—a lesson Chabad took to heart.[15] As Schneerson likely knew, refusing the position was the best way to enlist support. There were rumors, too, that despite Schneerson's apparent recalcitrance, behind the scenes he was not so passive. For Barry Gourary the episode proved so distasteful that he became permanently estranged from his uncle and from the movement. To Shmaryahu Gourary and his supporters, it must have seemed absurd that this aloof individual, who spent years playing at being a university student, was now touted as the next rebbe of Chabad.

In later years Schneerson claimed that he accepted the position out of necessity; with his father-in-law dead, the fate of the movement hung in the balance. Would Chabad Hasidism, a tradition that survived both Soviet and Nazi persecution, perish on American soil? Would the community of Hasidim wither away after remaining loyal to Yosef Yitshak for so long? What would become of Yosef Yitshak's insistence that it was the responsibility of their generation to bring the Messiah? As most Hasidim understood, Schneerson was the only person capable of shouldering such a burden. And although he insisted that Yosef Yitshak was still the rebbe, rather than himself, he never recognized Gourary as the rightful heir. He might have acknowledged Gourary's competence and loyalty, but his rival seemed to lack the charisma and vision that he himself had. Perhaps, as Plato wrote, the best motivation for a reluctant leader is the fear of being ruled by someone worse.

* * *

As the year went on, the balance of support solidified around Schneerson. He, too, was coming around to the idea. While he continued to formally deny the possibility of leadership, he began taking on more significant roles, including counseling petitioners who sought his advice both in writing and in late-night meetings. "People come to him every day, until late at night, and he answers them all firmly and decisively, even in matters of literal life and death," Kahn wrote to his father in June.[16] Around the turn of the Jewish New Year, Schneerson gave up his modern style of dress for a rabbinical frock coat, and on the holiday of Simhat Torah he was called to the Torah with the title of "our master, our teacher, and our rebbe," to which he gave no protest.

By the beginning of January 1951, the community was growing restless. On the second day of the month a group of senior Hasidim presented Schneerson with a letter reading, "We, the undersigned, truly and wholeheartedly accept upon ourselves the leadership and authority of the son-in-law." In response, Schneerson began to cry, insisting, "This does not have any relevance to me," and he asked that they leave the room.[17] The Hasidim had already informed the press that Schneerson was the new rebbe, and two days later three Yiddish newspapers ran stories announcing the succession. Schneerson insisted that the Hasidim call the newspapers to issue a denial, but they refused, and no retraction was published.

Finally, he acquiesced. On the morning of January 17, a group of Hasidim entered his study and presented him with another letter dedicating themselves to him. This time Schneerson said, "You all have to help me."[18] He spent the rest of the day at Yosef Yitshak's grave, reading the notes he had been given and weeping. That night, members of the Lubavitch community gathered in 770 to commemorate the first anniversary of Yosef Yitshak's passing. At least one hundred people were present—a substantial crowd for the space—and they included many of the movement's senior figures. At about 9:45 p.m. Schneerson began to speak. Once again he stressed the continuing presence of Yosef Yitshak and the mission he had given to spread the teachings of Hasidism. Schneerson continued: "Here in America they love to hear an announcement, a 'statement,' something new, and preferably exciting. I don't know if it's necessary, but when you come to a place you do according to its custom." He went on: "The three loves—the love of God, the love of Torah, and the love of the [Children of] Israel, are all one . . . When one sees a Jew who has the love of God and he doesn't have the love of Torah or the love of Israel, one must say to him that the love of God alone doesn't last. On the other hand, when one sees a Jew who just has the love of Israel, one must try to bring him to the love of Torah and the love of God . . . And through this redemption will come."[19]

In time this idea would inspire his efforts to return wayward Jews to religion through expressions of love and sympathy. For the Hasidim present, a mere "statement" was not enough. After about an hour, Avrohom Sender Nemtzov, one of the oldest Hasidim there, stood up and shouted: "Speeches are fine, but the congregation wants a Hasidic discourse! The rebbe should say Hasidus!"[20]

In Chabad tradition, a rebbe delivers two types of talks. The first, a *siha*, is informal, and can encompass nearly any subject. The more formal discourse, a *ma'amar*, is limited to the mystical regions of Hasidic thought and is also referred to as *divre Elokim Hayim*, or "words of the Living God"—a transmission from the Divine, channeled through the rebbe. It is preceded by a special melody sung by the Hasidim, who stand throughout its recitation. The rebbe chants the ma'amar in a singsong tune with his eyes closed and a handkerchief clasped in his hands to keep his soul tethered to the earth. After he delivers the ma'amar, it will be reviewed by its listeners and is often tran-

Although Schneerson's talks would eventually be attended by
thousands of people, crowds were small at the beginning of his
time as leader. The man to the left of Schneerson with the tilted gray
hat is Shlomo Carlebach, who became famous as a composer and
performer of Jewish music. (JEM, The Living Archive)

scribed for publication. Aside from certain works written and
published by Chabad rebbes, these discourses form the core of
the movement's doctrine.

Schneerson had often edited his father-in-law's discourses
for publication. A year earlier, on the day before Yosef Yitshak's
death, Schneerson had prepared a ma'amar originally delivered in
1923; to mark its publication, Yosef Yitshak replaced the opening
sentences with a new paragraph, beginning with a verse from
Song of Songs: "I have come into my garden, my sister, my
bride."[21] Using a midrashic play on words, Yosef Yitshak used
the verse to express one of the fundamental teachings of Chabad
Hasidism. At the beginning of creation, the *Shekhinah*, the Divine presence, was located in this world. Because of human sin,
starting with Adam and Eve and continuing for another six generations, the Shekhinah departed for celestial realms. With the

arrival of Abraham, the Divine presence once again began to descend until it was finally brought back to earth by Moses, the seventh generation from Abraham. (For "all sevenths are beloved," Yosef Yitshak declared parenthetically, once again quoting the Midrash.) On earth the Shekhinah found a home in the tabernacle, in the temple in Jerusalem, and within each person.

"And the point is," Yosef Yitshak continued, spelling out what might be the most important idea of Chabad thought, "that the ultimate intention in the creation of the worlds was that the Holy One Blessed Be He desired to have a dwelling in the lower regions, for there to be a revelation of Godliness below through the service of man . . . [He desired] that the soul should descend to be clothed in the body and the animal spirit, which hide and obstruct its light. And yet, despite all of this, the soul will accomplish the purification and refinement of the body and the animal spirit, together with its corresponding portion in the world."[22] It seems unlikely that Yosef Yitshak knew this would be his last statement to his Hasidim, but he couldn't have picked a better message.

Now, when Nemtzov beseeched Schneerson to deliver a ma'amar, Schneerson had his theme at hand. Switching to the traditional singsong tune, he spoke on the subject addressed by Yosef Yitshak. Citing a succession of his predecessors' teachings, Schneerson explained that the Shekhinah was not a monolithic instantiation of the Divine but a prismatic phenomenon that began in the original Divine illumination and echoed through each level of creation. In the midrash quoted by Yosef Yitshak, he said, *Shekhinah* did not mean the lowest level of Divinity, as it often does in kabbalistic teachings, but the "essence of the Shekhinah," that is, "the beginning of the revelation of the light of the Infinite," which preceded the process of Divine concealment.[23] The Shekhinah's presence in the world, therefore, was not a matter of mere revelation; it was the essence of transcendent Divinity expressed in the fabric of reality. And, Schneerson noted, citing Yosef Yitshak's parenthetical comment, the reason why Moses merited returning this "essential Shekhinah" to earth was because he was the seventh, and "all sevenths are beloved." This role "was not dependent on his choice, his desire, or his worship, but because he was seventh, which came as a matter of birth . . . The entire greatness of the seventh is that he is a seventh from the first, that he can carry out the service and mission of the first . . . that he draws down the essence of the Shekhinah, and even more, that he draws it down to the lower worlds."[24]

As his listeners understood, Schneerson wasn't just speaking about biblical characters or events long ago. He was speaking about himself and about everyone present. Just as Moses was the seventh patriarch after Abraham, he was about to become the seventh rebbe of the seventh generation of Chabad. Nor did it take long for Schneerson to make this comparison explicit. "[And] this imposes a demand on every one of us, the seventh generation. The fact that we are in the seventh generation is not because we chose it, and not because we worked for it, and in certain ways it is possibly against our wishes," he said, referring transparently to his own ambivalence. "Nonetheless, all sevenths are beloved. We find ourselves in the era of the footsteps of the Messiah, at the end of the footsteps, and our service is to complete the drawing down of the Shekhinah—not just the Shekhinah, but the essence of the Shekhinah—and to the lower worlds, specifically."[25]

Schneerson paused and instructed the Hasidim to sing a song beloved by Yosef Yitshak, then a tune from the fifth rebbe, Shalom Dov Ber. As they started singing, Nemtzov jumped on a table, raised his cup, and recited the blessing thanking God "who has given us life, sustained us, and brought us to this day," to which the congregation responded "amen." Schneerson, smiling, asked Nemtzov to get off the table. Then, returning to the ma'amar, he spoke again about Yosef Yitshak, this time in explicitly messianic language. "My saintly father-in-law, our master and teacher, who 'bore our sicknesses and endured our pains,' who was 'wounded by our sins and crushed by our iniquities'— just as he saw our suffering, so, speedily in our days and in our time, he shall redeem the sheep of his flock from both spiritual and physical exile . . . Now the matter is dependent only on us, the seventh generation. And we shall merit seeing the rebbe here in a body and below ten cubits—and he shall redeem us."[26]

The crowd again began to sing; the ma'amar was complete, and it had been a virtuoso performance. Although the speech seemed impromptu, Schneerson clearly had planned it in advance. He not only used Yosef Yitshak's last published discourse as a departure point, emphasizing the continuity of leadership, but structured the discourse to include a series of teachings from each of the previous rebbes, situating himself in the chain of transmission. The identification of Yosef Yitshak as the Messiah, made at the moment of his inauguration, was a claim he would continue to make over the coming decades, and it would inspire his followers to make the same claim about him. Most importantly, the talk was a manifesto, a proclamation of the vision he would pursue for the rest of his leadership.

Still, Schneerson wasn't finished. In Chabad, he declared, each Hasid was responsible for fulfilling his mission himself and couldn't just rely on the rebbe. "I am not excusing myself, God forbid, from helping, from helping with all my ability," he said. But "each person needs to act for himself, to fulfill his mission . . . and the purpose of creation will be fulfilled—that there will be a dwelling for God on earth." He concluded by calling for unity between all those who had been loyal to Yosef Yitshak, "and then God will help fulfill the goal that the Rebbe gave to us and passed on to us, the ultimate good that is possible."[27] Now, at almost 12:30 a.m., Schneerson left the room surrounded by a throng of admirers. The Hasidim had convinced him to become rebbe, and they were not disappointed. He may not have envisioned himself as a leader or been enthusiastic about the responsibilities it entailed. But he did have ambitious ideas for the future of Chabad, and becoming rebbe was the best chance to make them come true.

What happens when the Messiah comes? Will redemption arrive gradually or all at once? Will the messianic era be a new utopia or the restoration of a golden age? Will there be miracles and wonders or just a refurbished political order? Will the laws of the Torah still apply, or will a different law take their place? Will redemption be preceded by an apocalypse, or will there be a peaceful transition from one stage to the next? Will there be two Messiahs, as some sources teach, or only one? Will the Messiah be a human being or a metaphor for Divine action? Will redemption mark the beginning of a new historical era or the end of history altogether?

Jewish tradition has never given clear answers to these questions. Since biblical times, prophets, sages, and theologians have tried to reconcile conflicting descriptions of the future while offering visions of their own. In the earliest biblical uses of the word, "messiah," or *mashiah*, describes someone who is anointed at the direction of God, such as a king or a high priest. Over time its meaning came to refer, not to any king, but to the king who will come at the end of days. But the timing of redemption, the identity of the Messiah, and the events that will precede and follow his arrival have eluded agreement. In the visions of Daniel, according to some interpretations, the Messiah is pictured coming "with the clouds of heaven"; in Zechariah he is "lowly and riding on a donkey."[28] In some accounts the third temple—or perhaps the entire city of Jerusalem—will descend from heaven fully built, whereas other authorities believed that the Messiah would build the temple himself. Some sages, fearing that redemption would be accompanied by suffering, did not wish to see it; others said that the righteous would be spared the horrors of apocalypse. Many rabbinic teachings prescribe specific acts to hasten redemption; some warn against pressing for the end. One Talmudic passage says that the Messiah will come only when the Jewish people have repented of their sins; another states that the Messiah will come regardless. A third view posits that if the Jewish people merit the redemption, it will come quickly, but it will otherwise arrive at its predestined time. According to one famous teaching, "The son of David will come only in a generation that is entirely innocent or entirely guilty."[29] Many believers hoped the Messiah would enact the miraculous visions of the prophets; for others "the only difference between this world and the days of the Messiah is the subjugation to [gentile] kingdoms."[30] In the view of one Talmudic rabbi, "There is no Messiah for the Jewish people, for they already enjoyed him during the days of Hezekiah."[31]

Despite such profligate speculations, certain ideas gained consensus. The most important codification of these, and the most conservative, was that of Maimonides, who provided his views at the end of his code of Jewish law. Belief in the Messiah, he wrote, was a biblically ordained obligation, and, reiterating traditional teachings, he stated that the Messiah's primary tasks would be to restore the Davidic monarchy, rebuild the temple, and gather the dispersed people of Israel from exile. In contrast to those who preached that the messianic age would be characterized by miracles, Maimonides taught that one must not expect the Messiah "to perform signs and wonders and to innovate new things in the world."[32] How, then, would the Messiah be known? "If a king arises from the house of David who is steeped in Torah and engages in the commandments like David his father . . . and compels all of Israel to follow its ways and fortifies [the Torah's] breaches, and fights the wars of God, he is presumed to be the Messiah. And if he does this and is successful and builds the temple in its place and gathers the dispersed of Israel, he is definitely the Messiah."[33] However, Maimonides continued, if the messianic candidate "is not successful, or is killed, we will know that he is not the one the Torah promised."[34] In the true messianic age, he concluded, "there will be no hunger and no war, no envy and no competition . . . And the endeavor of the world will only be to know God."[35]

If Maimonides put a floor under messianic belief by defining its essential elements, he was less successful at imposing a ceiling. Despite his immense authority, few thinkers limited themselves to his minimalist criteria. But it wasn't until the sixteenth century, during the kabbalistic efflorescence in the Galilean town of Safed, that the messianic idea received a truly new meaning. In the cosmogony of Isaac Luria, the first act of creation was tsimtsum, the Divine contraction that allowed the world to exist. God then emanated the sefirot, the attributes through which He would become manifest, and sent a ray of Divine light to take shape within them. But the vessels were not capable of containing the light, and they shattered, sending sparks of Divine radiance to be embedded in "shells" of materialistic impurity. This was the original rupture, and the task of humanity—and of the Jewish people in particular—was to repair God and creation by restoring the sparks through the rituals of religious observance. When this effort succeeded, the apparent separation between God and the world would be overcome, and all beings would exist in a state of spiritual wholeness, otherwise known as the messianic age. All other events and prophecies associated with redemption would follow as a matter of course.

This doctrine, known as *tikkun*, or "repair," is among the most astounding ideas of Kabbalah. It teaches that the Jewish people, their actions, and their exile, are not only at the center of history but also at the center of an immense cosmic process. It teaches that the suffering of Israel is not hers alone but a burden shared with God. And it gives the commandments of the Torah—whose functions are often inscrutable to human reason—a purpose of incalculable significance. Yet this doctrine also created a new and troubling possibility. If the point of the law is to achieve tikkun, what happens when tikkun is achieved?

The rabbinic literature on this question, as on other aspects of messianism, abounds in cryptic and contradictory statements. According to some teachings, the commandments will stay in force, but their esoteric meanings will become known. In the view of the anonymous author of the late-Zoharic work *Ra'aya Meheimna* (Faithful Shepherd), in the messianic age the "Tree of Knowledge of Good and Evil," which governs our fallen world, will be replaced by the mysterious "Tree of Life," whose imperatives are as yet unknown.[36] One radical midrash uses Hebrew wordplay to declare that in the future God will not only "release the prisoners" (*asurim*) but also "permit the forbidden" (*isurim*).[37] For kabbalists of the sixteenth century, such as Isaac Luria, such ideas were purely theoretical; so long as redemption remained a perpetually awaited event, they were without practical consequence. But wittingly or not, the doctrine of tikkun gave life to a distinctly antinomian possibility in Judaism.

It did not take long for a messianic movement to make use of the new Lurianic teachings. Since the late second temple period, and especially after the temple's destruction, there had been no shortage of messianic aspirants among the Jewish people. In 132 CE the sage Rabbi Akiva believed that the military leader Simeon Bar Koseva—known in Christian sources as Bar Kokhba—was the Messiah, only to be disappointed when Bar Kokhba's revolt against Rome ended in humiliating defeat. In accordance with a tradition that the Messiah would arrive four centuries after the destruction of the temple, messianic figures emerged in fifth-century Crete and Babylonia. In the eighth century there were messianic outbursts in Persia and Syria, and a swell of messianic enthusiasm broke out during the period of the Crusades. Between 1087 and 1172 there were at least nine messianic contenders, appearing in Spain and France to the west and Babylonia and Yemen to the east. The most notorious of these, David Al-Ruhi, or Alroy, was beheaded by his father-in-law while launching an uprising against Caliph Al-Muqtafi in Baghdad. In sixteenth-century Europe the messianic adventurer David Reubeni arrived in Rome claiming to be the representative of a kingdom of three hundred thousand Jews in northern Arabia who could help retake the Holy Land from the Ottomans. His machinations earned him an audience with Pope Clement VII and a papal endorsement in his behalf for King John II of Portugal before he was exiled back to Spain and burned in an auto-da-fé. None of these—except for Jesus of Nazareth—achieved the success of Shabbetai Tsvi.

Born in 1626 in Smyrna (now Izmir, Turkey) to a merchant family, Shabbetai Tsvi began his life as a gifted scholar of Talmud and Kabbalah. While still a young man, he seemed to entertain messianic fantasies and, according to some historians, exhibited signs of what we would now call bipolar disorder. In his manic, or "illuminated," states, he performed antinomian acts, such as pronouncing the tetragrammaton, the not-to-be-spoken four-letter name of God. Eventually this led to his excommunication by the city's rabbis, and in the early 1650s, he was banished from Smyrna. After wandering in Greece and Thrace he wound up in Salonika, where he was again banished by the local rabbis. From Salonika he went to Constantinople, Cairo, and finally Jerusalem, where he gathered a new circle of followers.

According to Shabbetai Tsvi's later testimony, he received his mission in 1648, when "the holy spirit and a great 'illumination' had come over him."[38] But his messianic career did not begin in earnest until April 1665, when, on a trip back to Jerusalem from Cairo, he met Nathan Benjamin Halevi, better known as Nathan of Gaza. Nathan was a kabbalist and a reputed healer of souls, and Shabbetai Tsvi sought him out to soothe his troubled psyche. Instead, Nathan convinced his visitor that he was in fact the Messiah and that the world would soon be redeemed. After Shabbetai Tsvi announced his newly confirmed status, he was threatened with excommunication by the rabbis of Jerusalem, so he made his way back to Smyrna. That December, after declaring himself anointed by God, he predicted that redemption would take place on the fifteenth of Sivan: June 18, 1666.

In the meantime, letters from Palestine, Egypt, and Turkey made their way to Jewish communities around the world, proclaiming imminent redemption. Dispatches to Holland, England, and Germany in the summer of 1665 reported the return of the ten lost tribes of Israel, who were about to conquer Mecca or, in other versions, Persia. Reports about Shabbetai Tsvi that arrived in Europe that autumn were filled with fantastic accounts of the would-be Messiah's deeds. Within the year his reputation had spread to nearly every corner of the Jewish world. Nathan's calls for repentance were answered by lengthy fasts, the cessation of commercial activity, mass prophesying by men, women, and children, and sightings of the prophet Elijah. Special prayers were instituted for Shabbetai Tsvi, and poems were composed in his honor. A new calendar was inaugurated, starting from "the first year of the renewal of the prophecy and the kingdom." Many people believed that they would be miraculously transported to Palestine; others prepared by selling their possessions. Wealthier adherents rented ships on which entire communities might be brought to the Holy Land.

At the end of 1665, Shabbetai Tsvi left Smyrna for Constantinople, where, according to Nathan's prophecy, he would place the sultan's turban on his own head. Instead, he was intercepted in the Sea of Marmara and imprisoned in Gallipoli, though he was well treated and was able to make the prison a new center for his activities. Then, in September, the bottom fell out. After being denounced by a messianic rival, Shabbetai Tsvi was brought before the royal vizier in Adrianople, where he was given the choice between conversion to Islam and death. Unwilling to face martyrdom for the hysteria he had instigated, Shabbetai Tsvi, along with his wife and several hundred followers, chose conversion. Although his compliance earned him royal support, his continued messianic antics resulted in his banishment to Dulcigno (today Ulcinj, Montenegro), where he died in 1676. Surprisingly, the Sabbatian movement he started did not.

Historians have been at pains to explain the scale and span of Sabbatianism, which remained vigorous well into the eighteenth century. Some point to messianic tensions that had been building for centuries: the fall of Constantinople, the expulsion of Jews from Spain and Portugal, and the Khmelnytsky massacres of the mid-seventeenth century had all raised hopes of imminent redemption. But as one scholar, Gershom Scholem, argued, it was the spread of Lurianic Kabbalah, with its messianic and antinomian potential, that prepared the ground for the Sabbatian outburst. Just as importantly, it gave the movement a way to cope with disappointment and crisis.

Even before Shabbetai Tsvi's apostasy, Sabbatianism was characterized by a paradoxical theology used to justify the would-be Messiah's strange behavior. During periods of mystical inspiration Shabbetai Tsvi would commit public transgressions of Jewish law, including the vocal recitation of the tetragrammaton and the consumption of forbidden foods. In Salonika in the early 1650s he performed a marriage ceremony between himself and a Torah scroll; during one ecstatic period he celebrated the holidays of Passover, Shavuot, and Sukkot in a single week. In 1665, Nathan of Gaza repealed the fast of the seventeenth of Tammuz, which was to become a day of celebration; Shabbetai Tsvi later abolished the fasts of the tenth of Tevet and the ninth of Av, the day of the destruction of the temple, which he claimed as his birthday. At the height of the movement Shabbetai Tsvi signed his letters "firstborn son of God," "the bridegroom of the Torah," and even "the Lord your God Shabbetai Tsvi." Upon performing his "strange acts" he often pronounced a blessing to "the Lord of the Universe, who permits the forbidden."[39]

Like other messianic movements, Sabbatianism preached

not only that redemption was at hand but that it had, in certain respects, already arrived. Because of this belief, Lurianic Kabbalah provided a convenient explanation. If Shabbetai Tsvi was the Messiah, and the messianic age had begun, then tikkun was accomplished and the commandments needed to be examined in a new light. In a clever reworking of the Lurianic scheme, the Messiah was no longer merely the herald of tikkun but the one who would accomplish the final and most perilous tikkun of all. He might even do it—perhaps could only do it—by descending to the lowest depths to redeem the sparks therein. Thus, Shabbetai Tsvi's "strange acts" were part of the special mission of the Messiah, even to the point of apostasy. Rather than elevating the sacred from the mundane, Sabbatianism sanctified sin.

Given this traumatic history, the early Hasidic movement was, not surprisingly, suspected of harboring Sabbatian tendencies. Although its immanentist theology was distinct from Sabbatianism, it, too, was characterized by separatist behavior, veneration of its leaders, and a mystical outlook that carried antinomian currents. Some Hasidic leaders were even influenced, albeit unwittingly, by Sabbatian books and ideas. Nonetheless, as Scholem argued, the overall tendency of Hasidism was to "neutralize" the messianic impulse. Whereas Lurianic Kabbalah emphasized repair of the world, Hasidism taught the absorption of the individual into God. Although everyone was expected to study the Torah and fulfill its commandments, the elevated states of devekut and bittul—the "higher unity," in kabbalistic terminology—were the true goals of spiritual struggle.

Even these quietist activities contained messianic content; through them the individual achieved personal liberation and thereby contributed to the liberation of the world. Moreover, the traditional belief in redemption remained central to Hasidic theology, leading to occasional messianic excitements. In the early nineteenth century some Hasidic leaders saw Napoleon's invasion of Russia as the pre-messianic war of Gog and Magog referred to in the book of Ezekiel. In 1814 three Hasidic leaders were said to have made a pact wherein they would collectively try to force the end; instead, all three died within the year. Nahman of Bratslav, a tsaddik of the late eighteenth and early nineteenth centuries, believed himself—and was believed by his followers—to be a messianic figure and a reincarnation of Moses. But Hasidic messianism was largely consistent with rabbinic attitudes. Even the Ba'al Shem Tov's meeting with the Messiah implied a deferment of his coming until Hasidism "spread outward." The enlightenment of the individual became paramount, and collective redemption was postponed.

If this was true of Hasidism generally, it was particularly true of Chabad. Although Shneur Zalman occasionally referred to the approaching redemption (and even predicted that the Messiah would arrive in 1842–43 or, according to other accounts, 1847–48), he also declared that there was "a long time yet before the time of redemption" and that "the messianic outcry is not yet heard."[40] The third rebbe, the Tsemah Tsedek, declared that "the exile continues, for all the purifications are not yet completed."[41] Yet the teachings of Hasidism did add new meaning to messianic doctrine. According to Shneur Zalman's dialectical theology of Divine concealment and revelation, the messianic age signified not only the repair of the world but the ultimate revelation of the Divine. Although it was axiomatic that direct, unmediated revelation was impossible, redemption allowed for the transcendence of this impossibility. Just as God could encompass a unity of opposites, so could the messianic state. Moreover, this ultimate revelation would not obliterate the world but would take place within and through the world. Citing Isaiah 40:5—"And the glory of God will be revealed and all flesh shall see together that the mouth of the Lord has spoken"—Shneur Zalman taught that in the messianic era the revelation of Divinity would be perceived by all humanity through

the physical senses. This idea—that the messianic age would constitute the ultimate union of the world and God—received great
emphasis from Schneerson, starting with his first discourse, in
which he identified the return of the "essential Shekhinah" as
the task of his generation.

While such ideas gave the messianic idea yet another layer
of significance, they did not solve the antinomian dilemma. In
the early years of Hasidism this remained a theoretical concern,
as it had during the time of Isaac Luria. But as the twentieth
century dawned, the quietistic stance of Chabad gave way to
activism. For the fifth Lubavitcher rebbe, Shalom Dov Ber, the
threat of modernity and Zionism, which contained its own messianic implications, was a clear sign that the messianic advent
was nigh. Whereas his predecessors taught that the purifications necessary for redemption had not yet been completed, he
declared that "now is the most final purification" and that "ours
is the generation of Messiah."[42] In a 1900 talk to the students
of his yeshiva he explained that the ideologies of enlightenment
and Zionism were no more than a prelude to the messianic age,
which he and his followers would bring about through their
spiritual efforts. He declared again in 1907 that "this present
generation is the generation of Messiah, without any doubts
whatsoever."[43] Messianic expectancy increased again under Yosef
Yitshak, who said in 1927 that the Messiah would come in his
lifetime. His rhetoric reached a fever pitch during the Holocaust, when he declared that with repentance, the Jewish people
would be saved from destruction.

For Schneerson, the Messiah was a long-standing obsession.
In a 1956 letter to Israeli President Yitzhak Ben-Zvi, he claimed
that "from the day I went to school, and even before then, there
began to form in my imagination a vision of . . . the redemption
of the Jewish people from its final exile."[44] Messianism continued to be an abiding concern during his precarious years in
Western Europe and intensified under the influence of Yosef

Yitshak. Even after his predecessor's death, Schneerson's commitment did not waver; since Yosef Yitshak was spiritually alive, his promise of redemption in his lifetime was still good.

This development, though counterintuitive, was somewhat predictable. In a 1956 study, *When Prophecy Fails*, the sociologists Leon Festinger, Henry Riecken, and Stanley Schachter theorized that when faced with prophetic disappointment, believers become more fervent and more enthusiastic about proselytizing their beliefs in order to reduce cognitive dissonance. "If more and more people can be persuaded that the system of belief is correct," they wrote, "then clearly it must, after all, be correct."[45] Although the study's methods and conclusions were contested by later scholars, they were widely applied to Chabad in the wake of Schneerson's death. However, the same speculation might be applied to Schneerson himself and to his exceptional messianic efforts. The only way to avoid the falsification of Yosef Yitshak's promise was to make it come true.

Even for Schneerson, messianism contained the old theological difficulties. There was the problem of antinomianism and the difficulty of maintaining halakhic observance amid a full-blown messianic campaign. Then there was the related issue of Maimonides. Although the philosopher's rationalist theology contrasted with the Kabbalah from which Hasidic writers drew their ideas, he was often quoted by Shneur Zalman and other Chabad masters, who tried to reconcile his teachings with kabbalistic ones. In regard to messianism, Maimonides's teachings were especially important because he included them in his legal work, giving them the force of law. But how could Schneerson reconcile Maimonides's view that the messianic age would not entail miracles with the kabbalistic belief in the world of tikkun and the Hasidic vision of revelation beyond comprehension?

This clash of ideas was not just a conflict between Maimonides and Hasidism but a contradiction within Maimonides's own views. In his commentary on the Mishna, Maimonides proclaimed resurrection of the dead to be a core tenet of Judaism. He also maintained that the afterlife was purely spiritual, without any trace of corporeality. But, as Maimonides's great rabbinical antagonist, Abraham ben David, asked, if the messianic age is not miraculous and if the world to come is incorporeal, when and where does resurrection happen? Furthermore, although there is a Talmudic opinion to support Maimonides's position, many rabbis said the opposite. How could Maimonides rule definitively against the sages who predicted miracles, especially when such prophecies are arguably biblical in nature?

To these problems Schneerson offered an ingenious solution. In a lengthy 1945 letter, which he later elaborated in several lectures, he drew on the teachings of Shneur Zalman to explain that existence in this world consists of three stages. The first is the one we are in now, in which there is a struggle between spiritual and material, good and bad. The second is the messianic age, when this struggle is essentially won, and humanity returns to a prelapsarian state. The rebuilding of the temple and the ingathering of exiles will take place, and it is this stage Maimonides refers to when he says that it will not be characterized by miracles. However, Schneerson continued, even at this stage evil is not entirely vanquished. Therefore, the task of the Jewish people during this era—a period of forty years, according to the *Zohar*—will be to perfect the world through study and worship. Then, in the final stage, the dead will be resurrected and the ultimate redemption will occur. The afterlife, in contrast, is merely a way station for souls until resurrection. Here the shadow of antinomianism remains—the commandments are yet to be transformed in the final stage—but its menace is removed. Since the still-awaited first stage of redemption requires full religious observance, there is no danger of anyone prematurely invoking the second and casting off the law.

Still, Schneerson emphasized, even the present age contains messianic qualities. Whereas traditional Jewish teachings state that wisdom decreases with each generation, for messianic thinkers the approaching redemption exercises a countervailing influence—not the influence of the past on the future but the influence of the future on its past. This, Schneerson argued, is because the future reward for any action is not arbitrary but the result of a kind of karmic cause-and-effect. Since redemption is "dependent on our actions and service the entire time of the exile," there is a transtemporal connection between present and future, between what we do now and what happens later.[46] If the messianic age results from human actions, those actions are messianic in nature. And if this principle is true for all human history, it becomes especially relevant in the period preceding redemption, when the connection is closest.

This type of argument had been made before, notably by kabbalists who insisted that the approach of redemption necessitated revealing secret wisdom. For Schneerson, Hasidism was the new revelation. As he explained in a celebrated 1965 talk, later published as "A Treatise on the Essence of Hasidism," the statement of the Messiah to the Ba'al Shem Tov that redemption would come when Hasidism "spread outward" implied a causal link between the two—a karmic connection between deed and reward. This, he said, was because Hasidic thought constituted the quintessence of the Torah, just as the Messiah represented the singularity of all existence. And just as the messianic age will cause revelation everywhere, so Hasidism must be all encompassing and not confined to its own milieu.

Here Schneerson's pragmatic nature came to the fore. Spreading Hasidism was not a theoretical idea but a task he expected his followers to perform. Just as the Messiah would bind together the spiritual and material in one overwhelming unity, so Schneerson wove a messianic vision that was at once philosophical and practical, esoteric and goal-oriented. As he told the

New York Times journalist Israel Shenker in 1972, "The Messiah will be a real human being. Don't translate Him as something abstract."[47] However spiritualized Schneerson's messianic vision became, redemption, to him, was entirely realistic.

7

―――――◆◗◆◖◆――――――

New Beginnings

THE CONTRAST BETWEEN the first and second halves of Schneerson's life is confounding. How did this private scholar become one of the most charismatic holy men of the century? How did a reserved student become a compelling leader and speaker? Despite Schneerson's intellect, his personality made the transformation seem unlikely. There was his explicit distaste for communal work and his aversion to public spectacle. Even his manner of prayer was inexpressive; like his nineteenth-century predecessor Dov Ber, he stood still with his eyes fixed on the prayer book, reading the words without movement or exclamation. A biographical note in the 1957 edition of his book *Today Is* begins simply: "He studied with great diligence and succeeded."[1] Joseph B. Soloveitchik, who knew Schneerson in Berlin, is reported to have said, "If you asked me who I thought was going to be successful, who was going to be a leader, the last one I would have picked would be Rabbi Schneerson."[2]

Schneerson's personality did have a certain charm. Throughout his life he was inclined to treat others with empathy, even—maybe especially—when they didn't share his views. In his youth he maintained a loving bond with his brother Leibel long after Leibel stopped being religious. In the 1940s he captivated the much younger yeshiva students in 770 with a mixture of seriousness and good humor, a significant factor in his elevation. In later years he forged connections with figures across the religious and political spectrum, attracting supporters beyond the Hasidic sphere. But there was more to his charisma than being personable. Under his composed exterior he was a man of fierce convictions. Before he became rebbe, he kept these feelings secret or shared them with only a few confidants. Afterward, he had a platform from which he could turn his ideals outward and demand the same commitments of his followers. What had been his interior life became public, while his public life was now largely private, confined to his home and family. By the time he turned fifty he was no longer Mendel Schneerson, an engineer from Ekaterinoslav, but the Lubavitcher rebbe, heir to a Hasidic dynasty.

The assumption of leadership had more prosaic effects as well. Although Schneerson had assumed certain responsibilities during Yosef Yitshak's lifetime, those burdens were now his alone. He was expected to give regular talks and discourses, meet privately with individuals seeking blessings and advice, respond to petitioners' written requests, and guide the Chabad movement spiritually and materially. As his stature rose, he met and corresponded with leaders throughout the Jewish world and opined on questions beyond his own community. In time, he would turn Chabad from a parochial Hasidic group into a Jewish outreach movement of unprecedented size, and Chabad's success turned him into one of the world's most influential rabbis. But such ambitions took time to realize; first, Schneerson had to rebuild Chabad itself. In his first decade of leadership,

Schneerson's primary role was caretaker of his tradition and shepherd to his flock.

Schneerson had always been meticulous, and he dealt with his new responsibilities through organization, routine, and nonstop work. Near the beginning of his tenure, he moved into a small office at 770, the same room he had occupied with Chaya Mushka when they arrived in America. It was located to the left of the building's main entrance and measured around ten by twelve feet, with wood-paneled walls and built-in bookcases, small windows looking onto Kingston Avenue, and a small glass chandelier. The only furnishings were a large mahogany desk, a brown leather chair, green metal filing cabinets, and a rotary telephone, which he used to communicate with his secretaries across the hall. Over time the room became cluttered with books and papers, which would be cleared out before he saw visitors. The novelist Harvey Swados, who interviewed Schneerson in 1964, described the office as "bleak and dingy," with nothing on the desk but a pad and a telephone.[3] Aside from his home and eventually the large synagogue next door, this was where Schneerson spent most of his time until his death.

Schneerson's schedule was orderly to a fault. Each day he arrived at 770 around 9 a.m. On most days he prayed the morning service by himself; on Mondays and Thursdays he joined a congregation in the next room for the Torah reading, and on the Sabbath he prayed with the rest of the community in the main synagogue. During his first decade in office, he walked to and from home by himself, always at a brisk pace. When crime began rising in the 1960s, he reluctantly allowed Yehuda Krinsky, the former student who was now one of his secretaries, to drive him. After prayers he studied and prepared lectures; starting in the early 1970s he spent the first hour of each day editing transcriptions of those talks. In the afternoon he began opening the mail, which was voluminous. Later in the day he visited his mother and had tea with his wife before returning to the office in the evening. When he got home, typically late at night, he ate dinner with Chaya Mushka before retiring. Often he took home from the office a brown-paper shopping bag full of unfinished correspondence, which he returned completed the next day.

His lifestyle was austere. Instead of breaking for meals, he nibbled dark chocolate and sipped hot water with milk from a thermos; he avoided eating chicken or meat except on the Sabbath. Like many rabbinic prodigies, he was reputed to sleep very little. According to one report, he went to bed from 2 to 4 a.m. and remained awake after that until the early morning, when he rested for another two hours. At the beginning of his tenure, he received a salary of approximately $420 a month, an amount that hardly budged over the years. Rabbi Joseph Telushkin, whose father served as Schneerson's accountant, recalled seeing one of Schneerson's tax returns from the 1960s, which attested to an annual salary of $6,000.[4] According to the journalist Sue Fishkoff, at the time of his death in 1994 his yearly salary was about $30,000.[5]

In the early 1950s, Schneerson occasionally traveled to other parts of the city to pay respects to a mourner or to officiate at a wedding, but those trips soon stopped. After 1954 he no longer attended weddings unless they were held at 770, and after 1963 he stopped accepting invitations altogether. Although he met with important donors, he refused to attend fundraising dinners for Chabad institutions, something Yosef Yitshak had done. During his entire period of leadership, he left New York City only three times, for visits to Chabad summer camps in 1956, 1957, and 1960. Most of the time he never left Crown Heights except to visit the grave of Yosef Yitshak at the Old Montefiore Cemetery in Queens, which he did once or twice a month during the 1950s and up to several times a week in later decades. There he prayed and read the requests for blessings he received from his followers, sometimes for eight or nine hours at a stretch. Unlike other Hasidic leaders who summered in resort areas north of the city or went south to Miami in the winter, Schneerson refused to take vacations, even at the urging of his wife and staff. For the duration of his leadership he worked unceasingly, as though the fate of the world rested on his shoulders. Perhaps he believed it did.

For Schneerson's followers, direct access to their rebbe came through personal meetings or written correspondence. Like his father-in-law, Schneerson felt obliged to reply to every letter he received, and as the years passed, the letters increased to a nearly unmanageable quantity. Hasidim requested his advice or blessing on career and job prospects, marriage and relationships, medical concerns, and issues relating to their spiritual lives. As his reputation grew, he corresponded with rabbinical authorities and Jewish leaders outside the Lubavitch community who sought his input on questions of communal policy and leadership. Although his letters often touched on halakhic issues, he did not consider himself a legal authority and referred such questions to other rabbis. He wrote letters to the entire community ahead of holidays and sent standardized letters to individuals at life-cycle events. According to an internal estimate, the volume of mail eventually reached between 250 and 300 pieces a day.

Schneerson's secretaries often marveled at his speed and efficiency at handling the mail. He would scan each letter, running a pencil down the page as he went, underlining the points needing a response. After reading a letter, he wrote a reply in shorthand or dictated one to a secretary. The draft was then typed and returned to Schneerson to review before he signed it. According to one of his assistants, Schneerson often began reading a new letter while still dictating a response to the previous one. On some occasions—perhaps on issues where he didn't want to be personally involved—the secretary signed the reply himself with his own name. As the volume of mail increased, Schneerson could no longer reply to everyone at length. In the 1940s he wrote many long letters expounding on Jewish thought and philosophy; after he became rebbe such statements were mostly reserved for public lectures. He responded to questions of communal policy or to his followers' personal concerns in writing, but those answers became increasingly concise.

For devoted followers and outside visitors who wanted to meet the famed Lubavitcher rebbe, a letter from his desk could not replace a private meeting, known in Hasidism as *yehidut*. For the first thirteen years of his leadership Schneerson held these meetings on Sunday, Tuesday, and Thursday evenings, starting around 8:00 p.m. and going into the early hours of the morning. Appointments were made weeks or months in advance, and as the community grew, so did the wait.

Schneerson's personality, as reflected in these meetings, depended on the person he was meeting with. For Hasidim, yehidut had strict rules of decorum. On the day of the appointment a Hasid would fast and go to the mikveh for ritual purification; for the yehidut itself he would dress in formal clothing and wear a gartl, the cloth belt usually worn during prayer. Schneerson was also known to dress formally in his coat and hat for each visit. Upon arriving at 770, the Hasid sat on a bench in the hallway and studied or recited Psalms while waiting, which could be for several hours. According to Hasidic custom, the visitor would write a note, or *kvitl*, with his name, the name of his mother, and the request or concern he wanted Schneerson to address. Often the petitioner offered a donation, although it wasn't required. Upon entering Schneerson's office the Hasid would give the rebbe the note but not offer his hand, sit down, or speak first. Schneerson would read the note before offering a brief response and a blessing. Throughout the meeting the Hasid stood in a state of intense concentration; in many cases, Schneerson would be the only one to speak. At the end of the yehidut, which typically lasted around five minutes, the Hasid backed out of the room, in order not to turn away from the rebbe. If the visit ran long, one of Schneerson's secretaries knocked on the door or sounded a buzzer to ensure that everyone waiting had a turn.

For Hasidim, these meetings stood at the center of their relationship with their rebbe. In a yehidut the Hasid revealed his doubts, fears, and innermost secrets, and Schneerson devoted himself to guiding the Hasid in his spiritual, intellectual, and worldly life. While the contents of a yehidut were often discussed among friends and family members, they were sometimes too personal to share. Afterward, the Hasid would try to remember everything the rebbe had said, sometimes writing it down for posterity.

Attitudes varied regarding the appropriate times to seek a yehidut. For some, Schneerson's blessing was a necessary part of any decision, large or small. Others felt it inappropriate to bother him with minor things and sought a yehidut only on special occasions or when confronted by something particularly important. It was common to have a yehidut on or around one's birthday and before getting married; in the latter case the couple went in together.

Not just Hasidim sought audiences with Schneerson. As his fame grew, intellectuals, artists, politicians, business leaders, and rabbis from outside the Lubavitch community came to seek his counsel. Although Schneerson was most comfortable speaking Yiddish, he was fluent in Hebrew, Russian, English, and French and could communicate with most visitors without a translator. (He presumably also knew German but was not known to speak it.) Although he remained politically nonpartisan, politicians seeking his blessing included New York Governor W. Averell Harriman in 1958; New York Mayors Robert F. Wagner in 1963 and John Lindsay in 1968; Attorney General Robert Kennedy in 1964; and future New Jersey Senator Frank Lautenberg in 1972.

For such dignitaries, the rules of yehidut were loosened, if not discarded altogether. Prominent visitors were granted much longer meetings and often spent hours with Schneerson in conversation. They also provided some of the most vivid descriptions of Schneerson's personal magnetism. In some cases, visitors reported transcendent experiences in which the laws of time and space seemed suspended. "Time . . . begins running at a different pace," wrote Elie Wiesel. "In his presence you come closer in touch with your inner center of gravity."[6] Many people remarked on the intensity of his focus, which could seem like an altered state of consciousness. "In the *yechiduyot* with him, it seemed that he was taken over by some sort of divine inspiration," wrote Adin Steinsaltz, a scholar, a writer, and one of Schneerson's prominent followers in Israel.[7] The experience, he said, was like being "marked by fire."[8] Yitzhak Rabin, expressing a common observation, remarked, "It was the eyes of the rabbi that impressed me, the blue, penetrating eyes that express wisdom, awareness, and deep penetration."[9] An encounter with Schneerson was said to be so intense that some people purposefully avoided it. "There's something about him that is quite literally indescribable, that has to be experienced, which is one of the reasons that I have always hesitated to be in the same room with him," the author Chaim Potok told Ted Koppel in a 1991 *Nightline* interview. "I worry about my objectivity being swallowed and overwhelmed by this charismatic man."[10]

In other instances, non-Hasidic visitors reported more relaxed experiences. Many were surprised to find a curious and informed interlocutor who asked them about their own lives and professions. Although he cajoled the less observant to change their views or take on religious commitments, he rarely seemed harsh or judgmental. "Instead of the serious expression and faraway look which the Rebbe habitually seemed to wear, we found ourselves conversing with a very cheerful, happy and friendly—albeit holy—person," wrote the British businessman Zalmon Jaffe in his 2002 memoir.[11] In another exchange, reported by a New

York City psychiatrist, Sholom Zev Applebaum, Schneerson argued that one's religious beliefs and personal philosophy were as relevant to one's mental health as anything else and urged Applebaum to read the work of the psychotherapist and Holocaust survivor Viktor Frankl. He then counseled Applebaum on the best way to marshal political and community support for a mental health clinic he was trying to keep afloat.[12] Journalists and writers who came to interview Schneerson found him interviewing them in return. Harvey Swados wrote that he was "flabbergasted" when Schneerson asked him about the relationship between his work and that of Upton Sinclair.[13] In one case, while talking with the Reform rabbi Herbert Weiner, Schneerson explained his own theory of yehidut. "When a man comes with a problem, there are only two alternatives," he said. "Either send him away, or try to help him. A man knows his own problem best, so one must try to unite oneself with him and become *batel*, as dissociated as possible from one's own ego. Then, in concert with the other person, one tries to understand the rule of divine Providence in this particular case. And, of course, if the man who comes to you shares your ideas and faith, there is immediate empathy."[14] It is no surprise that yehidut experiences, particularly those in the early years of Schneerson's leadership, have been characterized as a form of psychotherapy.

For Schneerson, such occasions provided an opportunity not only to expand his influence but also to step out of his persona. He especially enjoyed talking about the subjects that had once been a major part of his life, like science, mathematics, and engineering. Bentzion Rader, a British accountant and businessman who enjoyed many meetings with Schneerson in the 1960s and 1970s, recalled that he often brought up topics unrelated to Rader's personal interests, including, on one occasion, an explanation of rocket mechanics following the 1969 moon landing. For Schneerson, who had given up nearly all semblance of a private life and had seemingly disappeared into his role, a ye-

Schneerson was considered relatively young for a Hasidic rabbi
when he began his leadership. This picture was taken in 1957, when
he was fifty-five years old. (JEM, The Living Archive)

hidut with an educated and interesting person was an opportunity to relax, talk about something other than the usual Hasidic
subjects, and become, if only for an hour, the curious, scientifi-
cally minded young man he had once been.

If a yehidut was the best opportunity for an intimate encounter with Schneerson, the communal gatherings, known in
Lubavitch terminology as farbrengens, were his most important
public forums. Previous rebbes held such events rarely; the fifth
rebbe, Shalom Dov Ber, did so only three times a year. For
Schneerson, they were the primary way he instructed his followers. Since the early 1940s he had spoken to the congregation on
the Sabbath afternoon preceding each Jewish new month, and
after becoming rebbe, he maintained this practice and added to

it considerably. Although the frequency of his talks waxed and waned over time, he remained a prolific speaker until his final years.

These events, common to all Hasidic groups but practiced in a unique style by Chabad, were more than public lectures. In Yiddish to *farbreng* means simply to enjoy oneself, but Lubavitch farbrengens were communal experiences of a highly theatrical nature. Packed body to body in the hall at 770, the crowd would drink vodka ("If the wheels are dry, they don't turn," Schneerson occasionally remarked, quoting a Hasidic aphorism), sing songs, and participate in the kind of spiritual uplift for which Hasidism is famous.[15] The crowds quickly outgrew the synagogue at 770, and larger farbrengens were moved to rented halls around the neighborhood. At other times, gatherings were held in an outdoor space between 770 and an adjacent apartment block. After the movement purchased the next-door building in the mid-1960s, a series of expansions and renovations enlarged the main synagogue until it could hold crowds of well over a thousand. Women also attended Schneerson's farbrengens, although they sat in a separate room, watching from above through a smoked glass partition. At a 1972 farbrengen, the *New York Times* journalist Israel Shenker estimated the crowd at about fifteen hundred men, plus women and children.[16] And as the years passed, the crowds grew.

Although any group of Hasidim could farbreng among themselves for any reason, a farbrengen with Schneerson was a special occasion. It was an opportunity for Hasidim to greet the rebbe and for visitors to witness his acclaim. Over the years figures ranging from Isaac Bashevis Singer to Bob Dylan passed through Schneerson's farbrengens to satisfy their curiosity or to pay their respects. "I experienced something which moved and amazed me," wrote Singer of a farbrengen he witnessed in 1960. "I could not see the table because the hall was so packed full of Hasidim. Men sang. People clapped their hands and climbed up on windows and benches to see the rebbe."[17] During musical portions of the evening Schneerson energized the crowd by waving his arms and bouncing up and down in his seat, transforming the room into a roiling ocean of black hats and beards. At other moments his eyes roamed the crowd, catching the glances of individual Hasidim waiting with a toast. From 1955 to 1964, in late-night farbrengens on the holiday of Simhat Torah, Schneerson taught the crowd a song he knew from his youth, singing it first himself, stanza by stanza. For visitors and regulars alike, a farbrengen in Lubavitch was an opportunity to experience Hasidic spirituality in the old style.

The centerpieces of such gatherings were Schneerson's talks, which he gave in Yiddish and at great length. Sitting at the head of the room behind a long table covered with a white cloth, Schneerson spoke in bursts of half an hour or longer and might talk for three or four hours over the course of a gathering that could last five or more. As an orator, Schneerson was more like a long-distance runner than a sprinter. In place of a dynamic delivery, he relied on steady intonation and sustained, forceful clarity. He almost never used humor to win over his audience and, unlike his father-in-law, only rarely told stories. Physically he remained almost motionless; the only interruptions were the occasional stammer, stutter, or cough. Invariably Schneerson spoke without books or notes, yet his delivery was fluid, as though he were reading from a text.

The high point of a farbrengen was often the delivery of a ma'amar, which was accompanied by its own set of rituals. Schneerson composed and delivered 1,558 such discourses, but unlike previous Chabad rebbes, who used the ma'amar as their main vehicle for theological exposition, Schneerson was less renowned for these original discourses and eventually stopped giving them altogether. Instead, he preferred to deliver less formal talks, or *sihot*. These lectures, though considered a single genre of Hasidic teaching, were formally united only by the fact that they were spoken by a rebbe. In substance and style they ranged from lectures on the Talmud to speeches on matters of timely concern to lessons in long-running series on specific areas of interest. Starting in 1952, on Sabbaths between the holidays of Passover and Shavuot, Schneerson lectured on *Ethics of the Fathers*, a classic of Jewish wisdom literature. Following the death of his mother, in 1964, he began a series of lectures examining the medieval commentator Rashi on the weekly Torah portion. In these talks, which totaled around eight hundred lectures over twenty-five years, he sought to elucidate the unstated textual difficulties that had attracted Rashi's attention, the commentator's approach to earlier rabbinic sources, and the general principles that informed Rashi's methods and conclusions. Together, these lectures comprise one of the most significant Rashi supercommentaries of the modern period. In 1970, in homage to his father, whose notes Chana Schneerson had smuggled out of the Soviet Union, he began a series of talks based on Levi Yitshak's explanations of the *Zohar*. At most of his farbrengens one of the talks was directed toward women, and the evening usually included moral exhortations, policy statements on issues of the day, and directions for specific efforts he expected his followers to perform.

Aside from letters, Schneerson stopped composing his own written works after becoming rebbe, but his talks were dutifully transcribed by a small group of followers and were often edited by Schneerson himself. Despite their variety, these talks, which constitute the bulk of Schneerson's published work, demonstrate his unique style and sensibility. Years earlier, he had been influenced by his correspondence with the Rogatchover Gaon, Yosef Rosen, whose idiosyncratic system of Talmudic analysis relied on a vast grasp of the literature and a synthesis of wide-ranging sources. Schneerson's method of teaching was similarly broad, stretching across multiple genres of Jewish thought while striving toward synthesis and systemization. One of his guiding principles was the underlying consistency of the entire Torah; as he often stated, "Since the exoteric Torah and the esoteric Torah are one Torah . . . it cannot be that they contradict one another."[18]

In his most impressive performances Schneerson started the evening by asking a series of questions about a relevant text before moving on to tangential subjects seemingly removed from the initial topic. Yet in the course of the discussion, he answered the earlier questions one by one while tying together the disparate themes he had broached throughout the evening. Often the same principle that resolved a Talmudic quandary was the basis for a broader philosophical point or ethical lesson. "A problem in the laws of divorce leads us to consider the concepts of separation and unity and to a radical reinterpretation of the nature of exile," explained Rabbi Jonathan Sacks in the introduction to his own adaptation of Schneerson's talks. "A passage relating to the fruit of trees in their fifth year takes us through the levels of spiritual reality, an examination of the Baal Shem Tov's life, and a reversal of our normal understanding of holiness and sanctification . . . Each talk moves from the specific to the general, the finite to the infinite, and back again."[19]

Such structures, particularly when they concerned a complicated Talmudic, halakhic, or mystical issue, could be difficult even for scholarly individuals to absorb. Listening to Schneerson speak in the mid-1950s, Herbert Weiner observed that "very few of the Chasidim present could follow his words; after fifteen minutes or so had passed I noted that eyes were closing all around me, and not in mystical ecstasy."[20] For those who could keep up, such lectures demonstrated breathtaking virtuosity.

Naturally, some of Schneerson's ideas were more brilliant than others. At times his teachings seemed to consist of little more than a loose reading of sources designed to draw tenuous connections and arrive at predetermined conclusions. In earlier years his talks were structured and explicative; in later years he relied more on an associative collage of biblical and rabbinic quotations to gesture at familiar ideas. Although he stressed different issues at different times and articulated his positions in different formulations, his thinking evolved little over time. This could give his talks a certain sameness, and over decades of public speaking he often repeated himself. But through his unceasing emphasis on certain core ideas, he attained a clearness of thought that might have been absent from a more complex thinker. In contrast with the Kabbalah, which tended toward baroque elaborations of the Godhead and heavenly spheres, Schneerson's theosophy drove toward an essential simplicity, consistent with his belief in the ultimate unity of the Divine and its messianic revelation. Despite the scholarly heights he sometimes reached, his performances were never just demonstrations of intellectual ability; through consistency and repetition he conveyed an unambiguous message that his followers could enact without ambivalence. In cumulative effect Schneerson's talks, given in the heightened emotional and spiritual atmosphere of a farbrengen, set the policy, mission, and tone of the Chabad community. This was where he inspired his followers, raised his army, and rallied the faithful.

As Schneerson expected, or perhaps feared, his duties were all-consuming. He had once led a private life; he now had almost no private life left. This was partly enabled by his lack of children—a circumstance that pained him but that also allowed him to become almost completely absorbed by work. His immediate family consisted only of his wife and his mother, leaving him few domestic responsibilities. But his work ethic was a matter of choice. Like other Hasidic leaders, he could have maintained a more spacious existence by handing off duties to subordinates, declining to be quite so available in person or by mail, and not holding so many farbrengens. But he was not a man given to half measures. Being rebbe was not a job but a calling. To bring the Messiah was the responsibility of his generation, and no one could tell how much effort that would require. Coming up short was unthinkable.

Yet Schneerson was careful to maintain a regular home life. In 1955 he and Chaya Mushka moved from their apartment on New York Avenue to a freestanding three-story brick house at 1304 President Street, just a few blocks from 770. The ground floor consisted of a spacious living room decorated with dandelion-yellow wallpaper, a small dining room and kitchen, and an alcove whose table was generally strewn with newspapers and periodicals. On the second and third floors, up a set of stairs illuminated by small stained-glass windows, were the bedroom, another small dining room and library, and a study with book-lined walls and an armchair. Although Schneerson spent little time at home, he returned each afternoon to have tea with his wife, a routine he considered sacrosanct. He once said that having tea with Chaya Mushka was as important to him as putting on tefillin.[21] While his mother was alive, he visited her daily at her own home just down the block.

If Schneerson's personal life was confined to these few domestic rituals, Chaya Mushka's was the reverse. Throughout her life she declined to participate in official Chabad activities, which made her an enigmatic figure. She never went to her husband's farbrengens, although in later years she sometimes listened to them by telephone. (Schneerson's mother did attend.) Throughout his years as rebbe she never referred to herself as the "Lubavitcher Rebbetzin," but as "Mrs. Schneerson from President Street" or, occasionally, on the phone, as just "Schneerson." Even as Chabad women became more prominent in the movement, taking on roles as emissaries, public speakers, and leaders of women's groups, she chose to remain a wife and homemaker.

Despite her absence from organizational activities, Chaya Mushka did lead an active personal and social life. She did her own cooking and shopping, and Crown Heights residents occasionally saw her running errands. At other times she drove to other neighborhoods, where she was less likely to be recognized, sometimes stopping at 770 to pick up her sister along the way. She ate dinner with her husband most days, and until 1971, when her mother died, she and her husband ate holiday meals at Nehama Dina's apartment in 770. She also maintained a close circle of friends, including Necha Rivkin, whom she had known since childhood; her father's nurse, Mania Lotz; and her cousin, Hadassah Carlebach.

Although Chaya Mushka had grown up in a Hasidic dynasty with antimodern tendencies, she had received a secular education, and she continued to enjoy reading Russian literature. In Berlin and Paris she was able to expand her intellectual horizons, and in New York she was said to take in the city's cultural offerings, including art museums and possibly the ballet. In the early years of her husband's leadership, she was able to take a few trips abroad; she traveled to Paris and Zurich in 1953 and again to Switzerland in 1958. She was interested in fashion, and friends remembered her as a slight, immaculately groomed woman given to wearing stylish outfits.

Why Chaya Mushka never took a more public role in Chabad is unclear. Some observers have suggested that the presence of Nehama Dina made her concerned about usurping her mother's place, or perhaps she did not want to insult her sister, who had been denied a more prominent position when her husband did not become rebbe. Schneerson's mother, Chana, was present in the community until 1964, which also made a public role for Chaya Mushka less necessary. Others have argued that she saw her primary function as private and domestic; until Schneerson's leadership Chabad women, including the wife of the rebbe, did not have official roles in the movement.

Nonetheless, Chaya Mushka did engage with the Chabad community in an unofficial capacity. Neighborhood women sought her council and support, and young couples spoke to her before their weddings. In some cases, she served as an unofficial conduit to her husband for those who couldn't or wouldn't go through official channels. And although Schneerson's responsibilities prevented the couple from spending as much time together as they had spent when they were younger, they still had a close relationship. Schneerson often turned to his wife for her thoughts on his initiatives, and she weighed in with praise and criticism. Schneerson's doctor once referred to her as his "intellectual sparring partner," as the one person who "could take the Rebbe to task at home, as a good wife would, when she saw him going a little too far afield."[22] She was rumored to help her husband with research on politics and current events by reading newspapers and periodicals at home and making trips to the main branch of the Brooklyn Public Library, just a few minutes away by car. Throughout all the stages of Schneerson's life, from his youth in the Soviet Union, to his education in Berlin and Paris, to his new life as the Lubavitcher rebbe, she was at his side as his wife, confidante, and friend.

8

Breaking Out

IN A 1922 BOOK, *Economy and Society*—partly translated in 1947 as *The Theory of Social and Economic Organization*—the German sociologist Max Weber described three sources of social authority. The "rational" form rests on legal, bureaucratic, and democratic bases, as in a modern liberal democracy. "Traditional" authority derives from historically enshrined norms, as with an absolute monarchy. And the third form, the "charismatic," comes from nothing but the character of the person who wields it. Such a figure, Weber explained, commands the obedience of followers by virtue of being, or seeming to be, in touch with a deeper, truer, more fundamental reality, perhaps through supernatural means. Although charismatic leaders could arise in almost any context, they are often religious figures claiming Divine inspiration. And while charismatic authority might complement rational or traditional structures, it can also challenge and replace them with the leader's unique gifts.

There are few better examples of Weberian charisma than the Hasidic tsaddik. Since the time of the Ba'al Shem Tov and his disciples, Hasidim have believed the tsaddik to be intimately connected with the Divine. He was a cosmic savior, sent to retrieve the fallen sparks of holiness from the shells of impurity; an individual redeemer who connected his followers with God; and a miracle worker who channeled Divine blessings to his community. According to Shneur Zalman of Lyady, the tsaddik was not merely an exceptional individual but a soul that descended from a high celestial origin. Other people, no matter how pious they might become, could not aspire to this status. The tsaddik wasn't made but born.

As the Hasidic movement developed, the institution of the tsaddik suffered predictable scorn. Like other kinds of charismatic leaders, tsaddikim were opposed by traditional and bureaucratic officials who based their authority on scholarship, wealth, or family connections. As far back as the eighteenth century, tsaddikim were accused of fraud and charlatanism; after visiting the Maggid of Mezritsh's court around 1770, Salomon Maimon, a young Talmud scholar who became one of the early leaders of the Jewish enlightenment, accused the Ba'al Shem Tov and his followers of practicing "kabbalistic hocus-pocus."[1] Although the first tsaddikim were chosen for their scholarship and spiritual accomplishments, the position became dynastic, leading to the appointment of unsuitable characters. A few Hasidic leaders, like Israel of Ruzhin, proclaimed a kind of Hasidic prosperity gospel, practicing an aesthetic of "kingship" in which their luxury and wealth were of primary importance. Materialism, other forms of corruption, abuse of power, and feuds between Hasidic courts became commonplace. Over time Hasidism underwent what Weber called "the routinization of charisma"— the passing of authority from the original luminary to his family, staff, disciples, and office. But there still arose genuine charismatic figures who conveyed a sense of connection with the

Divine. Among twentieth-century tsaddikim, Schneerson was such a man.

Schneerson's conduct and abilities attested to his extraordinary nature. People remarked on his unusual memory, evidenced by his ability to give lectures without notes and to pick up conversations where they had left off years before. In keeping with Weber's description, Schneerson seemed to have no care for "rational economic conduct," amassing virtually no private wealth. His childlessness, which was likely a source of personal anguish, aligned him with the Weberian ideal of a leader who is "outside the routine obligations of family life."[2] His work ethic, physical stamina, productivity, and unceasing quest for accomplishment gave the impression that he was more than an ordinary human.

His official routines enhanced this mystique. Throughout his leadership he insisted that anyone who wanted to meet him had to do so at 770, within the environment of the Lubavitcher court. In 1979 he turned down a meeting in Washington with President Jimmy Carter, and then he declined a telephone call with the president, since it conflicted with a visit to Yosef Yitshak's grave. When visitors came to see him, he met them only in the evening or late at night, often forcing them to stay up for the audience and to leave at dawn, which reinforced the otherworldly atmosphere of the encounter. Within the movement there was little hierarchy; instead there was a fraternal spirit and a dependence on Schneerson's authority. At farbrengens, senior Hasidim jostled for a place alongside schoolboys and younger men. Adin Steinsaltz recalled once finding Shimon Peres—who was then Israel's foreign minister—sitting on a bench outside Schneerson's office, waiting for a yehidut along with two ordinary Hasidim.

Schneerson's followers described him unselfconsciously in Weberian terms. "We felt that here was a man who lives and feels the truth, a man who is the essence of truth himself," a Hasid

This photograph, taken at a farbrengen, or communal gathering, in late 1967, shows some of the Lubavitch community in that pivotal decade of rapid growth. (JEM, The Living Archive)

named Yossi Greenberg told Sue Fishkoff.[3] "I firmly believed that he possessed some sort of supernatural capability, and that he was in contact with another level of being—which I do not hesitate to call the Divine," wrote Steinsaltz.[4] For the new generation of Lubavitchers, living in his vicinity could be a life-changing experience. In the 1950s and 1960s, Crown Heights was bursting with excitement, hope, and purpose, and the Lubavitch community attracted everyone from Holocaust survivors trying to find a new sense of belonging to flower children searching for spiritual meaning. Schneerson was at the center of it all, a tsaddik not in theory or in the mythic past but here and in the flesh.

The most important element of Schneerson's charisma was the sense of purpose he imparted to his followers—the conviction that they weren't just following a holy man but following him on a holy mission. In the aftermath of the Holocaust, many rabbis believed that the catastrophe constituted the birth pangs of the Messiah and that humanity was living in the end-times. Schneerson shared this position and added to it, saying that his era was not just the "footsteps of the Messiah" but the "footsteps of the footsteps of the Messiah."[5] In rabbinic tradition it had always been important to do all one could to merit redemption, but the timing and circumstances of that event were up to God. The Talmud recorded a prohibition against trying to "force the end," and legends were told of righteous men who tried to bring the Redeemer before his time and were punished. Schneerson believed he could succeed where others had failed. For the practical engineer he once was, faith, while necessary, wasn't enough. His was the generation of redemption; with one more push, and with the help of his followers, he could make it happen. All he needed was a plan.

In Judaism, redemption has traditionally been understood in collective terms. Although it includes every individual, the salvation of the nation—and the world—are at stake. Accordingly, episodes of messianic ferment tend to assume a political character; redemption entails not just spiritual revival but national rebirth. As the historian Gershom Scholem argued, Hasidism, with its inner-directed spirituality, "neutralized" that messianic impulse. This was also true of the Chabad movement, at least until the twentieth century. In speeches to Lubavitcher Hasidim and yeshiva students, the fifth rebbe, Shalom Dov Ber, emphasized the nearness of the messianic age and the special role his disciples would play in its coming. The urgency of bringing the Messiah increased with the wartime proclamations of Yosef Yitshak, who argued that redemption was a practical solution to the Holocaust. But neither of them inspired a messianic ferment to the degree that Schneerson did.

The seventh rebbe's messianism was not only more insistent than that of his forebears; it also represented a shift in the theological orientation of Chabad. Schneerson never disavowed the importance of inner-directed bittul (self-annihilation) and did emphasize the necessity of individual liberation as a precondition of general redemption. On many occasions he stressed that both inner- and outer-directed approaches to worship were necessary and that without sufficient bittul a Hasid was liable to "forget his mission."[6] Yet it was the active component—the "drawing down" of the Divine—that constituted the purpose of Hasidic efforts. "The ultimate aim is . . . not to withdraw from the world, but to make the world a vessel for godliness," Schneerson said in 1962.[7] Or, as he put it on innumerable occasions, paraphrasing *Ethics of the Fathers*, "Action is the essential thing."[8]

Most remarkably, Schneerson taught that self-sacrifice in the service of God meant forgoing not only material comforts but spiritual accomplishments as well. According to an analogy he used in reference to Yosef Yitshak, a king will not expend all his resources to win a limited war. But he will exhaust all his treasures, and even put his own life in danger, to achieve total victory. So, too, the current generation wasn't tasked with improving the world piecemeal but was engaged in a life-and-death struggle. For Schneerson, bringing the Messiah meant a complete transformation had to be achieved, despite the apparent spiritual cost.

To his followers, this reorientation did not represent a true change in the movement's direction but was instead a response to the approach of redemption, which had been foreseen from the beginning. True change or not, the shift in emphasis enabled the outreach and activism that became the hallmark of Schneerson's leadership. Chabad had once split the difference between spreading Hasidism and serving as an elite spiritual brotherhood. Now Schneerson turned it into an outreach empire. And if Schneerson's messianism inspired the movement's activism, the activism enabled its messianism. Early Hasidism neutralized the messianic impulse by emphasizing the salvation of the individual; Schneerson revived it by doing the opposite. With a focus on practical accomplishments, the door to historical redemption was again open. Bringing the Messiah was no longer the province of holy mystics, who might commune with God in the depths of their absorption, but the task of every Hasid, every Jew, who could go out into the street and make it happen.

Rabbinic literature is replete with acts that will bring the Messiah. These include the giving of charity, the love of a fellow Jew (to counter the dictum that the temple was destroyed because of baseless hatred), and the strengthening of basic religious observance, as Yosef Yitshak tried to do during the war. In accordance with the Ba'al Shem Tov's vision that the Messiah would arrive when Hasidism spread "outward," it was necessary to propagate the movement's teachings, an imperative that could assume hyperliteral form. In 1978, Schneerson instructed that Shneur Zalman's *Tanya* be published in as many cities as possible; it was consequently printed in more than five thousand places using a portable press mounted on the back of a truck. In Schneerson's view, studying the subject of redemption itself was necessary, and in 1984 he instituted a daily practice of studying Maimonides's twelfth-century code of law, the *Mishneh Torah*, which allowed participants to complete a review of the entire work in just under a year. In contrast with subsequent codes, the *Mishneh Torah* covered the entirety of Jewish practice, including subjects only relevant in a future messianic age. Learning those laws, Schneerson believed, was both a necessary preparation for the messianic advent and a symbolic enactment of the post-messianic dispensation.

But the most important act, as it had been throughout the history of messianic movements, was repentance. As the Talmud stated in the early centuries of the Common Era, "All the end-times have passed, and [redemption] depends only on repentance and good deeds."[9] According to Hasidic teaching, repentance was not just a matter of regretting personal sins and resolving to do better. Rather, it was a "return of the soul to the God that gave it," a metaphysical act of infinite significance.[10] Repentance had the power to raise the penitent's religious observance to a state of perfection and, according to the Talmud, transform even intentional sins into meritorious acts. Its power, which could affect the nature of past behavior and was therefore intrinsically unbounded by time, derived directly from God's essence and was, like the messianic state, "above boundary and limitation"—an embodiment of the Divine unity of opposites. According to the *Zohar*, even a single act of true repentance by a righteous person had the power to bring the Messiah immediately. "For through a complete repentance one draws down the revelation of the light of the Infinite without any boundary, and this revelation is in every place," Schneerson explained in a 1981 ma'amar, the last such talk to be published during his lifetime.[11]

In the hall of 770, Schneerson's exhorted his audience over and over, assuring them that redemption could happen in the blink of an eye. But religious fervor among the faithful was not enough. As the Ba'al Shem Tov had prophesied, the Messiah would come only when Hasidism spread "outward." Although repentance was primarily an individual task, it was also a communal undertaking. As Schneerson stated in 1981, all efforts to make the world a Godlier place were included in the category of repentance, since they "*return* the world to its state and situation at the beginning of creation."[12] Somehow, the message of repentance had to reach the millions of Jews who belonged to non-Orthodox denominations or were not religious at all. Yosef Yitshak preached the same thing during the war, to no avail. For Schneerson to succeed where his father-in-law had failed, he would have to try something new.

As in other areas, Schneerson walked the line between tradition and innovation. In the earliest years of the movement, Chabad developed a network of emissaries who collected charity for Hasidim in Palestine and provided religious services to Jews in remote areas. In the late nineteenth century Shalom Dov Ber expanded the network, drawing on yeshiva alumni to spread Chabad's influence across the Russian Empire. Chabad outreach increased again under Yosef Yitshak, who sent emissaries throughout the Soviet Union to fortify religious communities suffering from government repression. Upon arriving in America, Yosef Yitshak began rebuilding through organizations like Machne Israel and Merkos L'Inyonyei Chinuch and, after the war, by sending his representatives to places like Australia, Morocco, and displaced persons camps in Germany. In the United States he dispatched his followers to start Jewish day schools in New England and the Midwest, and yeshiva students to visit Jewish communities during the summer months. Locally, he took advantage of the Released Time program, which allowed public school students to receive religious education once a week at off-campus locations; by the late 1940s Lubavitchers were conducting weekly classes for thousands of students in the New York area. Just two months before his death, in the winter of 1949, Yosef Yitshak inaugurated what became a staple of Chabad outreach by sending Zalman Schachter and Shlomo Carlebach—two men who would become major Jewish figures in their own right—to Brandeis University. They arrived during a Hanukkah dance in the school cafeteria, where they tried to talk to students about Judaism and give them free pairs of tefillin. Although they were kicked out by school administrators and warned not to return, university campuses would provide fertile ground for Chabad activities.

If Chabad outreach was a long-standing tradition, it attained its modern form under Schneerson. On June 30, 1958, in a landmark farbrengen held on the anniversary of Yosef Yitshak's release from Soviet exile, Schneerson delivered a discourse based on God's words to Jacob in the book of Genesis: "Your descendants shall be as the dust of the earth, and you shall break out to the West and to the East, to the North and to the South."[13] Schneerson explained this as a messianic statement: when Jacob's descendants reach the level of dust, then the one who "breaks out"—that is, the Messiah, who reveals the infinite Divinity within the finite world—will arrive to raise them from their lowly state. However, Schneerson explained, "Since all the things that will be revealed in the days of the Messiah are dependent on our actions [now]," the "breaking out" of the messianic age had to become manifest in pre-messianic times.[14] In part, breaking out was accomplished by the righteous leaders of each generation, whose miraculous deeds constituted a rupture of the natural order. In a talk given a few months later Schneerson went further, saying that every person could "break out" by exceeding personal limitations—by studying and praying without looking at the clock, or by giving to charity without regard to financial considerations. Most importantly, "breaking out" meant physically going to the four corners of the earth and spreading Judaism in every place. The Hebrew word for "and you shall break out"—*ufaratsto*—became a slogan for Chabad ambitions and, rendered as a song, the march to whose rhythm Schneerson's followers settled in city after city, country after country. Outreach once meant preaching Hasidism to otherwise observant Jews, but never had that community shrunk to such a small and insignificant part of the Jewish people. Now it was necessary to reach every Jew a Chabad emissary could get to by plane, train, car, or boat. Although these efforts began as a trickle, they soon became a deluge.

By the time Schneerson's outreach enterprise got off the ground, the straitlaced 1950s were giving way to the counter-cultural 1960s, and a new crop of spiritual leaders were trans-forming America's religious landscape. Psychedelic gurus like Timothy Leary, Ken Kesey, and Carlos Castaneda drew audi-ences and acolytes on the West Coast and around the country. Shunryu Suzuki arrived in San Francisco from Japan and, in 1962, established the San Francisco Zen Center. Maharishi Mahesh Yogi, founder of the Transcendental Meditation move-ment, made his first visit to America in 1961 and later achieved renown for his association with the Beatles. The Hindu teacher A. C. Bhaktivedanta Swami Prabhupada founded the Inter-national Society for Krishna Consciousness in New York City in 1966, and its members, known as Hare Krishnas, became widely recognized thanks to their distinctive dress, chanting, and public proselytizing.

As a participant in this spiritual marketplace, Schneerson understood that if Judaism couldn't capture the interest of young seekers, they would turn elsewhere. In 1969 the first "Chabad House" was founded by Rabbi Shlomo Cunin on the University of California campus in Los Angeles, and over subsequent de-cades many other Chabad centers opened on college campuses around the country. Students were a natural target of Chabad outreach—young people exploring new ideas might be attracted to the kind of spirited, traditional Judaism lacking in the subur-ban synagogues they had attended growing up. They were also more likely to relate to Schneerson personally. Unlike other Ha-sidic figures, he was still relatively young, and he had a univer-sity background. Other rabbis saw youthful rebellion as a threat to tradition; Schneerson saw potential in its energy and idealism. The journalist Ascher Penn observed in 1958 that students in the New York area could often be seen coming to Schneerson for conversation and advice. "The fact is," he wrote, "American Jewish youth instinctively feel that in Rabbi Menachem Mendel Schneerson they have someone who understands them."[15] Although Chabad's model of strictly Orthodox Judaism differed from other philosophies of the era, it also appealed to young spiritual seekers, many of whom embraced its ritually demanding lifestyle.

Schneerson was not the only one trying to draw estranged Jews back to their roots. Other Hasidic leaders, like Levi Yitzchak Horowitz, the Bostoner Rebbe, attracted new followers by appealing to both non-Hasidic and non-Orthodox Jews, especially university students in the Boston area. In Israel, the Breslov Hasidic movement, whose rebbe, Nahman of Bratslav, had died in 1810 and was never replaced, enjoyed a resurgence through an influx of new devotees. Educational institutions such as Ohr Somayach and Aish HaTorah, both founded by Rabbi Noah Weinberg in the early 1970s, began catering to newly religious students. (Chabad opened its own yeshiva for newly religious men, Hadar HaTorah, in 1962 and a seminary for women, Bais Chana, in 1971.) Esther Jungreis, a Hungarian-born Holocaust survivor, author, and lecturer, drew large audiences under the auspices of the Hineni organization, which she founded at Madison Square Garden in 1973. Others figures, such as Shlomo Carlebach, who split from Chabad in 1955 to become a composer and performer of Jewish music, pursued their own brands of outreach, often drawing on elements of Hasidic spirituality.

All this activity coalesced into what became known as the *ba'al teshuva*, or repentance, movement and helped turn the tide in favor of a shrinking Orthodox population. Even if the revival was not all Schneerson's doing, he was a pioneering figure. Whereas most Orthodox communities were trying to preserve a way of life that was in danger of disappearing, Schneerson believed that the survival of Orthodox Judaism depended on a proactive effort. Short of bringing the Messiah, Chabad's aggressive outreach enterprise would be the most important achievement of his life.

It helped that Schneerson, despite his fundamentalism, endorsed a religious philosophy that was indulgent of its targets. Like most Orthodox rabbis, Schneerson viewed contemporary Jews as innocents who had grown up ignorant through no fault of their own. Non-Orthodox Jews, in his opinion, were merely asleep, spiritually speaking, and could be woken up with some friendly coaxing. Unlike other Orthodox organizations, Schneerson rejected an all-or-nothing approach to Jewish observance. While he insisted on not compromising in principle—and criticized more liberal streams of Judaism for doing so—he also taught that each religious act, each mitzvah, was of inestimable value and would lead to further commitments. As he told Herbert Weiner, "It's important to know that one must do everything, but at the same time we welcome the doing of even a part. If all we can accomplish is to save only one limb, we save that. Then we worry about saving another."[16] Although his methodical and demanding nature could make him seem like a perfectionist, he was unwilling to let the perfect be the enemy of the good.

Nor was Chabad outreach strictly concerned with ritual matters. In keeping with the doctrine that the highest level of divinity resides in the lowest places, Schneerson taught that it was the body, not the soul, that had the most intimate connection with God. The commandments of the Torah, after all, apply only to physical existence, not to a purely spiritual state. Whereas the connection of the soul to God is intrinsic, the connection of the body to the Divine comes only through God's will, which gives the body a more powerful connection to the Divine essence. Thus, "when a Jew lacks the needs of his physical body . . . it produces something like an exile, as it were, in the substance and essence of God."[17] Accordingly, Schneerson's emissaries not only taught Jews how to observe the Sabbath and keep kosher but also provided basic social services. Over time Chabad outposts in far-flung corners of the world became known for providing hot meals and holiday celebrations for young Israeli tourists who might not have had anything to do with Orthodox Judaism in Israel but who were glad for Chabad's hospitality in India or Peru. Like many religious organizations, Chabad found that the swiftest route to the heart is through the stomach.

Unlike the fire and brimstone of Yosef Yitshak's wartime rhetoric, Schneerson's style of outreach espoused a warm and welcoming optimism. This choice was largely based on the thirty-second chapter of *Tanya*, in which Shneur Zalman spelled out the metaphysical principle behind the commandment to love one's fellow as oneself. "Since [all souls] are congruous and of one Father, all of Israel are therefore called literal brothers, due to the root of their souls in one God—only their bodies are differentiated."[18] In other words, one must love others not because they are *like* oneself but because they *are* oneself, since all souls are extensions of the same Deity. Therefore, continued Shneur Zalman, "one must draw them with thick cords of love . . . and perhaps one will be able to bring them close to the Torah and the worship of God."[19] Moreover, Schneerson believed that all Jews, whatever their professed beliefs or choices in life, had a Divine soul, which was unsullied by earthly sin and inherently desired to be connected to its source. "Even the undesirable acts of a sinner are only a covering, not the essence of his nature, which is good and holy," he said.[20] In this spirit, Schneerson stressed that religious outreach must be done with love and compassion rather than reproof and condemnation. Emphasizing the preciousness and potential of Jewish souls was better than stressing the punishments people might suffer for their sinful ways.

Schneerson may have adopted a generous view of nonreligious Jews, but he had a different attitude toward his Hasidim.

Although the flowering of Chabad outreach took place in the peace-and-love context of the 1960s and 1970s, Schneerson—who had long been obsessed with military strategy—preferred metaphors drawn from war. Shalom Dov Ber had preached in 1900 that the students of his yeshiva were like "soldiers in the war of the House of David," an idea that Schneerson extended to all his followers, including women and children. "As soon as a Jewish child is born, he is immediately 'one who goes out to the army in Israel,'" he said in 1980.[21] The mobile outreach vehicles—originally envisioned as Jewish bookmobiles—became known in the 1970s as mitzvah tanks. His effort to encourage the lighting of Sabbath candles was called Neshek—an acronym for the Hebrew words "Nerot Shabbat Kodesh," or "candles of the Holy Sabbath," but also a Hebrew word meaning "weapon." And the Chabad youth movement, re-formed in 1980, was named Tzivos Hashem, or "Armies of God." On many occasions he preached the need to take the offensive against secularism and assimilation rather than wage a merely defensive war. As early as 1951, in an interview with *Jewish Life* magazine, he said, "Orthodox Jewry up to this point has concentrated on defensive strategies. We were always worried lest we lose positions and strongholds. But we must take the initiative and wage an offensive. This, of course, takes courage, planning, vision, and the will to carry on despite the odds."[22]

In the run-up to Israel's Six-Day War in 1967, Schneerson launched an effort to encourage Jewish men to put on tefillin, and starting in 1974, he expanded this initiative with nine more military-style "campaigns," each focused on a particular area of Jewish practice. These included the commandments of daily Torah study, hanging mezuzot on the doorposts of homes, stocking homes with Jewish books, and lighting Sabbath candles. The next year he launched campaigns to promote the Jewish dietary laws and the laws of family purity, and in 1976 he added Jewish education, giving to charity, and the obligation to love fellow

Jews. Many of these initiatives had specific religious significance—giving to charity and loving other Jews were singled out as messianic acts—while some efforts, like the education campaign, included larger policy goals, such as encouraging a moment of silence in public schools. These campaigns also allowed his followers' outreach efforts to take concrete form by focusing on specific ritual acts that could be performed on the street, in a synagogue, or in a mobile home.

In 1951, in his first talk as rebbe, Schneerson qualified his acceptance of leadership, saying that in Chabad "each one should work for himself, and not rely on the rebbe." In the case of his emissaries, this directive was taken literally. When emissaries went to start new Chabad centers, they might receive a bit of seed money, and would occasionally receive further resources or instructions from Brooklyn. But they were expected to do their own fundraising and become quickly self-sufficient. As the emissaries understood, they were not merely performing a job but were empowered to act in Schneerson's place. Nor was outreach limited to official emissaries. As Schneerson often stated, all people were responsible to have a positive effect on their environment, wherever that was. In response to such demands, Hasidim were encouraged to come up with their own initiatives, and many of the rituals now associated with Chabad were conceived by individual Hasidim and only later received Schneerson's blessing. When Schneerson began speaking in 1967 about promoting the mitzvah of wearing tefillin, a few young Hasidim came up with the idea of approaching people on the street to ask if they were Jewish and, if so, offering them the opportunity to fulfill the commandment. With Schneerson's approval the strategy went forward and remains one of the most visible aspects of Chabad proselytizing to this day.

While such aggressive methods drew criticism from other Jewish groups, Chabad Hasidim saw them as modern expressions of their long-standing philosophy. Every mitzvah a Jew performs connects them directly with the Divine and is therefore of infinite consequence. If any such encounter resulted in a moment of sincere repentance, that increased the spiritual power of the act and gave it greater messianic potential. Although some Orthodox leaders worried that Chabad's practice of sending emissaries to far-off communities posed an unacceptable spiritual risk, Schneerson understood that such activities could have a positive effect on the religious commitment of his followers. "Our Chasidism can be sent into any environment, no matter how strange or hostile, and they maintain themselves within it," he boasted in a 1955 interview.[23] Like the Mormons, Schneerson realized that active proselytizing, especially at an emotionally vulnerable age, only strengthened his followers' faith.

In hindsight it is easy to see Schneerson's efforts as carefully planned, with one campaign following in orderly fashion upon another—even, to borrow from his metaphorical stock, as a detailed strategy designed to lead to victory. But in practice his initiatives were more like guerrilla warfare. Schneerson impressed on his followers that their efforts must be performed with great urgency, since there was no telling when the Messiah might arrive. In a 1952 talk he compared the current situation of the world to that of a house on fire: a too-careful accounting would impede salvage efforts. An oft-repeated Yiddish motto, taken from the fourth Lubavitcher rebbe, was *l'khatkhile ariber*—meaning, idiomatically, that instead of reserving a last resort until last, it was better to use it first. Nobody knew how much was still needed for the Messiah to come. But so long as the Messiah had not yet arrived, more was necessary.

Schneerson's messianic mission inspired many of his followers, but his demanding leadership style didn't please everyone. For older Hasidim who had grown up under Yosef Yitshak, transferring allegiance to a new rebbe would have been difficult in any case. Many of them favored the older and more familiar

Shmaryahu Gourary and were reluctant to accept Schneerson's ascendancy. Yosef Yitshak's widow, Nehama Dina, was reportedly appalled at the treatment of her older son-in-law, and in an act of symbolic resistance she refused to hand over Yosef Yitshak's fur hat, or *shtrayml*, which symbolized his leadership. In response, Schneerson abandoned the practice of wearing a shtrayml and appeared for the rest of his life in a wide-brimmed black fedora. Although Gourary eventually accepted Schneerson's leadership, his son Barry became estranged from the movement and criticized the direction it had taken. "Chabad started out as a spiritual and philosophical movement," he told Jerome Mintz. "Nowadays ChaBaD stands for charisma, blessings, and dollars, especially dollars."[24] When Barry got married in 1953, Schneerson was not invited.

Even those who accepted Schneerson's leadership sometimes found him a difficult man to follow. Although Schneerson leaned heavily on Yosef Yitshak's legacy to establish his authority, his style of leadership was a sharp departure from that of his predecessor. Yosef Yitshak was reputed to be a warm, congenial person, and his Hasidim viewed him with filial affection. Schneerson was more demanding and less generous with praise. Upon completing a task, followers were rarely thanked or congratulated but instead were challenged to accomplish greater things. His militant conception of the movement extended not only to the names of organizations or efforts but to the loyalty he demanded from his Hasidim. He was not just their rebbe but their commanding officer, and a Hasid, like any soldier, was duty bound to follow orders. When confronted with complaints about the difference between his methods and those of his father-in-law, Schneerson replied, "My way of doing things is different."[25]

Even younger Hasidim who didn't have much experience of Yosef Yitshak's leadership could resent Schneerson's domineering attitude. Despite Chabad's early focus on university students—and despite his own studies—Schneerson usually instructed his followers not to pursue a higher education and discouraged the teaching of secular subjects in Chabad schools. This was perhaps based on the concern that such influences would weaken his followers' attachment to Hasidic life and on a desire to re-create the kind of educational institutions that had existed in prewar Europe. It also left his followers without the ability to pursue most professions in the secular world and with few options other than religious career paths, such as outreach. Although becoming his emissary was a welcome opportunity for many of them, some balked at the prospect of spending their lives far from family, friends, and other Orthodox Jews. In such instances, Schneerson's rebuke could be harsh. When President John F. Kennedy established the Peace Corps in 1961, Schneerson berated his followers; a non-Jewish president understood the concept of sending emissaries to far-flung places, Schneerson argued, while Hasidim were slow to embrace a similar idea. When a family objected to sending their son to some remote posting, Schneerson responded with a stinging letter. "I had thought he was my soldier, and I could give him a mission . . . but it appeared that before he decided, he had to hear what his mother and family would say. It is self-evident that the [proper] conduct of a soldier is not to make conditions, [such as] how long, and then to ask his family for their opinion about it."[26] The letter, which was widely circulated within the Chabad community, was a shot across the bow. If Hasidim wanted to remain in Schneerson's good graces, they had to do what he said.

Schneerson stressed that Hasidim needed to assume responsibility for themselves and couldn't just rely on the rebbe. But it was clear that any latitude existed only within the boundaries he set. Such restrictions occasionally became an issue with individual emissaries, who felt that the times demanded a more flexible approach. Shlomo Carlebach believed that Jewish assimilation represented such a grave threat that certain strictures, particularly regarding coed activities, had to be relaxed. Rather than comply with Chabad's insistence on gender segregation, he left to pursue his own style of Jewish outreach. When Zalman Schachter-Shalomi began exploring spiritual paths outside Chabad, eventually starting the Jewish Renewal movement, he still felt a deep connection to Schneerson and lamented that his former friend and mentor refused to engage with his ideas. As Schachter-Shalomi understood, Schneerson was willing to offer advice and instruction but not to receive any in turn. He was eager to give but reluctant to take.

For most of his followers, however, Schneerson's demands strengthened their faith in him and in their mission. In time these efforts would produce remarkable results, as Chabad emissaries and institutions spread across the globe. But their most immediate effects were on Hasidim themselves, who were electrified by Schneerson's messianic message. For them he became the paradigm of a contemporary tsaddik. They found in Schneerson not a tyrant but a resolute leader with boundless aspirations. His demands on them were not only justified but, as many Hasidim believed, helped them discover their true potential. His confidence made him seem Divinely inspired and convinced his followers of their ability to transform the world. For many, this impetus led them to spend their lives in remote locations, far from their families or other Orthodox communities. Under Schneerson's leadership, the lives of his Hasidim, their families, and the institutions of Lubavitch were all turned toward redemption.

9

Expanding Influence

IN MARCH 1972, in an interview with the *New York Times* on the occasion of his seventieth birthday, Schneerson was asked whether he saw his movement as conservative. Schneerson replied that he did not. "My explanation of conservative is someone who is so petrified he cannot accept something new. For me, Judaism, or halacha [Jewish religious law], or Torah encompasses every new invention, every new theory, every new piece of knowledge or thought or action. Everything that happens in 1972 has a place in the Torah, and it must be interpreted, it must be explained, it must be evaluated from the point of view of Torah even if it happened for the first time in March of 1972."[1]

For Schneerson, this was not a new idea. Since his youth he had fostered a belief that Judaism was all-inclusive, that nothing escaped its purview. As a young man he had been fascinated by astronomy and had tried to reconcile modern astronomical science with the astronomy described by the Talmud. As a university student he had drawn comparisons between his scientific studies and Hasidic concepts: they were, as he saw them, parallel structures in the material and spiritual realms. Later in life, he continued to follow developments in certain scientific fields, as well as political and military affairs in the United States and Israel. Because of these interests, he was not averse to offering his thoughts on everything from the age of the universe to the social welfare state. Unlike some Hasidic leaders, Schneerson wasn't content to be a mystical sage or to limit his teachings to purely religious matters. Just as everything fell under the umbrella of Torah, so, too, no issue was beneath his notice or beyond the scope of his authority.

This conviction led him to espouse some insightful ideas, as well as a few that were a bit strange. Like other modern theologians, Schneerson grappled with the apparent contradictions between scientific materialism and religious dogma, and with his background in physics he believed himself uniquely qualified to address those issues. Unlike other thinkers, however, who tried to reconcile traditional beliefs with scientific verities, Schneerson refused to budge from the literal statements given in the Bible or the Talmud. Previous authorities—including, most prominently, Maimonides—had acknowledged that the rabbis knew only what the science of their age could tell them; Schneerson clung to the idea that the Talmud was Divinely inspired and therefore infallible. If there was a mistake, it wasn't on the part of the Torah. Rather, science had gotten it wrong.

Despite this general position, Schneerson did not hesitate to make more specific arguments when it suited his purposes. In contrast to those commentators who conceded that the account of creation in Genesis should not be taken literally, he believed that it should, and that assertions to the contrary relied on improperly understood observations. "Scientists know very little of the atoms in their pristine state," he wrote in a 1961 letter. "In advancing such theories, they blithely disregard factors universally admitted by all scientists, namely, that in the initial period of the birth of the universe, conditions of temperature, atmospheric pressure, radioactivity, and a host of other catalytic factors, were totally different from those existing in the present."[2] Regarding the fossil record, he argued that "the discovery of the fossils is by no means conclusive evidence of the great antiquity of the earth . . . In view of the unknown conditions which existed in prehistoric times . . . one cannot exclude the possibility that dinosaurs existed 5722 years ago, and became fossilized under terrific natural cataclysms in the course of a few years."[3] He wrote to another correspondent on the same issue: "If you are still troubled by the theory of evolution, I can tell you without fear of contradiction that it has not a shred of evidence to support it."[4]

Schneerson's arguments were not limited to well-worn subjects like evolution or the age of the universe. As a student he had tried to substantiate the theory of spontaneous generation, which held that living organisms regularly emerge from nonliving matter, since the rabbis of the Talmud believed it to be true. Similarly, he insisted on upholding a Ptolemaic view of the solar system, asserting that the sun orbited the earth, and not the other way around. Here, too, he provided a modern rationale. "One of the conclusions of the theory of relativity is that when there are two systems, or planets, in motion relative to each other—such as the sun and the earth in our case—either view, namely the sun rotating around the earth, or the earth rotating around the sun, has equal validity."[5] Neither the convoluted orbital mechanics that a theory of geocentrism requires nor the fact that relative motion undercut the Talmudic position as much as it did the Copernican seemed to bother him at all.

Schneerson's goal was not to reconcile science and faith, however, but to cast doubt on scientific conclusions in order to give religion room to breathe. Underlying all his arguments was the contention that science was a valid means of investigation, but it had to be tempered by its own admissions of uncertainty. Since the advent of quantum mechanics, "the principle of probability now reigns supreme . . . science must reconcile itself to the idea that whatever progress it makes, it will always deal with probabilities, not with certainties or absolutes."[6] As he told another questioner, "Science formulates and deals with theories and hypotheses, while the Torah deals with absolute truths."[7] Despite a preponderance of evidence for a scientific theory, one had to remain faithful to the traditional view, even if there was no evidence for it whatsoever.

As such arguments demonstrate, Schneerson did not see himself as hostile to science per se, but only to claims he thought were overconfident. According to his Hasidic beliefs, nothing in the world existed without a Divine purpose, and that included the scientific revolutions of recent centuries. In several talks he argued that just as Hasidic teachings heralded the messianic age, so, too, scientific and technological developments served a similar purpose, particularly since the messianic revelation would take place in and through the physical world. Radio, he taught, was not only a practical way to teach Hasidism to listeners— Chabad scholars taught *Tanya* and other texts for years on stations such as the Yiddish-language WEVD—but radio waves physically embodied the spreading of Hasidism "outward," even if there was no listener listening and no receiver receiving. This, he said, was a fulfillment of Isaiah's prophecy that in the messianic age "the earth will be filled with the knowledge of God."[8]

Most importantly, the revolutions in theoretical physics of the early twentieth century seemed to parallel on the physical plane the teachings of Hasidism on the spiritual one. Hasidism taught that the apparent diversity of the world was a manifestation of the ultimate unity of God. Similarly, referring obliquely to Einstein's theory of special relativity, Schneerson argued that modern physics taught that both "quantity" (matter) and "quality" (energy) were ultimately the same. Just as Hasidic teachings were a foretaste of the messianic Torah, such insights were also of a messianic character.

A religious fundamentalist rejecting scientific orthodoxy was hardly unusual. But Schneerson's scientific ideas illustrated a pattern of thought that repeated itself in other areas. From one perspective, his stance was entirely consistent with his religious worldview. While he may have expressed unusual beliefs, he couldn't be accused of inconsistency or hypocrisy. From another perspective, Schneerson's positions could seem opportunistic or even in bad faith. He was eager to accept scientists' admissions of uncertainty but not to credit their assertions of confidence, let alone admit any doubt in his own nonempirical beliefs. This tendency repeated itself across political and cultural realms. Wherever he saw an idea that benefited his cause he was keen to take advantage of it. But he was not willing to grant that idea its own legitimacy or to reckon seriously with its implications.

Politically, Schneerson tried to keep Chabad scrupulously nonpartisan. He did not endorse candidates for office (though he did instruct his followers to vote), and he discouraged his emissaries from wading into controversial issues. Such involvements, even in service of worthy goals, would only alienate potential supporters. Although his traditionalism often brought him into alignment with the Republican Party, his religious beliefs did not map neatly onto any political identity. This could, at times, produce idiosyncratic positions.[9]

As early as the 1980s, Schneerson spoke in favor of solar energy production as a means of freeing the United States from a dependence on foreign oil and as a safer alternative to nuclear energy. He did not address the question of gun control, but he opposed gun ownership, even for self-protection, saying that it demonstrated a lack of trust in God. He was against not only mass incarceration but incarceration generally, arguing that it dehumanized imprisoned people and deprived them of the ability to fulfill their obligations to humanity and God. "Whatever his standing or situation, even if he sinned . . . he is still obligated to fulfill his task and mission in life," he explained in 1950. "Therefore, imprisonment is impossible, because this would deprive him of the ability to fulfill his task and mission."[10] Rather, Schneerson argued for a justice system that prioritized education and rehabilitation over incarceration and punishment.

Unlike President Ronald Reagan, with whom Schneerson seemed to agree on broad sociocultural issues, and with whom he shared a warm, albeit formulaic, correspondence, Schneerson supported a strong social safety net, and unlike most social conservatives, he saw no conflict between leftist politics and religious values. The poor were not liable to abuse government aid, he said, and there was "no contradiction between the good of the group and the good of the individual, but on the contrary—they complement one another, attaining a wholeness both for the individual and the group."[11] In a 1963 letter to the editor of a Yiddish newspaper he said that in his youth he had known many socialists who were religious Jews and that this posed no contradiction. Still, Schneerson addressed such questions only occasionally and emphasized that Judaism was not aligned with any party or ideology. A political philosophy independent of religion would have been unthinkable to him.

Yet Schneerson did take public and controversial positions on some issues, often angering liberal segments of American Jewry. Like many postwar Jewish leaders, Schneerson held the United States in unreservedly high regard. For most of his peers, this sense of American exceptionalism was rooted in the Constitution, particularly in the separation of church and state enshrined by the Establishment Clause of the First Amendment. Although Jews still faced discrimination, they could no longer be considered interlopers because of their religion. After cen-

turies as second-class citizens in Christian and Muslim societies, Jews in the United States were as American as anyone else.

Schneerson disagreed. Although he often referred to the
United States as a "country of kindness," the constitutional division between church and state did not, in his view, account
for America's special place in the world. Rather, like many Christian conservatives, he viewed the United States as a fundamentally religious country. As he said in a 1975 talk, "The nation
was founded on faith in God, and not faith in a transcendent
God, merely found somewhere in the seventh heaven . . . rather
the manner of [the founders'] faith was such that it permeated
their day-to-day lives, and their day-to-day conduct."[12]

Consequently, Schneerson's guiding political principle was
that religion in the public sphere was a good and necessary thing
and that the secularization of American society was harmful for
its Jewish citizens and everybody else. Although the framers of
the constitution had trusted the checks and balances of the democratic system to safeguard citizens' rights, Schneerson felt that
the only guarantee of public morality was a higher, Divinely
ordained law. Faith in that law was what distinguished the United
States from the atheistic communism of the Soviet Union and
what protected it from becoming another Germany, where he
had witnessed the rise of Nazism despite its democratic government and cultured society. As he wrote to one of his followers, "If in a previous generation there were people who doubted
the need of Divine authority for common morality and ethics . . .
our present generation has, unfortunately in a most devastating
and tragic way, refuted this mistaken notion. For it is precisely
the nation which had excelled itself in the exact sciences, the
humanities and even in philosophy and ethics, that turned out
to be the most depraved nation of the world, making an ideal of
murder and robbery, etc."[13] For Schneerson, the best way to ensure the safety and prosperity of American Jews was to encourage, rather than restrict, religious faith.

Politicians and public figures were regular visitors to
Schneerson's farbrengens. Pictured here in 1975 is Robert Abrams,
the longtime New York attorney general who was then borough
president of the Bronx. (JEM, The Living Archive)

Most of all, Schneerson believed that America's status as a
world superpower was of messianic significance, and its theistic
character was therefore even more important. He publicly recognized the country's role in freeing Yosef Yitshak from Soviet prison and later in rescuing him from German-occupied
Poland—acts that positioned it as an instrument of Divine providence. In the postwar era he saw America as the new center of
the Jewish people, eclipsing even the State of Israel. As he told
the journalist Ascher Penn, "The greatest concentration of our
energies is found here in America. We must lead the smaller Jewish communities in other countries and continents, even in the
Land of Israel, which must strongly rely on American assistance
for their economic and spiritual survival."[14] Schneerson's belief

in the United States as a new spiritual center wasn't just a matter of the country's power and wealth. Rather, it was America—the "lower half of the globe" in kabbalistic parlance, where the Torah had not originally been given—that needed to be infused with Judaism before the Messiah came.

Schneerson's belief that the United States had a messianic role was not limited to the part played by its Jewish population. Although his focus in the early years of his leadership was on the Jewish community, he became increasingly outspoken on matters of national interest. By the mid-1970s he had an emissary in Washington, DC, who lobbied lawmakers and government officials on his behalf. He was a strong anti-isolationist and argued repeatedly for the beneficent role America should play on the world stage. "When we speak of a great nation that in recent years has gained the ability to affect the entire world . . . it is also certain that this imposes a special responsibility and merit, both with regard to itself and also with regard to its global influence," he said in 1975. "This is a counter to those who mistakenly claimed in previous generations that we can isolate and limit ourselves, letting domestic concerns suffice."[15] In a full-page ad taken out in the *Washington Post* in September 1978, he praised President Carter for demanding that recipients of foreign aid uphold a high standard of human rights, and advocated that such aid go to educational, cultural, and economic causes, rather than military ones.

Yosef Yitshak had declared that "America is not different." Schneerson believed that America *was* different, and not just because of its material wealth or religious toleration. America had a messianic role to play. The motto on its great seal and currency was *E pluribus unum*—"Out of the many, one"—a phrase that could just as well describe Hasidic theology. As the colonial preacher and theologian Jonathan Edwards put it, salvation "would begin in America."[16] Schneerson seemed to agree.

* * *

Schneerson's political convictions were not merely theoretical. He also pursued policy outcomes, which put him in conflict with civil liberties groups and most of the American Jewish establishment. Like Jewish leaders throughout history, Schneerson believed that the future of the Jewish people rested on the education of its children, and he made the establishment and support of educational institutions one of his highest priorities. Here, much to his chagrin, he ran into his first open conflicts with the rest of the American Jewish community.

In the 1940s, Schneerson had directed the Merkos L'Inyonei Chinuch, an organization that led Chabad's educational efforts outside of the movement's school system. To this end the organization participated in the Released Time program, an effort begun in the early twentieth century to provide public school students with a religious education. With parental permission, students were allowed to leave school for religious instruction, usually at a different location. In New York most Jewish children attended public schools, providing a large target population for Chabad's activities. In 1943 more than 100,000 children and 272 schools in New York participated in Released Time; at the peak of Chabad's involvement in the late 1940s, the program drew around two million students across the country.

Not everyone saw this as a good thing. Despite the apparent separation between public schools and the instruction provided by religious teachers, the program was opposed by Jewish groups on church-state grounds, particularly when instruction took place during school hours or on school property. Objecters included the National Community Relations Advisory Council (an arm of the Council of Jewish Federations), the multi-denominational Synagogue Council of America, and the Reform movement's Central Conference of American Rabbis. In 1948, in *McCollum v. Board of Education*, the Supreme Court ruled against Released Time, although in that instance the program was making use of school facilities. Four years later in *Zorach v.*

Clausen the court clarified its ruling, stating that the program was constitutional so long as it took place off school grounds, did not use government funds, and was noncompulsory.

The fight over Released Time was Schneerson's first involvement with the question of public support for religious education, and one of his few major successes. As an Orthodox leader, he supported government aid to parochial schools, a development that would have lightened the financial burden on religious parents and communities. When the Kennedy administration determined that such aid would be unconstitutional, he joined with the Roman Catholic Church in protest. Although he never attained this concession, he remained incensed by the resistance to it, which came not just from nonreligious, non-Jewish Americans but also from Jewish leaders and organizations. Their opposition, Schneerson felt, was not just to government support for religion but to Jewish education as such. "The clear majority of Jewish antagonists to parochial schools are philosophically opposed to the very *idea* of parochial schools," he wrote. "Many of these individuals have the chief voice in how Jewish Federation funds are distributed, and resist support of Hebrew day schools or rabbinic academies, either by giving them miserable token funds, or by totally denying them any allocation."[17] Moreover, Schneerson denied that government support posed a constitutional problem. "The intention in that which is inscribed in the Constitution . . . is that no one shall be forced to adopt the beliefs of another, and that no priority shall be given to one over another," he said in 1975. "But God forbid that it shall be said to mean that the nation can provide funding for anything, and the singular exception for which state funds cannot be used is to bring the call to young people . . . that there is a God."[18]

Chabad's involvement in Released Time and the quest for public funding for religious education focused on Jewish students and Jewish schools. But Schneerson's concern for the religious fabric of the country exceeded parochial boundaries. With the increasing secularization of the postwar years, he believed that the country was failing its children by neglecting to provide them with religious direction.

The issue came to the fore in 1962 when a group of Jewish parents sued the Union Free School District No. 9 in Long Island, New York, over recitation of the Regents' Prayer. The prayer, which had been approved for use in New York public schools, read: "Almighty God, we acknowledge our dependence upon Thee, and we beg Thy blessings upon us, our parents, our teachers and our country." After the prayer was upheld in New York State Court and the New York Court of Appeals, the case went to the Supreme Court, where Chabad submitted an amicus brief in support of retaining it. Nonetheless, the court ruled 8–1 in *Engel v. Vitale* that the prayer contravened the Establishment Clause and banned it from public schools.

Most of the Jewish community saw the decision as a necessary corrective. Along with the parents who brought the suit, groups opposing the prayer included the Synagogue Council of America, the National Jewish Community Relations Council, B'nai B'rith, and the American Jewish Committee. In their view, inserting prayer into public schools not only violated the constitution but came uncomfortably close to the historical experience of religious coercion. Whatever the Constitution said, Christianity was by far the dominant religion in America, and school prayer could all too easily lead to the indoctrination of children in Christian beliefs. The Jewish community's opposition to the Regents' Prayer was so pronounced that it raised the ire of Christian groups. In the September 1, 1962, issue of the Jesuit magazine *America*, an editorial warned "our Jewish friends" that their position on school prayer could provoke "heightened anti-Semitic feeling."[19]

Schneerson, though not speaking the same thuggish language, agreed with the Jesuits and declared that all means should

be employed to reverse the decision. While other Jewish leaders worried about state-sponsored religion, Schneerson felt that
their anxieties were out of touch with the moment. "In our day
the world is suffering from an excessive indifference to religion,
or even from a growing materialism and atheism," he explained
in a 1964 letter. "Thus, if separation of Church and State [is]
necessary, it is not at all the answer to the problems of our contemporary youth."[20] Moreover, he argued, the nondenomina-
tional nature of the prayer was enough to allay any worries about
Christian proselytization.

Jewish students weren't Schneerson's only concern. All children, he believed, needed to be reminded of a higher power for
their moral well-being and the country's. They might once have
received such instruction at home, but that was no longer the
case. "The crux of the problem lies in the success or failure of
bringing up children to an awareness of a Supreme Authority,
Who is not only to be feared but also loved," he wrote in the same
1964 letter. "Under existing conditions in this country, a daily
prayer in the public schools is for a vast number of boys and
girls the *only* opportunity of cultivating such an awareness."

Despite Schneerson's efforts, the court ruling was never re-
versed, and the prayer was never reinstated. Still, Schneerson
never let the issue go. Along with Christian leaders like the evan-
gelist Jerry Falwell, he sought to find a compromise acceptable
to both the courts and the American public by proposing that
schools establish a daily moment of silence. "A child now hears
in his home nothing about the Creator and Ruler of the world,"
he said in 1984. "The institution of a 'moment of silence' in
schools is for the *good* of the country's citizens, affording their
children the opportunity to think about a spiritual value."[21] The
proposal suffered a setback in 1985, when the Supreme Court
ruled in *Wallace v. Jaffree* against an Alabama law mandating a
minute of silent meditation or voluntary prayer. The court upheld an earlier law, however, mandating silent meditation only,

and since then, a moment of silence in public schools has largely been upheld by the courts. Though he was far from the most prominent supporter of the idea, the legal decision in its favor was still a victory in Schneerson's battle against American secularism.

The issue of school prayer lay largely beyond Schneerson's control. The most Chabad could do was submit amicus briefs in Supreme Court cases. But in other areas Schneerson encouraged his followers to take direct action affecting the religious consciousness of the country's non-Jewish population. The clearest and most unusual of Schneerson's efforts to encourage a godly society was his campaign for observance of the Noahide laws.

Jews have rarely, if ever, proselytized to their gentile neighbors. Not only was it practically unfeasible, but Judaism does not mandate that non-Jews observe Jewish laws or accept Jewish belief. According to Judah Halevi, author of the twelfth-century philosophical work *The Kuzari*, Jews and non-Jews were not just given different tasks and allotted different destinies by God but were fundamentally different kinds of human beings. Just as animals occupied a different plane of creation from that of plants, so the Jewish people were distinct from the rest of humanity. This idea was taken up by kabbalists of later centuries and was emphasized by Shneur Zalman of Lyady. Whereas Jews possessed a Divine soul that was "a part of God above" non-Jews possessed only an "animalistic soul" that made them human but did not connect them to God in the same way.[22]

Despite this belief in an ontological difference between Jews and non-Jews, several Chabad rebbes had made overtures to non-Jewish leaders and audiences. The first two leaders of the movement were required to explain elements of Hasidic thought to secular authorities in order to absolve themselves of charges brought by the Mitnaggdic community. In the case of the second rebbe, Dov Ber, this included an explanation to the governor of Vitebsk of the providential role played by gentile leaders.

Other Hasidic sages—notably Nahman of Bratslav—taught that the conversion of gentiles would be part of the messianic process, although such a project was never undertaken.

Schneerson adopted this kernel of an idea and grew it to an unprecedented extent. According to the Talmud, only Jews are obligated to observe the 613 commandments of the Torah. But all humans are required to keep the seven laws given by God to Adam and, later, Noah. In Maimonides's view Jews are obliged to compel obedience to those laws on pain of death, though his position was rejected by other authorities. A gentile who accepts and performs these commandments, Maimonides continued, is one of the "pious among the nations of the world" and receives a share in the world to come.[23] According to the rabbinic exegesis of Genesis, these laws include prohibitions against idol worship; blasphemy; murder; adultery, incest, and other forms of sexual immorality; theft; and eating the flesh of a living animal. The seventh is a positive injunction to establish courts of law.

For Schneerson, this common set of obligations was congruent with his vision of Judaism as a universal religion. Just as the Torah was applicable in all times and places, so, too, was it relevant to all people. While it might accord Jews greater ritual responsibilities and spiritual status, non-Jews found their role in the Noahide laws. This idea also resolved a sticky problem with Schneerson's civic vision. If non-Jewish Americans were to embrace a theistic faith, what form would it take? While Schneerson seemed to support the halakhic position that Christianity was not a form of idolatry, advocating publicly for and accepting the value of Christian observance would have been a bridge too far. The Noahide laws provided a sanctioned—and in his view, obligatory—framework within which to promote religious consciousness among the American population.

As early as 1929, Schneerson had already been thinking about these laws and their application. In a letter to the Rogatchover

Gaon dealing with the prohibition on accepting charity from non-Jews, he noted that the prohibition was not applicable in the case of gentiles who had accepted the Noahide laws, since "they are among the pious of the nations of the world and have a portion in the world to come."[24] Not until the early 1980s, however, did he begin calling on his followers to encourage the observance of these laws by the general public. Though no Jewish community had attempted such an effort before, this was not a question of principle, he argued, but a matter of practicality. In the past, proselytizing to gentiles would have been dangerous and was therefore not required. Now that the danger had passed—another sign of the coming redemption—the original law emerged in full force. Moreover, by encouraging non-Jews to observe the Noahide laws his followers would lay the groundwork for the messianic age, in which all humanity would acknowledge the sovereignty of God. It was therefore their responsibility to promote God's will among non-Jews just as they did among Jews.

This call, though unusual, enjoyed a measure of recognition. President Reagan mentioned the Noahide laws in letters he exchanged with Schneerson, and in 1982 he praised Schneerson for providing "a vivid example of the eternal validity of the Seven Noahide Laws, a moral code for all of us regardless of religious faith."[25] Since 1978, Chabad had convinced Congress and the president to designate Schneerson's birthday "Education Day U.S.A.," and it often managed to work references to the Noahide laws into those declarations. The 1989 proclamation issued by President George H. W. Bush, stated, "The principles of moral and ethical conduct that have formed the basis for all civilizations come to us, in part, from the centuries-old Seven Noahide Laws."[26] In 1991, Congress declared that "these ethical values and principles have been the bedrock of society from the dawn of civilization, when they were known as the Seven

Noahide Laws."[27] The irony of honoring a leader who opposed secular education among his followers with a national Education Day was not remarked upon.

Of all Schneerson's initiatives, the Noahide campaign was perhaps the least successful. Despite its recognition in high offices, and lip service from Chabad emissaries, it was never prioritized to the same degree as Jewish outreach. While virtually no corner of the Jewish world has not been touched by Schneerson's emissaries, the number of non-Jews committed to Noahide observance number, at most, in the thousands. Schneerson's maximalist vision encompassed all of humanity, but there was only so much that he could accomplish.

If Schneerson's efforts in support of school prayer put him at odds with the rest of the Jewish community, the issue was just a foreshadowing of the conflict that would erupt over what became one of Chabad's signature outreach practices. In 1973, Schneerson launched a campaign promoting the mitzvah of lighting Hanukkah menorahs, a ritual intended to publicize the military victory of the Maccabees against the Seleucid Empire around 164 BCE, the rededication of the temple in Jerusalem, and the miracle by which a jar of lamp oil sufficient for one day lasted instead for eight.

The commandment was especially salient in the context of Schneerson's American outreach campaign. The Maccabean war had been a struggle against not just an external invader but also the Hellenization of Judean Jews. The lighting of Hanukkah menorahs in America symbolized the persistence of Jewish identity against a backdrop of Christmas decorations. That year the movement estimated that it distributed sixty thousand menorahs in Jewish community centers, synagogues, and college campuses. Within two years Chabad estimated that it was distributing nine hundred thousand Hanukkah menorahs on five continents. On the holiday itself a fleet of RVs bearing 10-foot-high menorahs on their roofs streamed out of Crown Heights, spreading holiday cheer throughout New York City. And in Philadelphia the local emissary, Avraham Shemtov, found an even more explicit way to follow Schneerson's instructions: erecting a small wooden menorah at the foot of the Liberty Bell.

As with other methods of Chabad outreach, public menorah lightings didn't originate with Schneerson, but he approved of the idea and encouraged it. In 1975 the Philadelphia menorah was followed by a 22-foot-high steel and mahogany structure in San Francisco's Union Square, sponsored by the music promoter Bill Graham and nicknamed "Mama Menorah." In 1979 the movement erected a 30-foot-tall menorah across from the White House and prevailed upon President Carter to light it. The next year Schneerson issued a directive encouraging public menorah lightings, which was followed by an official menorah lighting campaign.

Although Chabad intended the menorahs to instill pride in Jews who would not otherwise see their traditions represented in public spaces, Jewish and civil liberties groups soon realized that Chabad's efforts were yet another encroachment on the church-state divide. In 1978, Rabbi Joseph Glaser, head of the Reform movement's Central Conference of American Rabbis, wrote to Schneerson that the Jewish community's "considerable success in recent decades in preventing Christmas displays, crèches especially, on public property, and in preventing religious assemblies and prayer-periods in public schools," was being endangered by Chabad's activities.[28] Schneerson wrote back, arguing that the menorah lightings were justified "since the general acclaim and beneficial results have far exceeded our expectations." He dismissed the constitutional question by asserting that nobody's "loyalty to the Constitution" was compromised, and "in all cases permission was *readily* granted by the authorities."[29] Neither argument addressed the constitutionality of the practice or the dangers of mixing church and state.

As with the conflict over school prayer, debates over policy and principle eventually moved to the courts. In the winter of 1986, a group of Jewish organizations and the American Civil Liberties Union (ACLU) brought a suit challenging the erection of an 18-foot-tall menorah at the Pittsburgh City-County Building next to a 45-foot-tall Christmas tree and a "Salute to Liberty" sign. The ACLU also objected to a nativity scene placed by the Holy Name Society of Pittsburgh on the grand staircase of the Allegheny County courthouse. The presence of all of these at government buildings, the ACLU argued, violated the First Amendment.

Over the next three years—while a similar suit wound its way through the courts in Vermont—the case made its way to the Supreme Court. On July 3, 1989, in *County of Allegheny v. American Civil Liberties Union*, the court issued a 5–4 ruling against the crèche, reasoning that the "Government may celebrate Christmas in some manner and form, but not in a way that endorses Christian doctrine." However, in a separate, 6–3 ruling, the court allowed the menorah to remain, arguing that unlike the nativity scene, the menorah, Christmas tree, and "Salute to Liberty" sign in combination were secular holiday celebrations rather than religious symbols. "The display of the menorah is not an endorsement of religious faith but simply a recognition of cultural diversity . . . conveying the city's secular recognition of different traditions for celebrating the winter holiday season."[30] That the significance of the menorah to the Hasidim who erected it was entirely religious was apparently overlooked. But the decision, which rested on the menorah's placement next to an assortment of holiday decorations, left Chabad's other menorahs in dispute, and over the next few years further cases were brought in cities around the country. Despite such opposition Chabad persisted, winning some of its cases on free speech grounds. And while many of their menorah displays—particularly those situated on government properties—remained in legal limbo, Chabad continued to erect them, and their opponents eventually gave up trying to get rid of them.

Still, not everyone was won over to Chabad's point of view. Over centuries of exile Jews had learned what it meant to live as a small religious minority and knew the ways the majority might use state-sanctioned religion against them. The United States, with its constitutional protections and history of religious freedom, provided a haven from such treatment. The appropriate response, most Jewish leaders believed, was to remain vigilant in defense of these safeguards, not compromise them at the first opportunity. As Marc Stern, an attorney for the American Jewish Congress put it, "To Lubavitch, the public menorah balances out the public Christmas tree. To the American Jewish Congress, the menorah on public lands clears the path for the crèche and the cross."[31] Even other Orthodox groups disapproved of Chabad's methods. "Ideally, we would prefer no displays of any religious symbols," Sheldon Rudoff, then president of the Orthodox Union, told the *Forward* newspaper in 1992.[32] Following Chabad's successful efforts to erect menorahs, Christian groups used them as an argument to display nativity scenes. And in 1990, when Chabad obtained a federal court order allowing the placement of a menorah in Cincinnati's Fountain Square, the Ku Klux Klan used the same ruling to hold a rally and erect a 10-foot cross. When the city banned privately funded displays in 2002 to stymie the KKK, Chabad took the case to court. "One has to question the sanity of Chabad," Stern commented. "They're so hellbent on putting up menorahs that they're willing to run the risk of [KKK actions]."[33]

For Schneerson, such concerns were misguided. Past oppression, he reasoned, was not sufficient cause to react apprehensively to a new and different situation. Moreover, Jewish safety, both physical and spiritual, was endangered more by a cringing and self-conscious attitude than by proud demonstrations of culture and religion. Trying to hide only breeds suspicion, he argued, and had been proven unsuccessful by history. Rather, drawing on biblical and Talmudic dicta, he taught that the only way to ensure Jewish safety was to be Jewish visibly and openly. American Jewry suffered from an "inferiority complex," he said; restoring a sense of pride in Jewish identity and tradition was a necessary countermeasure.[34]

In a way, Schneerson was right. As Shaul Magid has argued, although Schneerson's opponents never conceded his dismissive views on church-state separation or his conception of the United States as a fundamentally religious country, he understood something about American multiculturalism that most Jewish leaders overlooked.[35] Like civil rights activists from the same era, Schneerson knew that the way toward toleration and acceptance lay not through quiescence and accommodation but through assertive claims of one's rights. If Orthodox Judaism was going to have a resurgence in America and draw non-observant Jews to its ranks, it had to do so loudly and with pride.

The pluralistic tendencies of American society served Chabad interests and ambitions, but other liberalizing aspects of the country ran contrary to the movement's traditionalist ethos. From the second decade of his leadership on, Schneerson was forced to confront rapidly evolving cultural and political mores on issues such as gay rights, abortion, birth control, and feminism. Here he was largely in agreement with conservative Christian leaders. He believed that homosexuality is a mental illness and should be treated medically. Like many Orthodox leaders, he discouraged birth control, blaming its use on a self-centered culture that viewed children "not as sources of joy and happiness, but rather as burdens and impediments to pleasure and 'fulfillment.'"[36] Abortion is a complicated issue in Jewish law, and while Schneerson's attitude was governed by halakhic strictures, he did not champion a public antiabortion stance. On such issues he was relatively quiet. When it came to feminism, he was outspoken, and had his own superficial view of the movement. Re-markably, under his leadership women took more active roles in Chabad than ever before.

Hasidism has historically been a patriarchal culture. In Chabad women were the wives and daughters of Hasidim but were not Hasidim themselves, and—aside from a few high-profile exceptions—were not afforded the scholarly or ritual opportunities of Hasidic life. Schneerson viewed Chabad women as Hasidic followers in their own right. In a 1955 letter to the Chabad women's organization, he wrote that women's status as Hasidim is "self-evident."[37] According to one famous anecdote, he objected to an issue of the Chabad children's magazine be-cause it had an illustration of boys on the cover but no girls. Women, he realized, needed to be included in the community and represented in its self-image if they were going to contrib-ute to its transformative mission.

Here, too, Schneerson followed and exceeded the prece-dent set by his father-in-law. In the late 1930s, Yosef Yitshak had encouraged the formation of study groups for young women in Riga and New York that were analogous to similar groups for young men. The women in these groups studied Hasidic texts along with the Yiddish writings of Yosef Yitshak—an unprece-dented development in the history of the movement. In 1942, Yosef Yitshak founded a network of girls' elementary schools; by 1946 there were twenty-six of them. Women participated in the activities of Machne Israel, which included a separate divi-sion to promote the laws of family purity, Sabbath observance, and religious education. Such efforts and institutions represented a new front in the Orthodox struggle against assimilation. Like the Beis Yaakov school movement, started by a Krakow seam-stress, Sarah Schenierer, in 1917, these initiatives recognized that without the traditional Jewish education given to men, young women were defecting from Orthodoxy at a prodigious rate. Even if rabbinical institutions like Lubavitch's Tomkhei Temimim succeeded in creating new generations of scholars and activists, they would have limited prospects without a corresponding female population with whom to marry and raise families. Just as the male yeshiva structure arose in response to the challenges of modernity, a similar effort was required for women.

Schneerson continued and expanded these activities at the beginning of his leadership. In 1952 the Agudat N'shei u'Banot Chabad, the Organization for Chabad Women and Girls, was founded at his direction in Australia and Israel, then in the United States and elsewhere, with the goal of "studying Jewish law relevant to [women], discussing Jewish education, studying the talks of the rebbes and stories about tsaddikim."[38] In 1958 the organization began publishing a quarterly journal, *Di yidishe heym* (The Jewish Home), ostensibly a publication by and for women, although the contributors were predominantly men. A girls' high school was founded in Crown Heights in 1955 and a teachers' seminary in 1962.

Traditionally, women's education was limited to practical matters relevant to their religious observance, a position reiterated by Shneur Zalman in his code of Jewish law. But like the prewar study groups organized by Yosef Yitshak, Lubavitch girls' schools taught their students Hasidic texts. In a 1954 letter to the principal of the Beth Rivkah school of Yerres, France, Schneerson made the novel argument that since women are obligated to keep all commandments related to faith in God, they should study *Tanya* and other works that facilitate such devotion. Schneerson's expectation that women would be able to study and understand Hasidic thought was underscored by his practice of directing one talk at most of his farbrengens to the women in the audience and by his periodic addresses to the Chabad women's organization and classes from the girls' high school in the main synagogue in 770.

If Schneerson's inclusion of women in Chabad educational and outreach activities served practical goals, it was also informed by a mystical and messianic conception of gender. The Kabbalah taught that the "male" power—represented by the higher Divine emanations—constituted the active, influencing force in the world, while the "female" power—represented by the this-worldly Shekhinah—was passive and receptive. The male symbolized loving-kindness; the female, restrictive judgment; the male, spirit and form; the female, matter and body; the male, disclosing and revealing, the female, veiling and concealing. In Hasidic thought the male was the tsaddik, the female his followers; the male was God, the female the Congregation of Israel. In the messianic age, however, "the female will encircle the male"—that is, there would be a reversal of gender roles, and the receiver would become the giver. As Schneerson taught in his first discourse, although the feminine Shekhinah is usually associated with the lowermost aspect of the Godhead, it originates in the essence of Divinity. If in exile we are privy only to the lowest part of the Shekhinah, redemption entails the re-emergence of that essence. And it is the body and its materiality, Schneerson repeatedly taught, that is the locus of the greatest sanctity. Thus, in the messianic state the "female" would occupy a higher and more profound station than the "male."

Such ideas had a long history in kabbalistic thought but were rarely of practical significance. The aspects of the Godhead described as the forces of "male" and "female" were barely related to human men and women, and if they were, only to mythical patriarchs and matriarchs. Such teachings might apply to a messianic future, but in exile they were relevant only to emphasize women's inferior status. For Schneerson, however, the impending redemption, and the heightened revelation that accompanied the pre-messianic period, entailed real-world consequences. If women would wield superior spiritual capacity in the soon-to-arrive messianic age, their power should be used to bring the messianic age closer. His position was bolstered by rabbinical affirmations of women's roles in previous episodes of redemption, including the biblical exodus from Egypt and the salvation of the Jews in the Purim story. So, too, Schneerson taught, the final redemption would be thanks to "the merit of righteous women."[39]

As the Chabad outreach enterprise expanded in the 1960s and 1970s, women began to occupy increasingly important positions in the movement's activities. In addition to the male emissaries sent to cities around the world, there were female counterparts—usually part of husband-and-wife teams—whose role was sanctioned by Chabad institutions and Schneerson himself. Women were involved in Schneerson's mitzvah campaigns, particularly those related to other women. Where boys might approach strangers on street corners asking them to put on tefillin, girls would approach women with a gift of Sabbath candles. Such forms of religious activism, despite going against centuries of Hasidic practice, were effective; it is hard to imagine how Schneerson could have succeeded without involving his female constituents. As he likely understood, Chabad could not become a world-changing religious movement in the twentieth century while engaging only half its members.

If Schneerson had a more inclusive attitude toward women than other Orthodox communities, the reason was not because of sympathy with modern-day feminism. Instead, Schneerson attacked the feminist movement, insisting on the gender essentialism of traditional Hasidic society. Feminism, he insisted, was no more than an ill-conceived effort by dissatisfied women to solve their frustrations by imitating men. The movement "has completely nullified the importance of the woman as woman, and the value of her unique mission, and set her up to imitate a man and his role," he said in 1984. "The result of this for women is to diminish the recognition of their inherent value and to give them the desire to nullify their essence and do everything possible to be like someone else—men."[40] Instead, he argued, women would be better served by embracing their inherent inclinations to fulfill themselves as wives and mothers. Although nothing was intrinsically wrong with women having jobs, careers, or professional success, their primary role was as homemaker. It apparently did not occur to him that the categorization of professional, intellectual, and communal accomplishment as "male" and domestic duties as "female" was itself a problem that feminism was trying to overcome. Even in the area of outreach, where women could distinguish themselves as activists and public figures, their role was, to his mind, still rooted in their supposed qualities as nurturers and caregivers. As he stated in a 1975 letter to the twentieth annual N'shei convention, "The work of drawing Jews close to Yiddishkeit specially concerns women, for it is understood that this work requires a special approach of empathy, good-heartedness, loving-kindness and the like. These qualities are to be found to a greater measure among women than men."[41]

Although Chabad envisioned a broader and more significant role for women than other fundamentalist groups did, the traditional distinctions between male and female roles were in many ways reinforced. Women might receive an education superior to that of some of their religious peers, but it was not comparable to that given to Lubavitcher boys and men, nor were girls' schools afforded the same level of social or material support. Women might participate in outreach activities along with their husbands and brothers, but their primary responsibilities were to be wives and mothers. As Ada Rapoport-Albert has argued, Schneerson's empowerment of Lubavitcher women constituted "a militant brand of counter-feminism that denounced the goals of women's liberation and equal rights, which he saw as a denigrating subversion of women's inherently powerful nature and crucially important God-given tasks."[42] If feminists critique gender roles and power dynamics in society and seek to act on those critiques, Schneerson sought to preserve those roles and stifle the critiques. If feminism is a struggle for women's liberation from patriarchal power structures, Chabad remained one such structure.

Seen in broad perspective, Schneerson's engagement with issues beyond his immediate sphere had a double-edged quality. From Schneerson's own point of view, all his positions were consistent with his religious beliefs and were a natural outgrowth of his expansive theology. Although others might object to his goals or methods, he was never shy about trying to spread religious faith and practice as widely as he could and to apply his ideas to every area of life. Nobody could accuse him of being self-serving or disingenuous when his ideology was so clearly articulated and so meticulously pursued, no matter the issue or its consequences.

From another perspective, Schneerson's approach to broader issues could seem like exercises in opportunism and bad faith. He was happy to use scientific ideas when they supported his views but was unwilling to give them any credence when they conflicted. Culturally, Schneerson welcomed the upheavals of the 1960s and 1970s as another opportunity to reach the spiritually disenfranchised. But unlike other spiritual leaders of the period, he was unwilling to consider any kind of religious ecumenicism. When it came to feminism, he was eager to make use of women's freedoms to further his outreach projects but maintained his gender-essentialist views on the nature and role of women. Ironically, women's involvement in the movement became a means to attack feminist gains rather than bolster them.

Similarly, Schneerson praised American freedoms and democracy and thought of them as harbingers of redemption. But he rarely treated them as a system of political values with their own worth or, indeed, as anything more than a means to achieve religious goals. When a choice had to be made between supporting democracy and human rights for everyone or pursuing Chabad's particular outreach mission, the latter invariably took precedence. In consequence, despite Schneerson's praise for democracy, Chabad emissaries have been all too willing to toady up to illiberal regimes. In 1987, Schneerson's followers invited the Chilean dictator Augusto Pinochet—a man who interned, tortured, and executed tens of thousands of political opponents— to sign a scroll of honor commemorating Schneerson's eighty-fifth birthday. Pinochet used the opportunity to praise his regime and was praised in turn by the president of Chabad in Chile. When confronted about bestowing such an honor upon Pinochet, Avraham Shemtov, who originated the scroll and represented Chabad in the White House and on Capitol Hill, claimed that "political science and current political goings-on in all parts of the world are not really my field."[43] Schneerson himself didn't hesitate to employ as his chief secretary Chaim Mordechai Aizik Hodakov, a man who had led a crackdown on Latvia's secular Jewish schools under the country's authoritarian leader Kārlis Ulmanis. Although Schneerson understood the possibilities of American democracy, his politics resembled a kind of theocratic opportunism rather than a support of the democratic principles he claimed to celebrate.

For Schneerson, everything he did was an outgrowth of his maximalist belief system. From his perspective, there was never any disparity: every idea, action, or aspect of life fell under Judaism's purview, which was meticulously self-consistent. To some observers this made him a broad and exciting thinker who was willing to take on the most important ideas, to advance where others retreated, to stand up for Jewish tradition. But Schneerson's conception was also very narrow. Everything lay within the scope of Jewish teaching, but that meant everything had to be understood only insofar as Judaism—and Schneerson's interpretation of Judaism—permitted. The entire universe was encompassed by Schneerson's vision, but he met the world only on his own terms.

10

A Heart in the East

"BUT THE LAND you are crossing into to possess . . . is a land the Lord your God cares for; the eyes of the Lord your God are continually on it from the beginning of the year to the end of the year."[1] In letters and talks Schneerson quoted these verses from Deuteronomy constantly. While the affairs of the United States were a high priority, and he understood the possibilities of Jewish life in America as few others did, his ambitions were not limited to one country. His correspondents and visitors came from all over the world, and he took an interest in any place Jews lived. If this was true of remote Asian or South American outposts, it applied even more to the historical homeland of the Jewish people. Though he lived in Brooklyn, and almost never left New York, his attention was often focused on the Land of Israel, half a world away.

Unlike nearly every other Jewish leader of his generation, Schneerson never visited Israel. When challenged by the Israeli general and politician Ariel Sharon as to why he didn't immigrate, like a commander leading his troops into battle, Schneerson responded that the better analogy would be to the captain of a ship. So long as there were Jews in the diaspora who needed his leadership, he could not abandon them. Another explanation, which he gave to the Ashkenazi Chief Rabbi Shlomo Goren, was that as a Chabad rebbe he had to be near the grave of his predecessor, Yosef Yitshak. In a 1964 interview with the Israeli legislator Geulah Cohen he proclaimed that he would be in Israel "one minute before the Messiah comes."[2] Other observers have suggested that his reasons were more practical. In the multicultural tumult of Israeli Jewish society, he could not command the same authority or project the same charisma as he did in the Lubavitch stronghold of Crown Heights. But whatever his reason was for staying away from Israel, Schneerson was deeply invested in its society, politics, and military conflicts. From his office in Brooklyn, he exercised a controversial, and occasionally decisive, influence on the country's affairs.

Like most of Schneerson's positions, his attitude toward the Jewish state had precedents in Hasidic thought. For Chabad leaders, the holiness of the Land of Israel lay not in its geographic confines but in its metaphysical quality, which could theoretically be attained anywhere. According to a midrashic teaching, attainment of this quality would occur naturally in the messianic age, when the Land of Israel would "spread out over all the lands."[3] Conversely, exile was a spiritual rather than a physical state and could exist within the Holy Land as well as the diaspora. In a 1925 letter urging his followers not to leave the Soviet Union, Yosef Yitshak related a story about the third rebbe, the Tsemah Tsedek, in which he told a follower who wanted to emigrate to Palestine that "one must make here into the Land of Israel."[4]

If Chabad maintained a dismissive stance regarding emigration to Palestine for spiritual reasons, doing so for the sake of secular nationalism was out of the question. When Zionism emerged at the end of the nineteenth century, the fifth rebbe, Shalom Dov Ber, was at the forefront of religious opposition. In letters, talks, and polemical tracts he argued that not only was Zionism a heretical secular ideology but it impinged brazenly on God's messianic prerogative. According to a Talmudic passage often quoted by anti-Zionist thinkers, the Jewish people had made three oaths to God: they would not "ascend the wall [from exile]"; they would not "rebel against the nations of the world"; and they would not "force the end." (In recompense the other nations of the world were forced to swear that they would "not oppress Israel overly much.")[5] Thus, Shalom Dov Ber argued, even if the Zionist movement were suddenly to become "submissive to the Lord and His Torah . . . we must not listen to them in this matter, to achieve redemption by our own power, for we are not permitted to hasten the end even by reciting too many prayers, let alone by material powers and plans, that is, to set out from exile by force."[6]

This was a common position among Orthodox leaders, but it was not universal. Other rabbis, most notably Abraham Isaac Kook, who in 1921 became the first chief rabbi of British Mandate Palestine, took the opposite view. Although traditional messianists believed that redemption was in the hands of God, Kook argued that it could be—and perhaps must be—realized by human effort. Although traditionalists expected the messianic revelation "in the blink of an eye," Kook taught that it could dawn gradually. And although other Orthodox leaders condemned the intrusion of nationalist politics into the religious sphere, Kook bestowed such programs with the highest theological significance. The country he envisioned would not be a nation-state like any other but "the pedestal of God's throne in this world."[7] The Zionist enterprise might be carried out by nonbelievers, but it was a tool of the Divine: "dark clouds" that "will be the vessels of great light."[8] Even the appearance of a personal Messiah, a standard element of the redemption narrative, was deemed unnecessary, at least in the beginning stages.

Kook died in 1935, but for his students and followers the events of 1948 seemed to fulfill their dream. On May 14, David Ben-Gurion declared the independence of Israel, and after approximately ten months of fighting against a multinational coalition of Arab countries, the fledgling state emerged victorious. For the secular Zionist movement that had dominated the pre-state Jewish settlement and the newly formed government, it was an epochal event representing the end of exile and the vehicle through which to rebuild the Jewish people after the Holocaust. For Kook's successors it was nothing less than the beginning of redemption. The final stages would not be long in coming.

For most of the Orthodox community, the new state posed an unavoidable challenge. Previously, Zionism was an ideology. Now it was embodied in a political entity that could not be ignored. Some elements, including Hungarian Hasidic groups and parts of the ultra-Orthodox community in Jerusalem, continued to reject both Zionism and the State of Israel with unmitigated ferocity. In their view—most forcefully expressed by the Satmar leader Yoel Teitelbaum—not only was Zionism theological anathema but its fruits were the work of Satan. As Teitelbaum wrote, "The very idea of the people of Israel achieving independence before the coming of the Messiah represents heresy against the ways of the Lord, may He be blessed, for it is He alone who enslaves and redeems."[9] In his view Zionism and its unsanctioned effort to "force the end" had caused the Holocaust.

For other Orthodox factions, the state was accepted as a matter of reality. While their ideological opposition to Zionism did not explicitly waver, and they continued to resist army service or the celebration of national holidays, they welcomed government support for their communities and secured their interests by forming political parties, voting in Israeli elections, and electing representatives to the Israeli parliament, the Knesset.

Pragmatic acceptance was the path taken by Chabad, albeit with differences in tone and tactics. Like Shalom Dov Ber, Yosef Yitshak castigated Zionism as an affront to Judaism. In 1927, before his brief exile to Kostroma, he gave a widely publicized speech in which he declared, "We did not depart from the Land of Israel of our own free will, nor shall we return to the Land of Israel by virtue of our own capabilities. God, our Father and King, has sent us into exile. He shall redeem us."[10] Even during the Holocaust, Yosef Yitshak insisted that worldly nation-building efforts were a futile means of addressing the calamity. "Everything that is already built is equivalent to ruins, heaven forbid," he wrote in October 1943. "This is because the redeemer needs to come through 'those who turn back from sin.'"[11] In 1948, when Israel declared independence, he ignored it completely.

Yet Yosef Yitshak was sensitive to the needs of religious Jews in Palestine, and of Chabad Hasidim in particular. In 1945 he established the Refugee Relief and Rehabilitation Organization in Paris, which assisted Holocaust survivors and later helped them emigrate to the newly founded state. In 1949, with the help of Zalman Shazar—a journalist, historian, and politician who came from a Chabad family and who later became the third president of Israel—he supported the founding of Kfar Chabad, an agricultural village of Lubavitcher refugees in central Israel.

Schneerson continued in this vein, supporting Hasidic interests and promoting a religious revival in Israel, as he did everywhere else, but never disavowing the principled anti-Zionism of his predecessors. He desisted from using the terms "Israel" and "State of Israel," resorting instead to more traditional locutions like "Land of Israel" and "The Holy Land." Unlike religious Zionists, Schneerson granted no theological significance to the state and repudiated any association between Zionism and messianism. According to his eschatology, the ingathering of exiles that religious Zionists saw as the beginning of redemption would occur only after the Messiah arrived and the temple was rebuilt. Moreover, he feared that the founding of the state—especially a state as understood by religious Zionists—would divert attention from the real messianic quest, thus delaying true redemption. As he once put it, "The false redemption does not allow the true redemption to be revealed, [for] . . . those who think that they are already living in redemption . . . cause the prolongation of the Exile, the exile of the individual, the exile of the community, the exile of all Israel, and the exile of the Shekhinah."[12]

In fact, Schneerson argued, so long as the Messiah had not actually come, the persistence of exile was not a weakness but a strength. "It is a mistake if we conceive of the worldwide dispersal of the Jewish people as a catastrophe," he told Ascher Penn. "As a matter of fact, this very lack of concentration of the remnants of our nation was the source of our salvation throughout the centuries of persecution and pogroms."[13] For Schneerson, exile was a necessary stage of Jewish development whose potential had not yet been exhausted. He did not encourage his followers to settle in Israel except in isolated cases; when Hasidim expressed a desire to emigrate, he would—like his ancestor the Tsemah Tsedek—instruct them to stay where they were and strengthen their local Jewish community instead.

If Schneerson disagreed with Zionists over the significance of the Jewish state, he also parted ways with those who saw it as a sinful, even demonic entity. Rather, like most of the ultra-Orthodox world, Schneerson saw it in neutral terms, neither evil nor holy. But unlike those who were inclined to view Israel as they would any other country, Schneerson understood that it occupied a unique place in Jewish history. Every event, he believed, was a direct result of Divine providence, and Jewish sovereignty for the first time in thousands of years could hardly be an exception. As he told his followers, "After the Holy One, Blessed Be He, saw the suffering of His people Israel, that they were being slaughtered and massacred, heaven forbid, in horrible and awful persecutions, He gave them the opportunity *in the midst of exile* to conduct all their affairs according to their will, in an organized fashion, with their own institutions. Thus tens, hundreds, thousands, and tens of thousands of Jews came to a place of refuge in the Land of Israel."[14]

The emergence of Israel as the country with the second-largest Jewish population in the world, whose policies had the ability to affect the Jewish people as a whole, was reason enough for Schneerson to involve himself in its affairs. He was particularly concerned about the religious character of the state and lamented that it had not been founded as a theocracy. "If the people of Israel had captured the moment and acted properly, this would have been a wonderful opportunity for it to prove that it was already worthy of redemption," he declared. "Instead the leaders argued over whether to mention the name of God in the well-known Declaration [of Independence], and whether to be dependent upon Moscow or upon Washington . . . Thus, to our great sorrow, once again Israel did not succeed in rising above itself, to seize the opportunity and prove that redemption can indeed be revealed."[15]

Still, he did not hesitate to share his opinions on Israeli policies and try to influence them where he could. To that end he maintained relationships with many Israeli politicians and public figures through correspondence and through the visits they paid him in Brooklyn. These included David Ben-Gurion, who visited in 1954; Ariel Sharon, who visited in 1968 and 1969; Shimon Peres, who visited in 1966 and 1970; Yitzhak Rabin, who visited in 1972; and Menachem Begin, who visited as a sitting prime minister in 1977, shortly before the Camp David peace accords. Schneerson maintained an especially close connection with Shazar, who visited him thirteen times.

Despite Schneerson's attentiveness to the State of Israel, and his de-emphasis of the anti-Zionism championed by his pre-

Schneerson received regular visits from Israeli politicians.
Zalman Shazar, president of Israel from 1963 to 1973, was particularly
close. He visited Schneerson thirteen times. (JEM, The Living Archive)

decessors, the country's success presented a challenge to his own program of Jewish revival. If pre-state Zionism threatened to replace religion with secular nationalism, the existence of the state made that threat an ever-present reality. And if this was true from 1948 on, it became particularly pressing in the lead-up and aftermath of the Six-Day War.

In the spring of 1967, Egyptian President Gamal Abdel Nasser, with the backing of the Soviet Union, demanded that the United Nations withdraw its peacekeeping troops from the Sinai Peninsula, where they had been stationed since Israel's withdrawal in 1957. On May 19 the United Nations complied, and the next day 100,000 Egyptian troops, including two armored divisions, were stationed along Israel's southern border. Two days later Nasser declared the Straits of Tiran between the Sinai and Arabian peninsulas closed to Israeli shipping. Despite a frenzied diplomatic effort by Foreign Minister Abba Eban, Israel was unable to get other countries to intervene. On May 30, Jordan's King Hussein flew to Cairo, where he signed a military pact with Nasser placing Jordanian forces under Egyptian command. Meanwhile, the armies of Iraq, Kuwait, Algeria, and Yemen began deploying to Jordan. Together with the Syrian army to the north, Israel was surrounded by an Arab force of 250,000 troops, 2,000 tanks, and 700 fighters and bombers. For Jews it seemed that their greatest nightmare might come true: the State of Israel, less than two decades old, might be destroyed by its Arab neighbors and its people slaughtered in a second Holocaust.

Anticipating catastrophe, some Israelis and most visitors to the country made plans to leave. Schneerson told anyone who would listen to stay. To four students at a Chabad yeshiva in Jerusalem, he wrote: "Continue to study with diligence. It is an absolute certainty that 'The Guardian of Israel neither slumbers nor sleeps.' I await good news."[16] To another Hasid whose son was studying in Israel, he wrote: "There is absolutely no cause for concern . . . The verse 'I will grant peace in the Land' will be fulfilled."[17] Not only did he assure his Hasidim of their safety, but he predicted a victorious outcome for Israel. In a talk given on May 29, he said: "Our brothers and sisters in the Holy Land are now in a situation where the Almighty protects them and sends His blessings and salvation in a greater measure so that they will come out of the current situation successfully . . . God will lead each Jew and all Jews with an upright stature and upraised head to the true and complete redemption."[18] The talk, which was given before a crowd of thousands during a parade for the holiday of Lag BaOmer, was broadcast later that night on Israeli radio, giving Schneerson one of the widest audiences he had yet enjoyed. When asked privately how he could be so confident, he is said to have answered, "I felt in my heart that nothing would happen to the residents of Israel."[19] According to a story making the rounds of 770, Schneerson is said to have remarked, "I was at the grave site and my father-in-law took responsibility."[20]

Schneerson did have one recommendation for those worried about disaster: to put on tefillin and to encourage others to do so. On June 3, two days before the war, he cited a Talmudic teaching stating that putting on tefillin ensured long life and intimidated enemies. If his followers wanted to protect themselves and assure Israel's victory, they should get as many people as possible to fulfill the mitzvah. The tefillin campaign, as it came to be known, was the precursor to his subsequent "mitzvah campaigns" and—at least from Schneerson's point of view—accomplished its immediate goals.

On June 5, Israel seized the initiative in the looming conflict by sending its air force over the border and destroying most of Egypt's planes while they were still on the ground. Sorties sent against the air forces of other Arab states destroyed them as well. At the same moment a ground offensive was unfolding in the Sinai. Over the next four days three divisional task forces pushed through the desert along different axes while a separate reserve infantry brigade, along with an armored force and paratroopers, took the Gaza Strip. By June 8, after a battle involving some 1,000 tanks—one of the largest such engagements in history— Israel had taken the Suez Canal and, with the participation of its naval forces, reopened the Straits of Tiran.

On the first morning of the war the Jordanian military began shelling Israeli towns and villages in the middle of the country; in response, Israel pushed into the West Bank, encircling Jerusalem from the north and south. By the next day Israel had taken the cities of Ramallah and Jenin. On June 7, the third day of the war, Israel went for Jerusalem. Paratroopers, along with a small armored force, broke into the Old City at the Lions' Gate leading to the Muslim Quarter, and by 10:15 a.m. the blue and white Israeli flag was flying over the Temple Mount and the Western Wall. The Jerusalem Brigade continued south, taking Bethlehem and Hebron. Before long the entire West Bank was under Israeli control.

After such monumental victories, the last two days of the war were somewhat anticlimactic. On June 9 the Israel Defense Forces attacked the Syrian army on the Golan Heights; twenty-four hours later the area was in Israeli hands. By June 11 the Arab states had agreed to a ceasefire; the war was over. Israel had not only beaten back and destroyed the Arab armies but had seized considerable territory, including the Sinai Peninsula and Gaza from Egypt, the West Bank and East Jerusalem from Jordan, and the Golan Heights from Syria.

The victory had far-reaching political and social consequences. Israel had demonstrated its military superiority over its Arab neighbors and its willingness to use it. Territorial gains allowed Jews access to holy sites in Jerusalem, Hebron, and Nablus, including the Western Wall. The country's economy, which had struggled before the war, now began to expand thanks to tourism, donations, and oil extraction from the Sinai. The ensuing euphoria brought a baby boom, which lasted four years. Meanwhile, the seizure of territory and the control of large Palestinian populations would have long-lasting military, political, social, and diplomatic effects.

For world Jewry, Israel's victory was equally profound. The outcome of the war led to a renewed sense of Jewish pride and an embrace of the Jewish State. In the Soviet Union it awakened feelings of Jewish identity and a demand that the country's Jewish population be allowed to emigrate. There were retaliatory attacks against Jewish communities and expulsions in the Arab world, as well as a rise in antisemitism in Communist Europe, which led to a wave of emigration. In the United States and other liberal democracies, political and material support for the country swelled, along with a smaller, though still significant, number of emigrants.

For Schneerson, Israel's astonishing victory was not merely a military triumph but a miraculous display of providence. "This was a revelation from above the order of the [Divine] concatenation, which was not clothed in the ways of nature," he said that summer. "The proof is that all the nations of the world are standing awestruck, and it is still not understood how it happened."[21] He would reiterate this position in the coming years. In a 1974 letter responding to the events of the 1973 Yom Kippur War, he wrote that "there was no shortage of miracles, quite obvious ones, in the last war."[22] Israel might be a secular country, but its wars, he argued, were like the conquest fought by the biblical Israelites in the book of Joshua. Moreover, the 1967 victory seemed to affirm not only the prophetic nature of his own pronouncements but also the efficacy of his tefillin campaign. As world Jewry gloried in the small country's military success, Schneerson tried to turn the narrative to support his religious agenda.

Schneerson was enough of a realist—and self-styled military tactician—to acknowledge that it was not merely spiritual merit that won the war. In talks given in the summer of 1967, Schneerson cited the Talmudic teaching that military efforts would have no success were it not for the merit of those who study Torah. Nonetheless, he said, the soldiers who physically fought and risked their lives deserved the most credit. Those who died were particularly meritorious and had earned the highest spiritual rewards of the afterlife. In later years he continued to praise the accomplishments of Israeli soldiers, even allowing some of his Hasidim to join the Israel Defense Forces and ascend through its ranks. In response to the daring Entebbe raid in the summer of 1976, in which a team of Israeli commandos rescued the passengers of a hijacked Air France plane in Uganda, Schneerson singled out the "newlyweds, or those preparing for marriage, who flew for thousands of miles, putting their lives in danger, for the sole purpose of possibly saving the lives of tens of Jews . . . their portion in the Hereafter is guaranteed."[23]

While Schneerson's praise of Israel and its nonreligious soldiers may have ingratiated him to most Jews, it provoked the ire of anti-Zionist groups who were once ideologically indistinguishable from Chabad. Yoel Teitelbaum characterized the Israeli victories not as manifestations of Providence, much less a vindication of Zionism, but as tests of faith created by Satan. "There is talk and publicity about miracles of Satan which in fact have no basis in reality," Teitelbaum wrote. "They are nothing more than phony miracles that have been produced to fool the masses and to attract them to heresy and rebellion against G-d and his holy Torah."[24] Schneerson noted ironically that even Satmar Hasidim in Williamsburg prayed and recited Psalms during the war—prayers that would have been to no purpose if they hadn't asked God to bring about salvation and victory.

If Schneerson's praise of Israeli soldiers and military victories inflamed those on his right, his involvement in Israeli politics more often provoked those on his left. Like other Orthodox rabbis, Schneerson insisted that the Judaism of more liberal movements was inauthentic, and in 1956 he supported a pan-Orthodox ban on collaborating with other movements in rabbinical organizations. In a conversation with Herbert Weiner, a Reform rabbi, Schneerson commented that while it was important for Jews to observe Jewish law as much as they could, liberal movements erred by "sanctifying the compromise." No matter the level of a person's observance, he said, there had to be an authentic Judaism to which the person could return. Because of liberal movements, "a repentant Jew who wants to 'return' would not know what there was to return to."[25]

This position didn't make Schneerson unusual. What drew Schneerson into conflict was the "Who is a Jew?" question in Israel. The issue had its roots in the 1950 Law of Return, which granted every Jew in the world the right to emigrate to Israel and become a citizen. However, the law neglected to say who was considered a Jew. This oversight was seemingly rectified in 1958, when Interior Minister Israel Bar-Yehuda (who had once been Schneerson's tutor in Ekaterinoslav) declared that all those who considered themselves to be Jewish in good faith, and who were not members of another religion, were considered Jewish for purposes of the law. This included the children of Jewish fathers and non-Jewish mothers—a contravention of traditional Jewish law, according to which Jewish identity passes through the mother. The decision drew an immediate outcry from Israel's Orthodox parties, despite Bar-Yehuda's protestations that these criteria were civil definitions with no bearing on religious belief. To resolve the situation Prime Minister David Ben-Gurion wrote to fifty scholars, rabbinical authorities, and jurists seeking their advice. One of these was Schneerson. In a letter dated 8 Adar 1, 5719 (February 16, 1959), Schneerson responded: "My opinion is absolutely clear, in accordance with the Torah and the tradition that has been handed down for generations . . . a Jew . . . is only a person born to a Jewish mother or someone who has converted according to the exact procedures explained in the legal books of our nation from generation to generation."[26] He rejected the notion that Israeli civil registration had no bearing on religious belief, noting that Israel's policies influenced Jewish identity worldwide. In response to the onslaught of protest, Ben-Gurion decided to annul his minister's directions and to instruct the children of non-Jewish mothers to leave the nationality and religion sections of their registry and identity cards blank.

This compromise did not resolve the issue. In 1970, the Israeli naval officer Benjamin Shalit sued the Ministry of the Interior, arguing that his children, though born of a non-Jewish mother, should be registered as Jews. And in *Shalit v. Minister of Interior*, the Israeli Supreme Court affirmed that in the case of a non-Jewish mother the duty of registration officers was to record the details as provided to them for statistical purposes, not to determine their truth or falsehood. The decision soon became meaningless, however, because that year the Israeli government amended the Law of Return, extending the right of citizenship to anyone with a single Jewish grandparent, as well as to a spouse. At the same time, the Knesset included in the amendment a provision stating that a person would be considered legally Jewish if "born of a Jewish mother or converted to Judaism" and if "not a member of another religion." Despite this capitulation to the Orthodox position, the matter was still not settled. The law neglected to stipulate what counts as "conversion," leaving the door open to certification by any Jewish group. Once again, the Orthodox parties were outraged. By passing this amendment the Israeli government seemed to condone the liberal movements that Orthodox Jews considered invalid and whose conversions were therefore inadmissible.

Despite such setbacks Schneerson continued to speak out on the issue, considering it an existential matter for the Jewish people. If non-Jews, according to his definition, were considered Jews by the Jewish State and were assimilated into the general population, who would be able to tell in a few generations who was Jewish and who was not? His own outreach efforts were predicated on the notion that a Jew was a Jew—and could be relied upon to be such—no matter their level of observance. In street-intercept campaigns, Lubavitchers could rely on a simple "yes" when asking whether someone was Jewish. Now the Israeli government was putting that straightforward identification and trust in danger.

On this issue Schneerson agreed not only with the rest of the ultra-Orthodox world but with religious Zionists as well.

Even if his theology departed from theirs, his politics aligned closely with religious Zionist positions. Though he attributed no messianic significance to the Jewish State, he believed that God's biblical promise to Abraham gave the Jewish people a claim to the land. Together with his enthusiasm for Israel's military exploits and his attribution of Divine providence to its victories, this belief brought him closer to the Zionist position than Chabad had ever been. When it came to Israel's foreign policy, he was as hardline as anyone.

Starting almost immediately after the 1967 victory, Schneerson inveighed regularly against giving back territory taken during the war and encouraged settlement in the West Bank. While religious Zionists saw Israeli expansion as another step in the unfolding redemption, Schneerson's concerns were practical. Since his youth he had been interested in military strategy and tactics, and he was convinced that ceding territory would endanger Israel's security. Writing in the early 1980s to the British chief rabbi Immanuel Jakobovits, who supported the "land for peace" formulation, Schneerson wrote that his opposition had "nothing to do with the sanctity of Eretz Yisrael," the Land of Israel, but only with his conviction that such arrangements would pose a danger to the country. Returning territory would therefore be against Jewish law, since it endangered life. Should military experts conclude otherwise, then their advice should be followed, just as one would follow the advice of a doctor regarding a medical procedure. However, he wrote, "all military experts, Jewish and non-Jewish, agree that in the present situation, giving up any part of [the territories] would create serious security dangers."[27]

Such positions lacked the messianic zeal that informed the rest of Schneerson's worldview, but they bore dark chauvinistic overtones. While the welfare of Israel's Jewish citizens was a primary concern, Schneerson gave little thought to the well-being of Israel's Arab citizens or to the fate of the Palestinians who came under its control. More disturbingly, Schneerson is reported to have said that Israeli leadership squandered an opportunity by not driving the Palestinians out of the West Bank immediately after the war. Despite his apparent devotion to "acts of goodness and kindness," neither the horrors of ethnic cleansing nor the prospect of placing an entire population under indefinite military occupation seemed to bother him.

On the return of territory, as with the "Who is a Jew?" question, Schneerson's public talks and private lobbying were largely unsuccessful. In July 1977, Israeli Prime Minister Menachem Begin visited 770 before meeting with President Carter for negotiations that would eventually result in the 1978 Camp David Accords and the 1979 Egypt-Israel peace treaty. At the meeting Schneerson reportedly discouraged Begin from bending to American pressure for territorial compromise, a position Begin shared. Nonetheless, a little over a year later Begin made a series of agreements with Egyptian President Anwar Sadat, calling not only for the return of the Sinai Peninsula to Egypt but also for the return of all territories occupied by Israel in 1967 and the creation of an autonomous Palestinian entity in the West Bank and Gaza. Although the agreements were never fully implemented, Israel did return the Sinai to Egypt, eventually withdraw from parts of the West Bank, and, in 2005, remove its settlements from Gaza. Schneerson may have had an unusual degree of influence over certain Israeli politicians, but he did not dictate policy.

On at least one occasion, Schneerson did play a pivotal role in Israel's political direction. In Israel, as in America, he never explicitly aligned himself with a single political party. Chabad's interests in Israel were represented by the Orthodox Agudat Yisrael party, and Schneerson met regularly with the Agudat Yisrael legislator Menachem Porush. But as he wrote in a 1957 letter, "Since Lubavitch is active in all locations, we have adopted the

policy not to become entangled in any matter of factionalism . . .
The defining purpose of Chabad is nothing other than unadul-
terated Torah and *mitzvot,* devoid of any factional ideology."[28]

His hands-off approach changed in 1988 when non-Hasidic
elements tried to marginalize Lubavitch influence and in-
volvement within the religious parties. The effort was led by
Schneerson's chief rabbinical antagonist, Elazar Menachem Man
Shach, who split from Agudat Yisrael in 1984 to help found the
Sephardic Orthodox Shas party and who now started his own
party, Degel HaTorah, to represent the Mitnaggdic faction of
Israeli Orthodoxy. Shach's move was motivated by Schneerson
himself, whose outspoken messianism Shach opposed. When
Agudat Yisrael refused to dissociate itself from Schneerson and
Chabad, Shach dissociated himself from Agudat Yisrael.

The controversy also concerned the "Who is a Jew?" question, which had been raised again by an influx of immigrants
from the Soviet Union, many of whom were not Jewish by Orthodox standards. While Agudat Yisrael wanted to reopen the
subject and further amend Israel's Law of Return, other parties,
both Orthodox and secular, opposed re-politicizing the issue.
On Schneerson's instructions Chabad ran a vigorous campaign
for Agudat Yisrael in that year's elections, spending upward
of $1 million on the party's behalf. Partly as a result of those
efforts the party increased its Knesset seats from two to five.
Other Orthodox parties also increased their representation,
with Shas winning six seats and Degel HaTorah two. By that
time, Schneerson had come to recognize the damage that the
"Who is a Jew?" issue was doing to Chabad's image, and in a
1989 talk he told his followers not to involve themselves in it
or discuss it publicly. Nonetheless, Agudat Yisrael's additional
seats would prove decisive.

In 1990, two years after Chabad's successful sortie into Israeli electoral politics, Shimon Peres, who was then finance min-

ister, succeeded in forcing a vote of no-confidence in the government of Likud Prime Minister Yitzhak Shamir. The conflict was over potential negotiations with the Palestinians; Shamir, despite pressure from U.S. Secretary of State James Baker, steadfastly refused to consider the possibility. After defeating Shamir's government by a vote of 60 to 55, Peres struck a deal with Agudat Yisrael to form a new coalition. But on April 11, the day the new government was to be formed, two Agudat Yisrael Knesset members, Eliezer Mizrahi and Avraham Verdiger, went mysteriously missing. The cause of their disappearance, it turned out, was Schneerson's unbudging opposition to territorial compromise. Although Schneerson did not personally contact either legislator, it was later discovered that the two politicians had called Lubavitch headquarters to ask if Schneerson's position on the issue had changed. When told that it had not, they strategically absented themselves. Two months later Shamir succeeded in again forming a right-wing government, scuttling any potential peace deal with the Palestinians.

Boosting Agudat Yisrael and thereby preventing the formation of Peres's coalition was Schneerson's most exceptional foray into Israeli politics, but it came as the culmination of his involvement in the country and its affairs. Those who shared his views saw his outspoken positions as visionary, even prophetic. His predictions of Israel's successes in its wars, his support for its military and its soldiers, and his overarching concern for the Jewish character of the state made him an influential voice during the country's first four and half decades. For those who opposed his positions on territorial compromise and Jewish identity, his involvement in the country was harmful and obnoxious. Schneerson was the head of a movement that had historically been staunchly anti-Zionist, and he did not repudiate those views. He declined not only to move to Israel but even to visit. For him to assume influence over the policies and politics of the country was insufferable. As an editorial in the Israeli newspaper *Yediot*

Ahronot angrily complained, Israel's fate was "in the hands of a Rabbi who lives in Brooklyn, who has never set foot in Israel."[29] Or, as Shach memorably put it, he was "the madman who sits in New York and drives the whole world crazy."[30]

11

---◆◆◆◆---

Larger than Life

Schneerson's principal challenges during his first two decades of leadership were to gather his community, rebuild its institutions, and construct its outreach infrastructure. By the 1970s, his efforts were paying off. The Chabad population had grown thanks to a high birthrate and an influx of adherents. A generation of Lubavitchers, born in the early years of Schneerson's tenure, were becoming adults and promoting his message on their own. New outposts were springing up at a rapid pace. Schneerson, however, was no longer young. He was relatively youthful when he became rebbe at forty-eight, but decades had passed. Though his efforts showed no slackening, he had no successor, and his health and longevity were legitimate concerns. Then, on the night of October 3, 1977, while in synagogue celebrating the holiday of Shemini Atzeret, he had a heart attack. He was seventy-five years old.

The event was alarming to the Chabad community, an unwelcome reminder of its rebbe's mortality. Ironically, it also bolstered Schneerson's reputation for physical stamina and vitality. According to eyewitnesses, Schneerson began feeling chest pains around 10:30 p.m. and asked for a chair. Still, he stayed in the synagogue until the end of the service before retreating to his office. Doctors confirmed that he was experiencing a major cardiac episode and should be taken to a hospital. Schneerson refused to go. When his condition worsened during the night, his aides appealed to Chaya Mushka to authorize his sedation and hospitalization. Absent her husband's consent, she, too, refused. Instead, doctors were brought to him. A makeshift hospital room was set up in Schneerson's office, and by the end of the holiday he had recovered enough to give a short speech to his followers. Lubavitchers hailed his recovery as a miracle.

Schneerson remained under doctors' care at 770 for over a month before returning home. Although he seemed to have fully recovered, the experience left its mark. At his age most people would slow down, if not retire altogether, and he had suffered the effects of his relentless work load in a visceral way. Although he gave the impression of superhuman energy and endurance, the unforgiving pace of his responsibilities was exhausting. "It pains me to notice when he doesn't feel well and is very tired, although he tries hard to show me otherwise," his mother had observed over a decade earlier.[1] If he didn't want his life to be cut short, he had to make some changes.

Retirement was out of the question. Rebbes didn't retire, certainly not this one. He didn't even take a vacation. But he did make alterations to his routine that allowed him to assume a broader leadership role while putting aside much of the personal interaction with his followers. He had reduced private yehidut meetings from three times a week to two in 1964; when he returned to 770 after convalescing at home for five weeks, he curtailed them further, and within the next few years he ceased holding them altogether. Although these meetings provided countless people with inspiration and spiritual guidance, they were time and energy intensive. There were still occasional individuals who could get in to see him, but this aspect of his leadership had largely ended. At the same time, he increased the length and frequency of his farbrengens, which now lasted five or six hours. And in 1981, he invented the "general" yehidut, in which he would see groups of fifty people or more at a time. Though these meetings were no replacement for the traditional one-on-one yehidut, they were a way for him to continue a practice that was at the heart of Hasidic life and they allowed Hasidim to enjoy more intimate encounters with their rebbe than they could expect to have at public gatherings.

Schneerson's correspondence also diminished. Where he had once written substantive letters on a range of subjects, he now dictated short notes to inform questioners of his position on particular issues. In later years he simply circled or underlined a word to indicate his response. And while he had previously been closely involved with his emissaries and their efforts, much of the operation was now delegated to subordinates. Though emissaries were still required to seek his approval before setting out for new locations, and reported back once settled, he was no longer involved in their day-to-day affairs.

Although Schneerson's primary responsibility continued to be the leadership of his movement, now he focused on maximizing his impact and influence. Instead of the detail-oriented management he had excelled at his entire life, he played the part of a big-picture visionary, suggesting ideas and initiatives that his followers would implement on their own. His expansive theology and wide-ranging involvements made him a notable figure throughout the Jewish world and beyond; in the coming years filling this function would take up even more of his energies.

The growth of the Hasidic community and the resulting strain on its leader's time was an old problem. An essential part of Hasidic identity was the relationship between a Hasid and his rebbe. But how could a rebbe maintain that relationship when he could no longer meet with everyone individually? In the eighteenth century Shneur Zalman tried to solve the problem by publishing his teachings; he told his followers that instead of consulting him personally they could read his book. Schneerson had long surpassed his predecessor on that count. Chabad had published a variety of periodicals for decades, featuring highlights from Schneerson's teaching and occasionally his writing. Since the 1950s his lectures had been transcribed and published in Yiddish booklets; in 1978 they started to appear in English translation, and in 1981, in Hebrew. As of 1987 his talks were distributed by fax to Chabad communities almost as soon as they were delivered. Publication, however, was only the beginning.

Chabad had long been willing to use modern media to spread its message. Still, Schneerson had initially forbidden the use of recording equipment at farbrengens, though some reel-to-reel tapes were made discreetly nonetheless. That began to change in 1953, when one transcriber received permission to record his talks for personal use. Such recordings, which soon began to circulate within the Chabad community, were the start of a more organized recording and broadcast effort. Like many Chabad undertakings, the media operation came from the initiative of individual Hasidim rather than Schneerson himself. But he understood its potential and acquiesced to their efforts—at first reluctantly, then with enthusiasm.

On January 17, 1970, the twentieth anniversary of Yosef Yitshak's passing, Schneerson was scheduled to give his regular lecture. This time, however, a group of enterprising Hasidim had received permission to broadcast the talk via telephone to a group of listeners in Israel. The idea was not entirely new—Chabad had run educational programs on New York radio stations since the 1950s, and it would have been natural to broadcast Schneerson's talks as well. The idea was proposed as early as 1959, although Schneerson rejected it at the time. While he did not give specific reasons, his reluctance was understandable. Farbrengens were public events, but they were still relatively intimate occasions where he could speak freely to his community. Knowing that he was being broadcast to a wider audience would have changed the tenor of his words. Occasions when his speeches were played on the radio, as his 1967 address prior to the Six-Day War had been, were isolated events. In 1970, however, the limited proposal of broadcasting his talks to Hasidic audiences abroad was deemed acceptable.[2]

The arrangement was not straightforward. For the first broadcasts Schneerson's talk was simply picked up by a telephone and transmitted, via long-distance call, to the receiving end. Soon, communities in England, France, and Australia were added to the phone hookup, and as additional locations were included, the arrangement became increasingly complex. But for far-off Hasidim, the chance to hear Schneerson speak live was too good to miss, and additional phone lines were installed in 770 to meet the demand. By the end of the 1970s eight lines were dedicated for the purpose, some of them run from neighboring homes. By the early 1990s there were hundreds.

Over time the operation became more technologically sophisticated. In 1972 an equalized phone line was installed, allowing for high-quality audio and therefore radio broadcasts, which Schneerson finally allowed. Most of his talks were still aimed at an internal audience, but he used radio addresses to discuss political issues or subjects of general concern. Recordings of Schneerson's talks were also regularly being made and were later distributed on cassette tapes from a storefront on Kingston Avenue.

Schneerson's teachings and talks were not the only thing media was proliferating. Several amateur or semi-professional photographers had been documenting events at 770 with Schneerson's permission, and as photographic technology improved, so

Schneerson's image has been plastered on everything
from banners to bumper stickers, making him one of the most
recognizable rabbis on the planet. (Nick Russell)

did their output. Soon, pictures of Schneerson showed up on
posters and billboards in the United States and Israel, as well as
in nearly every Chabad home and institution on the planet. This
had some precedent in Chabad history—paintings ostensibly
showing the first and third rebbes appeared in the nineteenth
century and displaying them helped solidify Chabad leaders' authority during periods of schism and contested leadership.[3] In
the twentieth century the medium switched to photography, and
Yosef Yitshak took the unprecedented step of authorizing an official portrait. He also urged his followers to send their photos
to him, using the medium to strengthen the Hasid-rebbe bond.
After Yosef Yitshak's death, Schneerson encouraged Hasidim to
look at portraits of the late rebbe to strengthen their attachment
to him. But none of the previous rebbes could equal the seventh
for sheer recognizability. Even in non-Hasidic communities, a
picture of Schneerson in a home or business became something

of a good-luck charm, making him one of the most iconic rabbinic leaders of the century.

Print, radio, and photography were yesterday's technologies. Making full use of twentieth-century mass media meant going on television. Although Schneerson discouraged his followers from having TV sets at home, fearing the deleterious effects of American pop culture, he understood the medium's potential, and by the 1980s some of his farbrengens were being broadcast by cable or satellite. TV broadcasts were used to particularly good effect on special occasions, such as the annual "Hanukkah Live" events, in which lightings of Chabad Hanukkah menorahs around the world were broadcast sequentially as part of highly produced and widely publicized programs. Chabad even gained an Internet presence as early as 1988 on the online discussion group Fidonet before making the leap to the World Wide Web in 1993 with chabad.org.

The use of such media served multiple purposes. It allowed Schneerson to spread his message and maintain a connection with his Hasidim; though his followers could no longer consult with him personally or receive letters of substance, they were able to see and hear him up close, at their convenience and in the privacy of their homes. As Jeffrey Shandler has argued, the private setting and zoomed-in intimacy of television or film could make the experience seem more like a yehidut than being one of thousands in a jostling crowd at a farbrengen.[4] If this was true of men, it was doubly true of women, for whom physical access to Schneerson was always difficult and now nearly impossible. Although most Hasidim had lost the possibility of a personal relationship with their rebbe, he was now more a part of their lives than ever before.

If publications, broadcasts, and a cascade of still images allowed Schneerson to spread his message, connect with his followers, and become one of the most recognizable rabbis in the world, they were still no substitute for personal contact. Schneerson's solution to this problem became one of his signature innovations: it managed to be a way of maintaining access, promoting one of his religious priorities, and fundraising for Chabad all at once.

Around 10 a.m. on Sunday, April 20, 1986, Schneerson appeared outside the door of his office and began distributing dollar bills for charity. Word of his activity quickly spread, and soon a line of people were waiting to receive a dollar from his hand. The next week Schneerson returned to his post, and by the third week the seemingly spontaneous initiative was becoming a tradition. For the next six years, "Dollars" was a community ritual and one of Schneerson's most public functions. According to one estimate, he saw five thousand people each week over an afternoon and evening.

Like most of Schneerson's ideas, Dollars had precedents. In some Hasidic communities it was traditional for the rebbe to give his followers coins as good luck tokens, a practice now updated with American dollar bills. Like other Hasidic leaders, Schneerson handed out pieces of honey cake before Rosh Hashanah and distributed wine from his kiddush cup on festivals. Dollars brought a new scale and significance to both traditions. Even though Schneerson was the one handing out bills, it was not really Schneerson, or Chabad, that was doing the giving. And although the dollars were for charity, the recipients were not charity cases. Rather, by giving people money that they were expected to give away themselves, Schneerson was enlisting them as agents in a larger charitable effort. Most people kept the dollar as a memento (some enterprising Hasidim even set up a sidewalk business laminating the bills) and gave other funds—usually much more than a dollar—to charity. Although neither Schneerson nor his aides explicitly suggested that the money be given to Chabad institutions, many times the amount that Schneerson distributed found its way back into Chabad coffers.

More important to Schneerson was the act of giving to charity, which had enormous messianic significance. "Israel is only redeemed through charity," the Mishna taught.[5] As Shneur Zalman explained in the fourth section of *Tanya*, charity was associated with redemption because, unlike other commandments, it was an act without defined limits. Although the traditional instruction was to give away one tenth, or at most one fifth, of one's income, in theory there was no limit to the amount one could give. Charity therefore had the power to reach the Divine essence above boundary and limitation, and the ensuing influx of Divine energy could repair flaws in creation. From the beginning of Schneerson's leadership he had emphasized Shneur Zalman's statement that "the essential Divine service in these times of the footsteps of the Messiah is charity."[6] Now he found a new way to bring the idea to life.

Finally, Dollars allowed Schneerson to maintain contact with his followers without having to hold all-night yehidut marathons. Although each person had only a moment or two to speak to him as he handed them the dollar bill, they could ask for a blessing or word of advice. Many of those encounters were recorded, creating a lasting trove of Schneerson's interactions with the public. Over the six years of Sunday Dollars, visitors included everyone from Israel's Sephardic Chief Rabbi Mordechai Eliyahu to the comedian Jackie Mason. For Chabad Hasidim, receiving a dollar became a rite of passage, and the dollars themselves lasting reminders of their rebbe's mission.

By the 1980s, Schneerson's stature was at a zenith. Thanks to the work of previous decades and his expanding network of emissaries, he was one of the most influential and, with his now fully white beard, recognizable rabbis on the planet. For his Hasidim he was a holy, infallible figure, and many admirers outside the movement held him in high regard. Yet it was at just this time that one of the greatest challenges to his leadership emerged. Unlike his predecessors, Schneerson did not go to jail. But here, too, his vindication involved a court case and a non-Jewish legal system, this time the Federal Court of the Eastern District of New York.

Near the beginning of 1985, officials at 770 noticed that books were missing from the Chabad library—the same library that Yosef Yitshak had been at pains to take with him from the Soviet Union and retrieve from Poland after the Second World War. Given Yosef Yitshak's penchant for collecting, many of the missing items were quite valuable, including a fifteenth-century illustrated Passover Haggadah, medieval incunabula, and rare mystical works. More importantly, the books held immense symbolic value to Yosef Yitshak, Schneerson, and the movement at large.

Chabad had been one of the first Hasidic groups to embrace printing technology, using it to publish the works of their own rebbes and those of other Hasidic leaders. Shneur Zalman took the controversial step of publishing *Tanya*, setting a precedent that his successors expanded on. Yet many Chabad teachings remained in manuscript owing to the cost and difficulty of printing as well as a lingering sense of esoteric discretion. These manuscripts, which were passed down from one rebbe to the next through the generations of Chabad, comprised the heart of the Chabad library and its most valuable contents. The teachings in them constituted the core of the movement's theology and, because they existed only in manuscript, possession of them was a potent symbol of a rebbe's position and prestige. When there were schisms in the movement, ownership of the manuscripts conferred legitimacy upon whomever held them.

Not everything in the Chabad library was a priceless manuscript. In addition to the generational accumulation of handwritten discourses, many rebbes amassed significant collections of printed books, some of them having little to do with Chabad, Hasidism, or Judaism. Of all the Chabad rebbes, Yosef Yitshak was the most ardent collector. In 1925, after his father's printed library was confiscated by Soviet authorities, he bought the five-thousand-volume collection of Samuel Wiener, librarian of the Jewish Division of the Asiatic Museum in Leningrad, and he continued adding to it until he was forced to flee German-occupied Poland. By then it had grown to include approximately forty thousand books, along with about four hundred manuscripts. Chabad managed to retrieve most of Yosef Yitshak's collection after the war, although portions of it continued to be recovered until the late 1970s. When Yosef Yitshak died in 1950, the library remained in Chabad headquarters, split between his study and the basement.

The disappearance of books was understandably concerning. Not only were they valuable, but the library symbolized Yosef Yitshak's legacy and the leadership of Chabad. To find the culprit, a hidden security camera was installed; nothing showed up for weeks until one night in the spring of 1985, Barry Gourary—Shmaryahu and Chana Gourary's son, Schneerson's nephew, and Yosef Yitshak's only grandchild—appeared on camera late at night. He entered the basement library and left with a full shopping bag.

By this time, Barry was thoroughly estranged from Chabad. During the leadership dispute in 1950 he had sided with his father, which put him at odds with Schneerson, with whom he once had a friendly relationship. After attending Brooklyn College in the 1940s, he earned a doctorate in physics from Columbia University and moved to Silver Spring, Maryland. In 1953 he got married and moved to Pittsburgh, where he was employed by the Westinghouse Corporation. By the mid-1980s he was living in Montclair, New Jersey, working as a management consultant. Despite his estrangement from the movement, family ties kept him within the orbit of Lubavitch. His parents continued living at 770, as did his grandmother, Nehama Dina, until her death in 1971. He was therefore a familiar face in the building, whatever differences he might have had with Schneerson or the Chabad community.

When Chabad officials discovered Gourary's actions, they quickly cut off his access to the library and got a restraining order to prevent the further sale of the books. By then he had taken around 550 volumes and sold approximately 102 of them, fetching a price of around $186,000. Enraged, Gourary claimed that his actions were perfectly legal; the library didn't belong to Chabad but to the Schneersohn family. He was not just Yosef Yitshak's only grandchild but had received permission from his mother, Yosef Yitshak's oldest daughter, to take the books. Schneerson, and the rest of the Chabad community, disagreed.

The dispute was not a new one. During the contest over succession, control of the library was a main point of contention. And despite Schneerson's triumph in that battle, the library remained in the hands of the Gourary family and the collection's librarian, Chaim Lieberman. Although Lieberman furnished Schneerson with any materials he requested, and the two had a collegial relationship, Schneerson was never given independent access. Schneerson's response was characteristic: rather than publicly contest the status of the library, he started his own under the auspices of Merkos L'Inyonei Chinuch.

It was one thing to deny Schneerson the key to the library; it was another to dismantle the collection and sell it off piecemeal. This was not just a matter of the books or their value, but a question about the legitimacy of Schneerson's leadership. If, as Barry claimed, the library was his as the heir to Yosef Yitshak, Schneerson was, by implication, not the legitimate spiritual heir to the movement. During the ensuing trial Chana Schneersohn said as much. The Lubavitch dynasty died with her father, she said, and Schneerson was merely "doing his own thing."[7] Schneerson understood the dispute the same way. In a meeting of the Agudas Chasidei Chabad he said, "It should be understood that the conflict is not over the *seforim* [books] but over the seat."[8]

As the current leader of the movement, he felt that he had the primary claim to the previous rebbe's library, regardless of family heirs.

Although both Schneerson and his antagonists interpreted the conflict in those terms, at trial the case didn't concern Schneerson and his status as rebbe but the relationship between Yosef Yitshak, his library, and the Chabad community. As Judge Charles P. Sifton understood it, and as lawyers for both sides argued, ownership of the books rested on a simple but difficult question: Was Yosef Yitshak's library his personal property, or was it a communal asset entrusted to his care? As some witnesses for the prosecution argued, the question reached even further and touched on Yosef Yitshak's fundamental role as rebbe. Was he a private citizen who happened to lead a particular religious group, or was his entire life bound up with the group he led, in which case none of his property belonged to him? In Hasidic tradition, the rebbe was supported by his followers' donations; once received, the money could be spent however the rebbe liked. Yosef Yitshak used such funds for both personal expenses and communal needs. To Hasidic thinking, the public and personal lives of the rebbe were inseparable, so his finances were too. Historically, however, a rebbe's property was considered his own.

The trial, which began on November 27, 1985, lasted twenty-three days. Each morning a lottery was held in Crown Heights to determine who could attend, and the winners were transported to and from the courthouse by school bus. Schneerson spent the time praying at Yosef Yitshak's grave and received a summary of the proceedings at the end of the day from one of his secretaries.

Each side had its celebrity witnesses; scholars and writers like Elie Wiesel and Louis Jacobs testified on behalf of Chabad. Chaya Mushka, in a deposition taped at her home in Crown Heights, told the court that the books "belong to the Hasidim, because my father belonged to the Hasidim."[9] Chana Schneersohn and Chaim Lieberman testified on behalf of Gourary. But the decisive evidence was three letters written by Yosef Yitshak in the late 1930s and 1940s, identifying the books as property of Agudas Chasidei Chabad. In the last of the letters, written in 1946 to the Jewish Theological Seminary librarian Alexander Marx, Yosef Yitshak asked Marx to convince the State Department to retrieve his library from Poland because of "the great value of these manuscripts and books for the Jewish people in general and particularly for the Jewish community of the United States to whom this great possession belongs."[10] While Gourary's side argued that such statements were merely a stratagem to enlist the aid of the American government, the judge disagreed. "Not only does the letter, even in translation, ring with feeling and sincerity," he wrote, "it does not make much sense that a man of the character of the Sixth Rebbe would, in the circumstances, mean something different than what he says, that the library was to be delivered to plaintiff for the benefit of the community."[11]

On January 6, 1987, Sifton handed down his verdict. Although he believed that Yosef Yitshak could and did hold private property, the library belonged to Agudas Chasidei Chabad. The ruling was not made because of an intrinsic relationship between a rebbe and his Hasidim but because Yosef Yitshak had transferred ownership of his books to get them out of Poland. Although "both [the books and manuscripts] . . . were undoubtedly, in their origins, personal property of the Rebbe," Sifton wrote, "the conclusion is inescapable that the library was not held by the sixth Rebbe at his death as his personal property, but had been delivered to plaintiff to be held in trust for the benefit of the religious community of Chabad Chasidim."[12]

At noon, when news of the decision broke, the Chabad community erupted in celebration. Schools were let out early and the service lane in front of 770 was blocked off with trash cans. Hasidim spent the rest of the day dancing, drinking vodka, and playing music. Chabad followers from abroad got on last-minute flights to New York. At 4 p.m., Schneerson emerged from seclusion to pray the afternoon prayer in the downstairs synagogue before delivering a fiery speech. The victory was like the liberation of Shneur Zalman from tsarist prison, he said, making explicit a theme that was widely understood. "The obstacles we have faced . . . are no longer obstacles. They show us how far we can go in our devotion. They show us how hard we must work."[13] That work was not yet finished. If the victory was to be complete, he said, the books didn't just need to be recovered but to be studied. "The broader implication of the court's decision" is that "we must do more! We must now *expand* the library and make maximum use of its books. We must be filled with great joy which bursts all limitations and nullifies all restrictions on our spiritual life! This joy must infuse our actions and influence all that we do to become messengers of God and transform every Jew to be an emissary of righteousness!"[14] That day, the fifth of the month of Tevet, was added to the cycle of Chabad holidays and given the moniker "Didan Notzach"—"our side won."

The legal saga was not quite over. Gourary appealed the decision, but on November 17, 1987, the United States Court of Appeals for the Second Circuit ruled unanimously to uphold Sifton's verdict. A few days later an armored van was dispatched to retrieve 450 books in thirteen boxes from the warehouse where they were being kept. Chabad investigators managed to track down 94 of the 102 books Gourary had sold, repurchasing them at a cost of $433,000.

Whatever triumph the decision represented for Chabad, it created a permanent rift in Schneerson's family. During the trial Chana sided with her son while Chaya Mushka supported her husband. The two sisters, who had been close, never spoke again. Shmaryahu Gourary had become an increasingly marginal figure in the movement, especially after suffering a stroke in 1980. Nonetheless, he sided with Schneerson, not his wife and son.

Chana, during the last years of her life, went to live with Barry in New Jersey; her husband remained in 770 until his death in 1989. Following Chana's death in 1991, she was not buried alongside her parents but in a cemetery in Floral Park, New Jersey, belonging to the Munkatch Hasidic community.

For Lubavitchers, the verdict was evidence not only of Schneerson's legitimacy but of his power to influence the outcome of events. At the moment of the appeals court decision a convention of Chabad emissaries was taking place in Crown Heights. Rabbi Faivish Vogel, a senior emissary from England, commented on the victory: "What does the trial represent? Surely not the books, but also possession and title, which, in turn, is all about the Rebbe's capacity to influence the finite, material physical world."[15] To Schneerson's followers, he had emerged victorious not only in court but in history, both earthly and cosmic.

Vogel was not alone in believing that Schneerson had extraordinary powers. Hasidism had always placed great emphasis on the performance of miracles; traditionally, a rebbe was supposed to provide his community with children, health, and material sustenance, and many tsaddikim were renowned for their ability to fulfill such obligations through miraculous means. For early Hasidic leaders, who gained their authority through the exercise of charisma, the ability to perform miracles was a useful way to attract and maintain a following.

Chabad was an exception to this; Shneur Zalman had said he was a teacher and a spiritual guide, not a wonder worker. But he did not deny the possibility of miraculous deeds, and as the generations passed, Chabad came to embrace the miracle-working ways of other Hasidic groups. The fourth rebbe, Shmuel Schneersohn, was reputed to be particularly capable in this regard. While Yosef Yitshak was not renowned as a performer of miracles, he reported many dreams and visions involving his late father and other Chabad rebbes who preceded him.

Schneerson rarely spoke about dream visitations, though he did seem to have, or give some evidence of having, paranormal powers. During the long hours he spent at Yosef Yitshak's grave he was rumored to speak to the deceased rebbe and to receive messages in turn. Shortly after Schneerson assumed leadership, Shmaryahu Gourary reportedly said, "My brother-in-law, may he be well, is not given to exaggeration. If he says he will consult with the father-in-law at the [grave], then he will surely speak to him there."[16] When asked for a blessing, Schneerson often said that he would mention it at the gravesite.

Schneerson made fewer claims to more overt forms of miracle working. Nonetheless, stories associated with his advice and blessings were widespread. Such tales often had a rational veneer or were presented as coincidences too fortuitous to be chance. According to one story, a Jewish soldier fighting in the Korean War was saved from a shell that killed the rest of his unit because he went off to wash his hands before eating, as Jewish law required and as Schneerson had urged him to do. Schneerson often advised petitioners to strengthen their observance of certain commandments; in following Schneerson's instructions, the Hasid would discover a flaw in their observance. When the correction was made, the blessing was forthcoming.

In other cases, miraculous outcomes were more explicit. In keeping with a rebbe's responsibility to provide his followers with children, Schneerson was credited with helping childless women become pregnant. Diane Abrams, wife of New York State Attorney General Robert Abrams, related that she conceived a child when she was forty-eight years old, six weeks after receiving a blessing from Schneerson for "an addition to your family" during the holiday of Sukkot. When she returned the next year with her newborn daughter, he commented, "I see you have brought the addition to the family with you."[17] In another story, a woman reported getting pregnant after drinking wine given to her by

Schneerson from his cup; the same wine was subsequently used by a Chabad emissary to help other women get pregnant.

On many occasions followers consulted Schneerson before undergoing medical procedures and followed his advice over that of doctors. Adin Steinsaltz reported that his son was diagnosed with leukemia when he was fifteen years old; contrary to doctors' recommendations, Schneerson advised against a bone marrow transplant. In the end, Steinsaltz wrote, his son recovered, and the medical experts admitted they had been wrong. Another Hasid said Schneerson had told his brother not to get an operation for tuberculosis because the affected lung had already healed. "They make their living by cutting," he once said. "I make my living by not cutting."[18]

Similarly, Schneerson was thought to have a kind of precognitive ability. When his father died, it was reported that he had been sitting in his office with the door locked. When he emerged to find two Hasidim waiting with the news, he told them, "I sensed that my father was gone."[19] In July 1968, according to one famous story, Schneerson advised Ariel Sharon not to take El Al flight 426, on which he was scheduled to fly the next day. En route from Rome to Israel the flight was hijacked and taken to Algiers. When asked why he hadn't issued a warning to all the passengers, Schneerson responded enigmatically: "Do you really think I knew that they would hijack the plane? I didn't know. But when Sharon came to see me, I had the sense he should not go. So I told him to stay."[20] Publicly, his pronouncements on world affairs, including his assurances before the Six-Day War, were celebrated as prophetic utterances that proved his ability to predict, if not outright influence, future events.

Schneerson maintained a more ambiguous position regarding his powers. He would give blessings, as a Hasidic rebbe was expected to do, but he insisted that their success or failure lay with God. After his blessing failed to help a couple conceive a child, he wrote that it was "because they forgot that it is God who is the source of blessing . . . they placed their trust in the 'son of man,' in 'flesh and blood,' in me."[21] He told the Israeli diplomat Yehudah Avner that those "who ascribe to the Rebbe powers which the Rebbe does not ascribe to himself . . . are people who need crutches."[22] When asked by a college student whether he had supernatural abilities, he responded that everyone potentially has them if they are sufficiently devout.

Whatever his ambivalence, Schneerson had long been attracted by miracle working as an element of charismatic leadership. In a letter written to his father-in-law in early 1932, he questioned the reluctance of Chabad rebbes to use supernatural feats, especially to counter modern scientific materialism. And though he didn't claim credit for all the miracles ascribed to him, he didn't deny them, either. As he told Herbert Weiner in 1957, "We are, of course, all of us only flesh and blood, and I'm not responsible for all the stories you may hear. But you must approach the facts of the case without preconceived theories. Science, after all, means the willingness to observe facts and follow them to whatever conclusions they lead, not to try to push the facts into a desired pattern." When Weiner pressed further and asked, "Do you believe, then, that the Rebbe has special insight and can see things and know things beyond the comprehension of ordinary people?" he responded, simply, "Yes."[23]

For Hasidim, Schneerson's miraculous abilities were proof of his extraordinary nature, but they were only one aspect of a personality that had taken on mythic proportions. The attention he received from politicians, celebrities, and other public figures reinforced the perception that he was not one Hasidic rebbe out of many but a leader of the Jewish people—or even of humanity—as a whole. When Chabad emissaries spread his message, they went with the assurance that they were fulfilling the mission of a world-historical spiritual figure and that they acted on his behalf. In symbiotic fashion, their efforts enhanced

Schneerson's reputation, bringing his name, teachings, and image to every place they went. To Chabad Hasidim and their fellow travelers, Schneerson was no longer merely their rebbe, or even the Lubavitcher rebbe. He was, simply, "The Rebbe."

As his reputation grew, Schneerson became increasingly distant from his followers. Whereas the previous generation could be said to have known him personally, that was no longer the case. Until 1989 there was no biographical account of his life, and in the absence of factual information, stories, exaggerations, and myths abounded; before long nearly every aspect of his life assumed a legendary character. One journalist, writing in the early 1990s, compared him to Chairman Mao at the height of the Cultural Revolution. Under all the stories there was still a real person, somewhere. But as time passed that person became obscured by claims that he was not just a saintly person, or even a miracle worker, but a prophet of our time and even the Messiah himself.

The messianic speculation surrounding Schneerson was modeled on his rhetoric regarding Yosef Yitshak. From the moment of his father-in-law's death, Schneerson insisted that Yosef Yitshak continued to lead the movement from the beyond, a theme he returned to often in the first years of his leadership. Long after Yosef Yitshak's death, he referred to his late father-in-law as "the rebbe" of Chabad; the rebbe "whose soul is in heaven," in contrast, referred to Yosef Yitshak's father and predecessor, Shalom Dov Ber.

Such statements, though presented with unusual conviction, were not utterly beyond the frame of normative Jewish belief. But Schneerson ascribed to Yosef Yitshak an exceptional status that went beyond that of other holy men. His father-in-law, Schneerson proclaimed, was not only the rebbe of Chabad but the *nasi*, or prince, of the entire generation—a title that expanded Yosef Yitshak's role to encompass not just his community but

the entire Jewish people. While some historians have specu-
lated that the title was a response to the State of Israel, which
had its own secular nasi, for Schneerson the term carried messianic implications. As he wrote to Israeli President Yitzhak Ben-
Zvi in 1956, "Part of this brilliant future, and part of this redemption, will be 'a nasi who is the king, not the prince of a tribe,
but one who has none above him but God.'"[24] Similarly, in a letter
to Chaim Weizmann, Israel's first president, he wrote that "from
my youth I imagined a nasi as a Messiah."[25]

Unlike his statements regarding himself, Schneerson's identification of Yosef Yitshak as the Messiah was not coded or ambiguous but forceful, frequent, and overt. Drawing on a teaching of the fifteenth-century Italian rabbi Ovadia of Bartenura,
who wrote in his commentary to the book of Ruth that there
is a potential Messiah alive in every generation, Schneerson
repeatedly stated that the Messiah of our generation was Yosef
Yitshak. He often referred to his father-in-law as the "Moses
of our generation"; just as Moses had led the Jewish people out
of Egypt, Yosef Yitshak would lead them from their current
exile. In response to the problem of how Yosef Yitshak could be
the Messiah after death, when resurrection of the dead was not
supposed to happen until after the Messiah arrived, he postu-
lated that certain people would be revived earlier, Yosef Yitshak
among them. On at least one occasion he referred to Yosef Yitshak in nearly Divine terms, saying that the deceased rebbe
"governs the world in its entirety" and that "this is the essence
of God Himself, as He is put in a body."[26]

Schneerson confined such remarks to his father-in-law, but
they were suggestive of his own status. In Hasidic tradition each
rebbe was believed to "fill the place" of his predecessors; thus,
such statements would correctly be understood by Hasidim to
describe Schneerson himself. Just as his father-in-law was the
nasi, and therefore Messiah, of his generation, so Schneerson,
as the current nasi of Chabad, would be the Messiah of his own.

He stated in his first discourse that his merit was a matter of his position and place in history, but the merit was his, nonetheless. If the seven generations of Chabad were like the seven generations between Abraham and Moses, that would make Schneerson the Moses figure, not Yosef Yitshak, to whom he ascribed the role.

Chabad messianists weren't content merely to deduce Schneerson's status from his words. To convince others they had to show that their ideas were consistent with Jewish tradition. According to Maimonides, a presumptive Messiah must compel the Jewish people to observe the Torah and fight the wars of God, requirements that were difficult to square with Schneerson's life and accomplishments. Yet messianically minded Hasidim argued that Schneerson met these standards through his outreach efforts and militaristic mitzvah campaigns. Schneerson was believed to be a descendent of Rabbi Judah Loew ben Bezalel of Prague, maker of the legendary golem, who was reputed to be a descendent of the biblical King David, another messianic identifier. There was a long-standing tradition that the name of the Messiah would be Menaham, which Schneerson mentioned suggestively in his later talks. Even those unwilling to proclaim Schneerson the definite Messiah cited Ovadia of Bartenura to argue that there *must* be a potential messiah alive at all times. Who better, they contended, than Schneerson?

By the 1980s, belief that Schneerson was the Messiah in some form was widespread. Children in Chabad schools and summer camps were taught songs proclaiming Schneerson "our rebbe, our messiah." In 1982, in celebration of Schneerson's eightieth birthday, a book was published in Israel titled *The Anointed King and Complete Redemption* which proclaimed Schneerson to be "chosen by the Holy One Blessed Be He as His anointed and the redeemer of His people."[27] Even those who refrained from publicly proclaiming Schneerson the Messiah were loath to say he wasn't. As Yehuda Krinsky put it in a 1988 interview with *New*

York Newsday, "Our sages teach us that the Messiah will be a human being who lives among us. We believe that in every generation there is a person who has the qualifications to be the Messiah of the Jewish people. I don't know of anyone around now more suitable to fill the shoes of the Messiah than the Rebbe."[28]

As with Schneerson's paranormal abilities, his beliefs respecting his messianic status were ambiguous. When he spoke about Yosef Yitshak, was he really speaking about himself, as many Hasidim believed? Although his statements could be suggestive, he usually discouraged more overt ones. In 1965, when a Hasid in Israel dropped a pack of leaflets from a helicopter stating, "With great joy, we can inform you that King Messiah, for whom we have waited so many years, is . . . the holy Lubavitcher Rebbe," Schneerson instructed him to retrieve the flyers. "We were shocked by the letter and ask that you immediately cease distributing it. Gather and send to the secretariat all copies of the letter, every last one, and please confirm immediately that you have fulfilled this instruction."[29] Decades later, in 1991, when the editor of the Israeli magazine *Kfar Chabad* wanted to publish an article explaining why Schneerson should be considered the presumed messiah, Schneerson responded by telling him that shutting down the publication entirely would be preferable. In 1992, when told by an Israeli journalist that he was the Messiah, he replied simply, "I am not."[30] As he told the *New York Times* in 1972, "Because I am not a *tzaddik,* I have never given any reason for a cult of personality, and I do all in my power to dissuade them from making it that."[31]

In other instances, however, Schneerson seemed to tolerate or even encourage such statements, or else he responded vaguely enough that his followers could interpret his reaction as encouragement. And although his protestations were enough to dissuade some Hasidim from proclaiming him the Messiah publicly, they did little to shake his followers' faith in his messianic identity. Even his objections were usually about appearances and public relations rather than the claim itself. If, as he told the *New York Times*, he did everything in his power to discourage a cult of personality, here his powers failed him.

To Chabad's critics, the messianic speculation surrounding Schneerson and his unwillingness to quash it was proof that his religious fervor was a self-centered, self-aggrandizing ploy. Like other messianic pretenders, Schneerson was little more than a charlatan, they protested, whipping his followers into a frenzy for the sake of power and prestige. If not, why did he allow their extreme veneration to continue? Did he really believe himself everything they thought him to be?

Schneerson's ambivalence in this area remains something of a mystery. It seems unlikely that he wanted to foster a cult of personality—had that been his goal, he could have accomplished it far more efficiently. Yet he was reluctant to discourage his followers' messianic enthusiasms, even when they concerned him personally. Perhaps he realized that doing so would undermine their motivation and endanger the decades-long project he had invested so much effort in constructing. It was Schneerson himself who inspired his emissaries to accomplish their feats of devotion, effort, and self-sacrifice. No teaching, idea, or program could have done it. As his letters to Yosef Yitshak indicate, Schneerson was not naïve about the motivating power of charismatic leadership, including his own. And once the Messiah arrived, what would it matter? A cult of personality might have been distasteful, but it had its uses.

12

———◆·◆·◆———

End of Days

Schneerson never had any close friends. He was a loner by nature, and after he became rebbe the possibility of real friendship vanished completely. His Hasidim, even those closest to him, were followers, not friends. Though he had opportunities for casual conversation with people outside his community, his position and prestige precluded meaningful intimacy. The only person who could have been considered an intimate and a peer was his wife, Chaya Mushka. But like Schneerson himself, she was growing old.

In the summer of 1983, Chaya Mushka fell down on the terrace outside her home and broke her leg. After that, she required full-time help but was generally in good health. Her death in the early hours of February 10, 1988, a few weeks before her eighty-seventh birthday, was unexpected. After being hospitalized briefly for gastrointestinal distress, she suffered a sudden heart failure. For Schneerson, his wife's passing was the heartbreaking end of an era and the beginning of a new, final chapter.

At the time of her death Schneerson was at home, editing the talk he had given the previous week on the holiday of Tu BiShvat. He was told the news by phone; around 5:20 a.m. the body arrived at the house on President Street, where it was placed in the kitchen. Before the funeral he went over to the coffin to say goodbye. Schneerson was once known for sudden outbursts of emotion, but in later years that side of him became less visible. Now he wept.

The funeral took place that afternoon. Schneerson followed the coffin as it was carried up Kingston Avenue to Eastern Parkway. There it was placed in a hearse and taken to the Montefiore Cemetery in Queens, where Chaya Mushka was buried next to her mother and her grandmother. Schneerson returned to Crown Heights to observe the ritual seven days of mourning and contemplate the future.

For Schneerson's entire adult life Chaya Mushka had been his companion; her loss affected him deeply. "I saw the Rebbe just really kind of fold inward," his cardiologist, Ira Weiss, observed. "He was very much more withdrawn."[1] Chaya Mushka's death reminded him of his own mortality. His health was in decline: he suffered from sciatica, which caused him to walk with a stoop; he had a serious case of diabetes; and his eyesight was becoming impaired by cataracts. He had no children or successors, and there were supposed to be only seven Chabad rebbes before redemption. Appointing a new leader in other circumstances would have been difficult but conceivable. An eighth rebbe would be a repudiation of Schneerson's life's work. When asked in 1972 by a *New York Times* reporter, "Who is to be the eighth Lubavitcher rabbi?" he responded: "The messiah will come and he will take all these troubles and doubts . . . My intention is to live many years more . . . There's a very great deal to achieve."[2] Now he didn't have that many more years to live, the Messiah had not come, and there was still a great deal to achieve.

Schneerson was able to combine his messianic faith with mundane practicality, and he knew that his death before the Messiah's arrival was possible. On the day of Chaya Mushka's funeral, he summoned Yehuda Krinsky to the office on the second floor of his house. He wanted to establish a charitable fund in his wife's memory and to update the paperwork for Chabad's principal organizations. He also wanted to draft a will. In it, Schneerson specified that his personal property, after the payment of funeral expenses, should go to Agudas Chasidei Chabad. Krinsky was listed as executor, and the will was witnessed and signed a few days later. Instructions regarding the future of the movement were not included.

The next Saturday night, Schneerson addressed his followers. Without a rebbe as a final authority, he said, Hasidim should rely on local rabbinical courts to resolve communal and religious problems, including conflicts between Chabad organizations. Other rabbis could never replace a rebbe, let alone a charismatic leader such as himself. But as he had told his followers at the outset, Chabad Hasidim were expected to take responsibility for themselves. The recent legal dispute over Yosef Yitshak's library had emphasized the primacy of the community over any single leader. And just as he insisted that Yosef Yitshak continued to lead the movement after his death, the same would presumably be true of Schneerson when he died. Over the past ten years he had withdrawn from day-to-day management of the movement. Now he tried to prepare it to do without him altogether.

There were other signs that Schneerson was providing for his eventual death. Following Chaya Mushka's passing, he moved his office and activities into his home, taking a ritual usually reserved for a week and stretching it into a year. At the same time, he began cleaning out his office, which had become cluttered with books and papers. When the year of mourning was over, he disposed of some possessions, changed the locks on his house, and moved into 770, sleeping on a cot in his office. With his wife gone, and whatever passed for a domestic life with her, his identity was subsumed by his public role more than ever before.

In the preceding years Schneerson had stopped giving Hasidic discourses, and his long-running lecture series had been largely discontinued. Now he canceled weekday farbrengens, even on special occasions. Instead, he held them every Sabbath, rather than once a month. Although he had previously prayed in the smaller upstairs synagogue during the week, he now joined the rest of the congregation downstairs and frequently gave short talks after prayers.

Even at this late stage of his life Schneerson was launching new initiatives. On what would have been Chaya Mushka's eighty-seventh birthday, he introduced the "birthday campaign," encouraging people to celebrate their birthdays by committing to ever-greater religious accomplishments. He also began to accelerate the publication of his work. Before he had deemed it a low priority, arguing that there were enough books to study and more pressing missions to accomplish. Now he turned his attention to editing and annotating his talks and discourses. Already in 1987, he had instructed his aides to begin publishing his correspondence; during the remainder of his life twenty-two volumes were released, encompassing over eight thousand letters. Altogether, the last six years of Schneerson's life saw the publication of forty-seven edited volumes of his thought. Just as Shneur Zalman had tried to reduce the reliance of Hasidim on their rebbe by printing *Tanya*, Schneerson prepared for his absence by making sure his work was properly published.

Whatever arrangements Schneerson made for his death, his messianic faith did not waver. During the last years of his leadership he would have a single-minded focus: the "Moshiach campaign," which subsumed all his previous efforts. He didn't have much time left, and his most important mission, bringing the Messiah, had yet to be realized.

Like many Jews of his generation, Schneerson had once led a peripatetic existence, shuttling around Europe to pursue his future. Upon arriving in America, and especially after becoming rebbe, his travels came to a halt. The rest of his life was spent almost entirely at Chabad headquarters, his home, or the cemetery.

Why he lived this way is unclear. He kept abreast of current affairs and continued to meet and correspond with diverse leaders and thinkers. Though he spent most of his time in a single room, his mind spanned the globe. Yet it is hard to imagine that existing exclusively in his own milieu, surrounded by worshipful Hasidim, didn't have a calcifying effect on his thinking. When Chaya Mushka was alive, there was someone who could offer other viewpoints. Unlike his followers, she was a peer who could speak to him as an equal. On one occasion she is reported to have said, while listening to one of his farbrengens, "He thinks everyone cares about Moshiach as much as he does."[3] As his doctor remarked, she was his "intellectual sparring partner" who "could take [him] to task . . . when she saw him going a little too far afield."[4] Now she was gone. He still had a few family members, including his brother Leibel's daughter Dalia and her husband, Avner, who had occasionally stayed with him and Chaya Mushka when visiting from Israel. But they were spiritually and geographically distant. The dispute over the Chabad library had destroyed whatever relationship he still had with his sister-in-law and his nephew. Now there was no one in whom he could confide or who could put any brake on his fervor. Although he was surrounded by adoring Hasidim, he was alone.

The community was also experiencing a sense of isolation, albeit for different reasons. When Yosef Yitshak based his headquarters in Crown Heights, it had been an upper-middle-class neighborhood with a diverse Jewish population. In the postwar decades, central Brooklyn underwent demographic changes like those of many urban centers in America. New York saw an influx of new residents, including Blacks from the southern states and immigrants from the Caribbean islands. Many of them moved to Brooklyn and to Crown Heights, which was directly south of the historical Black neighborhood of Bedford Stuyvesant. Better-off white residents fled to the suburbs of New Jersey and Long Island or went further into Brooklyn, Queens, and Staten Island. The racial makeup of the neighborhood quickly changed.

Although racism was a factor in the rapid flight of white residents, the Jewish community had legitimate concerns. As the area changed, tensions grew between Black and Jewish residents, focusing on access to housing, perceived or actual political influence, cultural differences, and rising crime and violence. Attacks against Hasidic residents, including murder, arson, rape, and antisemitic harassment, contributed to the sense of siege.

Unlike other white residents of Crown Heights, Hasidic communities faced obstacles to relocation. Not just individual members but schools, synagogues, and other institutions would have to move. Leaving Crown Heights would be a communal endeavor, not a piecemeal leave-taking. Still, by the mid-1960s some groups were assessing their options. At one point Schneerson pleaded with the Bobover rebbe, Shlomo Halberstam, to stay in the neighborhood, but in 1968 the Bobovers moved to Borough Park. For Lubavitchers too, decamping elsewhere was an enticing prospect. Although Schneerson was still in 770, families began looking for safer and wealthier neighborhoods where they could raise their children.

Then Schneerson put his foot down. On the last day of Passover, 1969, in front of a crowd of three thousand people, he made the case to stay. First, he contended, Jewish law prohibited selling a home when the sale would harm other people. It was even worse to sell a synagogue or a yeshiva except under the most pressing circumstances, but not for the sake of a more desirable neighborhood. If affluent residents moved out, it would be detrimental to those who could not afford to go. Worst of all, allowing the neighborhood to unravel would undo the institutional and social bonds that constituted the spiritual life of the community. "When they lived in a certain neighborhood, each person was rooted in a particular Jewish circle," Schneerson declared. "But this spiritual legacy is often lacking in a new environment . . . the difficulties of resettlement require time and energy to overcome and it is not always easy or successful."[5]

Schneerson's thinking was informed by more than legal or practical concerns. Although 770 had been purchased because it was in a Jewish, well-to-do area—neither of which was still true—it had since taken on a freight of symbolic meaning. The building underwent several expansions and renovations over the years; adjacent structures had been purchased, and by the late 1980s the complex included office space, living space, a yeshiva, the Chabad library, and the large main synagogue. The location was more than just symbolic of the movement's success. In talks from the 1980s and 1990s, Schneerson assigned it a novel theological significance. Its address, to begin with, was uncannily auspicious. The number 7 is intrinsically significant in Judaism: there were seven days of creation ("the existence of the world") and seven branches on the menorah ("the purification of the world").[6] In Hebrew numerology the number 770 is equivalent to both *paratsto* ("you shall break out"), the messianically imbued word that inspired Chabad's aggressive outreach activities, and "house of the Messiah." And the number 7 represented the seventh generation, "the last of exile and the first of redemption."[7] Even the name of the neighborhood, Crown Heights, could be translated as *Keter Elyon*—the highest, most liminal aspect of the Godhead, bordering the unknowable En Sof itself.

Then there was the messianic purpose of the building, which Schneerson derived from his reading of rabbinic sources. The Talmud taught that wherever the Jewish people were exiled, God's presence went with them. Although the temple in Jerusalem had been destroyed, the synagogues and study houses in exile are "minor sanctuaries" where the Shekhinah still resides. According to a second sage, the Divine presence resides only in the "house of our master in Babylonia."[8] These opinions, Schneerson said, did not conflict. While the Shekhinah might dwell in any synagogue or study house, one of them was primary, just as the Jerusalem temple had been. In the Talmudic context the foremost sanctuary was the study house of Abba Arikha, or Rav, an early Amoraic sage. Now it was 770, home to the "nasi of the generation," Yosef Yitshak. Furthermore, the Talmud said that in the messianic future the minor sanctuaries would be relocated to the Land of Israel and, according to Schneerson's interpretation, incorporated into the temple complex. Their placement wouldn't be equal, however, but would privilege the principal sanctuary; the future temple was therefore, in a sense, already present at 770. Moreover, at the outset of the messianic restoration the Shekhinah would first be revealed in exile; 770, therefore, would be the locus of revelation. In other words, when the Messiah arrived, he would come to 770 first. How could Chabad abandon that spot for some place in Borough Park or Monsey?

Whatever Schneerson's motivation, his decision to stay in Crown Heights was characteristically bold. He would not be intimidated by changes in the neighborhood or swayed by the departure of other Jewish groups. Although the community sometimes struggled to maintain its foothold, they remained geographically unified and retained their headquarters as a religious emblem and pilgrimage site. In later years Schneerson would be credited with preserving one of the most racially integrated neighborhoods in the country; when other whites fled, Lubavitchers stayed. At the time, however, his insistence on staying in Crown Heights isolated the local community from other parts of the Jewish world. They had once been at the center of a bustling Jewish district, but they were now a small minority in the midst of a much larger Black and Caribbean population. And despite some intermittent bridge-building efforts, conflicts between Hasidim and their Black neighbors continued to escalate. Then, in the summer of 1991, the neighborhood exploded.

At 8:20 p.m. on Monday, August 19, Schneerson was returning to Crown Heights from Yosef Yitshak's gravesite. He was driven by Yehuda Krinsky in a gray Cadillac Brougham and was accompanied by a small motorcade, including an unmarked police car in front and a 1984 Mercury Grand Marquis station wagon in back, driven by a twenty-two-year-old Hasid named Yosef Lifsh. After Schneerson's car passed Utica Avenue along President Street, on the eastern border of Crown Heights, Lifsh continued through the intersection. Swerving to avoid a collision with another car, he careened onto the sidewalk, hitting Gavin Cato and his cousin Angela Cato, the seven-year-old children of Guyanese immigrants who had come to America the previous year. Gavin, who had been fixing the chain on his bicycle, was driven against a window grating and killed. Angela was severely injured. A crowd gathered, threatening the occupants of the station wagon. An ambulance from Hatzalah, the Jewish volunteer emergency service, arrived at the scene around the same time as three emergency vehicles from the city. The Hatzalah ambulance removed Lifsh and his two passengers, and the city ambulances took the Cato children to the hospital.

The ensuing three days of riots, looting, and marches saw approximately 152 police officers and 38 civilians injured, 27 vehicles destroyed, 7 stores looted or burned, and 225 robberies or burglaries; in the judgment of one historian, Edward Shapiro, it was "the most serious anti-Semitic incident in American history."[9] About three hours after the accident, Yankel Rosenbaum, a twenty-nine-year-old Australian scholar from Melbourne University, was surrounded and stabbed by a group of Black youths on President Street. An hour after being taken to Kings County Hospital, he died from his wounds.

At the time and afterward, some neighborhood leaders tried to quell the unrest and improve relations between the Black and the Jewish communities. Schneerson remained silent. Aside from vague remarks urging his followers to remain peaceful, he seemed oblivious to the chaos. Other neighborhood clergy complained that he wouldn't speak to them. "They say he is a spiritual leader and doesn't deal in these matters," the Reverend Canon Heron Sam, rector of St. Mark's Episcopal Church, told the *New York Times*. "I hate to remind him, but this is a spiritual crisis . . . He is doing a great disservice to this community not to meet with his counterparts."[10] On Sunday, August 25, in a public meeting with Mayor David Dinkins, Schneerson offered platitudes. "I am confident, that with the good people of all of our communities, both sides, we will come together and do those things necessary to protect everyone," Dinkins said. "We need to forget 'both sides,'" Schneerson responded magnanimously. "There is one side, one people, united by the management of New York City."[11] At no point did he offer condolences to the Cato family, let alone an apology, even though a car in his motorcade had killed their child.

In defense of Schneerson's apparent lack of interest, his driver, Yehuda Krinsky, argued that he was an international spiritual leader who couldn't be expected to concern himself with local disturbances. "The Rebbe is an international figure," he told the *New York Times*. "If there is an incident in Washington, D.C., should the President get involved with white and black leaders to settle the insurrection?"[12] Yet Schneerson was intensely interested in local issues in his own community. Perhaps he ignored the riots because they didn't fit his messianic vision. The time of trial and upheaval had passed, he taught; the current age was a time of peace, prosperity, and miracles on behalf of the Jewish people. But that faith was being tested at his doorstep. If riots on the streets of Crown Heights were supposed to be a messianic harbinger, Schneerson didn't mention it.

Schneerson was never concerned with conformity. Throughout his leadership he set Chabad apart, distinct and separate from other Jewish groups. This separation was partly based on the precedent set by the fifth and the sixth rebbes. When Agudath Israel, a political organization that included both Hasidic and non-Hasidic groups, was founded in 1912, Shalom Dov Ber declined to participate because of the organization's support for settlement in Palestine. In the United States, Yosef Yitshak, and Schneerson after him, refrained from joining the American branch of the Agudah, as well as other Orthodox umbrella organizations. Chabad, Schneerson seemed to believe, had its own legacy and mission that would be dissipated by the bureaucratic consensus-building of larger institutions. Whether by instinct or calculation, he understood that such affiliations would only weaken the fervor and focus of his movement and diminish his own exceptional status within it. In Chabad he was the seventh in a line of seven; in another organization he would be one leader of many. His charisma could not be channeled by a board, even one consisting of venerable rabbis.

Schneerson had admirers among his peers. When his mother died in 1964, he was visited by many of the most prominent Orthodox and Hasidic leaders in the country; decades later when Chaya Mushka passed away, condolence calls were paid by an equally impressive list of names. Rabbi Moshe Feinstein, the preeminent halakhic authority in America, was a particular admirer. Yet Schneerson's policy of ideological and organizational isolationism struck many Orthodox leaders as hubris. His mitzvah campaigns allowed little room for collaboration, and the visibility they gave Chabad could be irksome. It was one thing to encourage mitzvah observance—but who had put him in charge of Judaism? On the local level, Chabad emissaries could make as many enemies as friends when they swept into established Jewish communities and assumed representation of its Orthodox segment. Although his followers believed their vision encompassed all Jews, not everyone wanted to be held within the embrace of Chabad.

Other rabbis had more substantive disagreements. Schneerson, early in his leadership, had clashed with the Satmar leader Yoel Teitelbaum over Zionism and the State of Israel, as well as over Chabad's outreach methods. To more insular groups, Chabad's willingness to interact with secular Jews, non-Jews, and members of the opposite sex was contrary to their own desire for purity from outside influence. Similarly, Teitelbaum objected to Schneerson's embrace of modern technology. While Schneerson argued that the use of current media for sacred purposes was a messianic act, spreading the teachings of Hasidism "outward," for Teitelbaum it was nothing less than "an act of Satan."[13] And while Schneerson believed that any mitzvah performed by any Jew was of infinite significance, for Satmar and other Hasidic groups, putting tefillin on a stranger in the street degraded the holiness of the object and the act.

Hostility to Lubavitch, and to Schneerson personally, festered in other Hasidic neighborhoods of Brooklyn. Lubavitch mitzvah tanks that ventured into the Satmar stronghold of Williamsburg were pelted with stones; on Passover, when groups of Lubavitchers fanned out to spread their message in local synagogues, their presence in Williamsburg provoked physical altercations and thrown garbage. In 1975, on the holiday of Purim, an effigy of Schneerson was hung from a telephone pole and burned together with an Israeli flag in front of a large crowd. The same year, the Borough Park offices of the *Algemeiner Journal*, a Chabad-aligned Yiddish newspaper, were ransacked and burned to the ground. Such incidents, along with reported threats against Schneerson's life, convinced New York City Mayor Ed Koch to provide him with a police escort and to station a patrol car outside his home—an arrangement that became a point of contention between the Lubavitch community and its Black neighbors, who saw it as a sign of favoritism on the part of the city and the police.

Opposition to Schneerson extended beyond other Hasidic groups. In Israel, Elazar Menachem Man Shach objected to Chabad's outreach tactics much as Teitelbaum had. In contrast to Schneerson, who was inclined to view non-Orthodox Jews with indulgence, Shach condemned Israel's secular population and challenged the very idea of a Jewish identity bereft of Orthodox practice. Shach's antipathy to Chabad, which he termed "the infamous sect," eventually resulted in his split with the Agudat Yisrael party and the formation of another party, Degel HaTorah, in 1988.

Schneerson's outreach campaigns weren't all that disturbed rabbis like Schach. His messianism struck his critics as similar to the heresy of messianic Zionism in substance, if not style. Just as the followers of Abraham Isaac Kook believed they could bring the Messiah through their own efforts, so did Schneerson. Most of all, Schneerson's antagonists were concerned about the troublesome combination of his unrelenting messianism and his apparent cult of personality. Although reverence of tsaddikim was a core component of Hasidism, in Chabad that veneration went beyond normative bounds. Rabbi Eric Yoffie, president of the Union for Reform Judaism, asserted that the "worship" of Schneerson is "virtually blasphemous."[14] Although Chabad Hasidim found it unfathomable that Schneerson would die before the Messiah came, others worried about the consequences of that eventuality. Past messianic disappointments had led to heterodox beliefs and practices; there was no reason why it couldn't happen again.

Such concerns had existed for decades, ever since Schneerson told his followers that the seventh generation of Chabad would welcome the Messiah, seemingly casting himself in the messianic role. But as Chabad's messianic fervor built throughout the 1980s and 1990s, so did opposition to it. A 1988 article in the *New York Jewish Week* laid out the case that Chabad messianism was a more mainstream phenomenon than previously thought. Responding to Yehuda Krinsky's interview with *Newsday*, in which he claimed that Schneerson was the most suitable messianic candidate, one unnamed Orthodox leader was quoted as saying, "This is the final proof that what we've suspected all along is true."[15]

None of this criticism discouraged Schneerson. Just as Yosef Yitshak once castigated Jewish leaders for not responding adequately to his messianic pronouncements, Schneerson took them to task for neglecting the messianic idea, an article of faith according to all Orthodox traditions. Some groups did support his messianic campaign, arguing that praying and working for the coming of the Messiah was normative Jewish practice. And as the years passed, the messianic excitement grew.

Schneerson was a remarkably consistent thinker. Although his ideas varied in emphasis or expression over time, their substance hardly changed over more than four decades. Messianism had featured prominently in his worldview since he was young, and there was no time when he didn't talk about it often. But there had also been immediate concerns to address, followers to advise, public figures to lobby, institutions to create and guide. As he grew older, his rhetoric became more insistent and extreme. With his health deteriorating and mortality in view, the urgency of bringing the Messiah prompted him to approach positions that had once been taboo.

The Talmud decreed that those who calculate the end of days should be cursed, "as they would say once the end has arrived and he has not come, he will no longer come."[16] The medieval German Jewish sage Judah HeHasid put it more harshly: "If you see one making prophecies about the Messiah, you should know that he deals in witchcraft . . . for no one knows anything about the coming of the Messiah."[17] As Maimonides reasonably argued, predicting redemption was dangerous because if the Messiah failed to appear, the faith of those who believed would be tested. The Messiah is certainly coming, the faithful affirm. But beware of anyone who claims to know when.

Still, the rabbis did not always abide by their own admonitions. The Talmud taught that the first two thousand years of creation were characterized by chaos, the second two thousand by Torah, and the last two thousand by the coming of the Messiah. Since four thousand years had already elapsed, the delay could only be explained by humanity's sins. According to another tradition, each thousand years corresponded to one day of the creation, and the messianic age would coincide with the Sabbath. Other predictions were based on biblical exegesis, historically significant intervals, and astrological calculations. It was thought that the Messiah would come seventy years after the destruction of the Second Temple, since that was the duration of exile after the destruction of the first. When that date passed, redemption was pushed to four hundred years, the length of the biblical sojourn in Egypt. The year 1068–69 was similarly auspicious, marking one thousand years since the temple's destruction, as was the twelve-hundredth anniversary in 1268. Eleazar of Worms predicted the messianic age would begin in 1226; Abraham Abulafia—himself a messianic pretender—believed the Messiah would come in 1290. Rashi, basing his calculation on the book of Daniel, put the year at 1352 or 1478.

Messianic speculation was encouraged by the baroque symbolism and fluid interpretive possibilities of the Kabbalah. The *Book of the Zohar* predicted that redemption would occur around the year 1300. Abraham bar Hiyya, a Catalan Jewish mathematician, astronomer, and philosopher, forecast astrologically that the Messiah would appear in 1358. Periods of turmoil were particularly fruitful for messianic speculation, and the expulsions of Jews from Spain and Portugal in the late fifteenth century fostered a widespread belief that redemption was at hand. Abraham ben Eliezer ha-Levi, a Spanish kabbalist who emigrated to Jerusalem in 1514, said that redemption had begun in 1524 and would culminate in 1530–31. Isaac ben Judah Abarbanel, a fifteenth-century Portuguese Jewish philosopher and financier, authored an entire messianic trilogy in which he similarly foretold that the messianic age would reach its apex by 1531; his contemporary Abraham Zacuto wrote that the Davidic monarchy would be restored starting in 1504. Later that century, Isaac Luria and his school anticipated that the Messiah would arrive in the year 1575. Even Maimonides, who warned against predicting the end, couldn't help but mention, in practically the same breath, a tradition he received from his father according to which the gift of prophecy would be restored in 1210, after which redemption would swiftly follow.

All those predictions ended in disappointment, perhaps proving the wisdom of those who cautioned against making them in the first place. Schneerson had a different theory. Chabad leaders had also made messianic pronouncements. Shneur Zalman foretold the Messiah's arrival would be in either 1842–43 or 1847–48. Shalom Dov Ber specified 1905–6, and Yosef Yitshak made repeated statements about imminent redemption during the Holocaust. For Schneerson, the failure of these predictions did not mean they were false. According to the old argument, those dates had indeed been auspicious, but some flaw still needed correction. Nonetheless, such claims indicated that redemption was closer than ever. As the Talmud said, in a passage that Schneerson quoted incessantly, "All the end times have passed, and [redemption] depends only on repentance and good deeds."[18]

Schneerson desisted from giving concrete dates, but he repeatedly marked a year or time period as favorable. In 1981, at the start of the Jewish year 5742, he taught that the Hebrew letters designating the date should be read as an acronym for "the year the Messiah will come"; the next year became "the year of the revelation of the Messiah," and 1983–84 was "the year of the words of the Messiah." These announcements picked up again at the end of the decade. In 1989, at the start of the Jewish year 5750, he pronounced it to be "a year of miracles." It was also the fortieth year after Yosef Yitshak's death—the duration of the Israelites' desert wandering. When the Messiah failed to appear, he pronounced 5751 to be the year in which "I will show them wonders," and then 5752 to be the year in which "wonders arrived." Now it was two years past the forty-year mark, but forty-two was also an auspicious number, since it corresponded to the number of stops the Israelites made before entering the promised land. The passage of one year after another meant only that the moment of redemption was ever closer.

Schneerson's calculations weren't just based on wordplay or numerology. He always believed that nothing happened by chance and that every event was a manifestation of the Divine will. In the late 1980s and early 1990s, signs and portents abounded. There was Ayatollah Khomeini's death in Iran; the Tiananmen Square protests in China; the collapse of Communism in Eastern Europe and the fall of the Berlin Wall. A full-page ad in the *Jewish Week* read: "Any one of these phenomena by itself is enough to boggle the mind. Connect them all together, and a pattern emerges that cannot be ignored."[19] Schneerson, in his talks, returned over and over to current events, presenting them as incontrovertible evidence for his eschatological views.

The most messianically significant developments, from Schneerson's perspective, were the Gulf War in early 1991 and the collapse of the Soviet Union later that year. When Saddam Hussein began lobbing Scud missiles at Israel, hoping to provoke an Israeli counterattack that would fracture the international coalition trying to dislodge Iraqi forces from Kuwait, Schneerson urged calm, as he had almost twenty-five years before. While Israelis huddled in bomb shelters, Schneerson assured them of their safety. "The events do not have to disturb the spiritual and physical peace of a single Jew, because they are a preparation and preface for the actual coming of the Messiah."[20] Before the war he advised against the distribution of gas masks, he was so certain of the nation's security. When Israel emerged relatively unscathed, Schneerson's words were again celebrated as prophetic.

Not just the outcome but the war itself had a messianic quality. In his talks that year Schneerson returned repeatedly to a passage from the *Yalkut Shimoni*, a thirteenth-century midrashic compilation. "In the year that the Messiah will be revealed, the kings of the nations of the world will provoke one another. The king of Persia will challenge an Arab king . . . and all the nations of the world will clamor and panic . . . Israel will also clamor and panic . . . [God] will tell them: My children, do not fear. Everything I have done, I have done only for you. Why are you afraid? Have no fear; the time of your redemption has arrived!"[21] The two kings, Schneerson contended, were Saddam Hussein and Kuwaiti Sheikh Jaber al-Ahmad al-Sabah (or perhaps Saudi King Fahd bin Abdulaziz Al Saud), with Iraq counting as Persia since it had once been part of the Persian Empire. Not only were the two rulers fighting, but it was the year in which "I will show them wonders." And lo! wonders had been shown.

The Soviet collapse raised messianic expectations even further. On August 19, while riots were engulfing Crown Heights, a group of conservative hardliners launched a coup against the Soviet leader Mikhail Gorbachev. Chabad had just sent a group of young emissaries to the Soviet Union; once again Schneerson assured his followers that they would be safe. When the coup fell apart three days later, he was proved correct. On earlier occasions Schneerson pointed to faraway conflicts, arguing that the brutality of modern warfare made them clear harbingers of redemption. Now, the end of the Cold War seemed even more meaningful. When the United Nations Security Council met in January 1992 and later issued an Agenda for Peace, Schneerson cited these activities as an initial fulfillment of Isaiah's prophecy that "they shall beat their swords into ploughshares, and their spears into pruning hooks; nation shall not lift up sword against nation, neither shall they learn war anymore."[22] Schneerson had previously argued that rebuilding the temple would precede the ingathering of exiles and that emigration to Israel was not a messianic event, but he now taught that the exodus of Jews from the former Soviet Union was, at the very least, a foretaste of the messianic era. Like Francis Fukuyama, an American political scientist who saw the end of the Cold War as the "end of history" and the beginning of enduring peace and stability among liberal democracies, Schneerson saw the events of the period through a rose-colored lens. If there were inconsistencies in his statements, they were beside the point. The Messiah was coming. Everything, therefore, was a sign.

Schneerson tried to imbue his followers with the confidence that their generation was "the last of exile and the first of redemption." But with his own death approaching, maintaining belief was not enough. If the Messiah was going to arrive, he had to come soon. To avoid lapsing into doubt or disappointment, his followers' enthusiasm needed to keep growing. As with earlier messianic movements, predicting redemption didn't suffice; it had to become real. The Messiah couldn't just be about to come—he had to be here already.

In a sense, this idea was consistent with conventional Hasidic theology. From the human viewpoint, there would be a moment when everything changed. From God's perspective, nothing changed. The difference between the pre- and post-messianic periods was therefore one of perception. The Messiah didn't need to come; rather, people had to open their eyes and see him.

For Schneerson, however, the Messiah wasn't merely present as he always had been. In the messianic age, revelation wouldn't be restricted to the select few; everyone would perceive God with "eyes of flesh." Now, that unrestricted revelation was at hand. The reason, Schneerson explained, was because all the preparations were finished. He had emphasized repentance; thanks to the work of his emissaries, repentance had been performed. The Ba'al Shem Tov said that the Messiah would come when Hasidism "spread outward." That had been done too. Schneerson frequently referred to a statement made by Yosef Yitshak in 1928, that the only thing left was to "polish our buttons."[23] Now the buttons were polished. Even the last possible step, simply being ready to receive the Messiah, was done. What could be left? Schneerson didn't need to predict anything; it had practically already happened.

But of course, it hadn't happened. Schneerson, in his talks, oscillated between emphasizing the Messiah's immediacy—that he had, in a sense, "already come"—and expressing his vexation that somehow, despite everything, he had not. Days became weeks, months, and years, and the world was still unredeemed. World events heralded the Messiah's arrival, yet the Messiah did not arrive. Schneerson proclaimed with utter conviction that this generation would welcome the Messiah and that his father-in-law, more than forty years dead, would lead them. Now he himself was approaching ninety and his powers were failing. Schneerson's own faith was as unshakeable as it had always been, or so it seemed. But how much disappointment could he or his followers take?

Finally, a crack appeared. In the spring of 1991 messianic expectation reached a fever pitch. The war between the kings was over; miracles had been performed. Passover was the holiday of redemption; according to one teaching, the future redemption would happen at Passover. But the holiday came and went, and redemption did not.

Despite old age and declining health, Schneerson continued
to give regular talks to his followers, imploring them to do more
to bring the Messiah. (JEM, The Living Archive)

That Thursday, April 11, Schneerson spent the afternoon
at Yosef Yitshak's gravesite before returning to 770 for evening
prayers. After the service, he stood behind his lectern to address the congregation. The talk he gave stunned his audience.
"How is it that . . . despite everything, we have not brought the
Messiah?! It's completely incomprehensible . . . That it seems
acceptable, God forbid, that the Messiah will not come tonight,
or tomorrow, or the day after tomorrow, heaven help us. You
cry out for the Messiah, but if you really meant it, the Messiah
would have come long ago . . . I don't know what else I can do.
Everything I've done until now has been futile and fruitless. It
hasn't helped—we are still in exile . . . The only thing I can do
is pass the problem to you. Do everything that is in your power
to bring our righteous Messiah immediately and without delay,
literally!"[24]

The lecture, which became known as the "infamous sermon,"

wasn't shocking because Schneerson told his listeners it was their job to bring the Messiah. He always taught that Chabad Hasidim couldn't rely on their rebbe to fulfill their spiritual duties. He often referred to a teaching of Maimonides according to which a single righteous act could tip the balance of the world, and that act could be performed by anyone. Rather, the speech was shocking because of how Schneerson characterized his efforts. Was he really discounting his work and accomplishments? Were they really futile? They had not brought the Messiah, true, but did Schneerson really believe his labors were for nothing? In his frustration, he allowed his rhetoric to get away from him. The lecture was disturbing for another reason, however. Schneerson wasn't just charging his followers with a mission; he was blaming them for their failures. The Messiah's delay wasn't his fault, he claimed. It was theirs.

Schneerson said there was nothing else he could do, but there was something, and his followers were clamoring for it: declare himself the Messiah. As in the past, the simplest way to make redemption real was for the Messiah to identify himself. Whether or not Schneerson did so is still disputed.

"The appointment of David King Messiah has already happened," he stated in February 1991. "There only needs to be acceptance of his rule and attachment between the king and the nation with the completeness of revelation."[25] A few months later he said, "Since in our days . . . all the end times have passed, simply and literally, certainly our righteous Messiah will come imminently and immediately, and each and every person will point with his finger and say, 'Behold this one (King Messiah) has come,' for he has already arrived (in the past tense) in the moment before this moment." He continued: "The Messiah is present in the world in the time and place of exile . . . and he waits impatiently to be revealed."[26]

In June he said again, "The Messiah has *already come*, that is, we are already standing on the threshold of the beginning of the days of the Messiah, on the threshold of the beginning of redemption, and imminently and immediately will be its continuation and completion."[27] In a talk that September, he said, "Since in the last period it has been fulfilled in literal fact that it has been publicized in many newspapers around the entire world (and it should be increased and publicized even more) that 'behold this one (King Messiah) has come,' imminently— has already come—in literal fact, below ten cubits, revealed to the entire world, and all the more so to 'the eyes of all Israel,' imminently and immediately, literally."[28] A few weeks later he repeated that the Messiah had been revealed and only needed to be accepted.

According to conventional Jewish belief, prophecy had ended during the second temple period. However, in a remarkable talk given on August 17, 1991, Schneerson claimed not only that Yosef Yitshak was a prophet but that, following Maimonides, a prophet had the authority to appoint another prophet. Again citing Maimonides, he declared that it was obligatory to obey such a prophet and forbidden to question or test him. "We believe the words of the prophet, not because they are his words, but because they are God's words, through the prophet!"[29] This claim was further justified by Maimonides's statement that prophecy would be restored *before* the Messiah's arrival. Since the Messiah was about to arrive, it stood to reason that prophecy had been restored.

Perhaps the most explicit identification of Schneerson as the Messiah was not an oral statement but a written comment on the transcript of a talk given at the beginning of February 1992. In several of Schneerson's later talks he alluded to the tradition that the name of the Messiah would be Menahem. Now, commenting on the word *miyad* (immediately), which he read as an acronym for the names "Moses, Israel, and David," he added that it could also stand for the periods of Chabad leadership in reverse chronological order: "Messiah (his name is Menachem), Yosef, and Dov Ber."[30] Although it has been claimed that the comment was not made by Schneerson himself, it was written in his voice and has been republished several times by the official Chabad publishing house.

For Chabad messianists, such statements were clear: Schneerson was the Messiah and had identified himself as such. Yet Chabad theology demanded not only the traditional hallmarks of the messianic age but a complete revolution in human consciousness. While some people might have believed that such a revolution had occurred, Schneerson had not been convinced. For all his pushing and pleading, he was not insane. If he was the Messiah, that status did not come from inference or argument but revelation. In a conversation with an aide, Schneerson is reported to have said as much. "The one who is the Messiah will have this revealed to him from above." He confessed, "This has not been revealed to me."[31] Despite his best efforts, the Messiah had not come, and therefore he could not be the Messiah himself.

Or at least, not yet.

Like his more conservative followers, he seemed to believe that even if he weren't already the Messiah, it was reasonable to assume that he could be. Not only had he worked for redemption harder than anybody else, but the entire purpose of his leadership was to prepare for messianic revelation. On at least one occasion he seemed to state that he was the presumed Messiah, using a loose interpretation of Maimonides's criteria. Although he shrouded such claims in ambiguity, there was no mistaking his place in the eschatological drama.

Perhaps, in those waning years, with his wife gone and his health declining, such entreaties constituted Schneerson's final and most desperate effort. Being the rebbe wasn't a role he had aspired to, but when the need arose, he met the moment and accomplished great things. If bringing the Messiah meant becoming the Messiah, he would do that too. It was as far as he could go.

If Schneerson put his foot on the messianic tripwire, his Hasidim had long since tumbled over it. Schneerson had charged them with bringing the Messiah, and the key to fulfilling that responsibility was simple. Schneerson was the Messiah, and he needed to be revealed as such. If their rebbe tried to make redemption more real by insisting that it had arrived, their beliefs about him must have been true. While the Chabad community had been conflicted about publicly identifying Schneerson as the Messiah, now most of the hedging or equivocation was set aside. With Schneerson's apparent encouragement, the messianist hysteria—which by this point encompassed nearly everyone—became louder and more insistent. Posters, banners, and billboards with Schneerson's picture and the words "King Messiah" began appearing in cities around the world. Hasidim distributed pamphlets and advertised Schneerson's status in the media. A store opened on Kingston Avenue that called itself the Moshiach Store.

Such efforts were not directed only toward the public but also toward Schneerson himself. Just as he had been reluctant to become rebbe but acquiesced under pressure, now he could be convinced to reveal himself. In the spring of 1991, a group of Chabad rabbis issued a halakhic ruling declaring that Schneerson was the presumed Messiah according to Maimonidean criteria. At the end of the year another letter was presented, pledging to accept his sovereignty. Further petitions and declarations followed. On the Sabbath of April 20, 1991, shortly after the "infamous sermon," a Hasid from Israel publicly toasted Schneerson at a farbrengen using the messianist refrain "Long live our master, teacher and rabbi, King Messiah, forever and ever." The next year during Sunday Dollars, a representative of a Chabad women's group presented Schneerson with a tambourine decorated with the same slogan, telling him that "the women danced yesterday with this tambourine, with a joy that breaks through all boundaries, and with faith in the revelation of the Rebbe, King Messiah, immediately and actually to the complete redemption." To which Schneerson, handing her a second dollar, responded, "Presumably this is for the 'clanging cymbals,' as it says in Psalms. May it be at an auspicious time."[32]

That statement would be one of his last. On Monday, March 2, 1992, Schneerson left 770 for Yosef Yitshak's gravesite in Queens, accompanied by his aide and driver, Yehuda Krinsky. "At twenty to six in the afternoon, shortly before the time I expected him to leave the *ohel* (mausoleum), the Rebbe suddenly was not well," Krinsky recalled in a 2009 interview with *Mishpacha* magazine. "I tried to communicate with him, but he was unresponsive. I understood what had happened. I've seen stroke victims before. We were out in the cemetery alone and I knew it was extremely serious. I called the main office at 770 right away and told them to send *hatzalah* (an ambulance)."[33] Schneerson had in fact suffered a major stroke and would never speak again.

Knowing Schneerson's aversion to hospitalization, his aides directed that he be brought back to 770, where medical facilities were once again installed. This time there would be no miracles. For the next two years Schneerson remained paralyzed on the right side of his body and confined to a wheelchair, unable to communicate verbally. His exact condition, including his mental state, were kept secret.

At first the Chabad community tried to carry on as usual. Schneerson's ninetieth birthday, which fell a month later, was celebrated in grand fashion. His assistants, who were now his caregivers, tried to maintain his public presence. A balcony was built over the main synagogue in 770, where he could be wheeled out to overlook the proceedings. His first appearance was on the holiday of Shavuot, a few months after the stroke, though he would not be seen again until Rosh Hashanah, in September.

From then on, for more than year, he was brought out regularly; Hasidim in Crown Heights wore beepers to alert them when he was present. On some occasions groups were allowed to pass by as he sat in his wheelchair outside his room.

Under Schneerson's charismatic leadership Chabad did not have much of a formal bureaucracy or, despite his militaristic tendencies, a chain of command. With their leader incapacitated, his assistants began jockeying for power and position. Arguments broke out over everything from Schneerson's medical care to the ideological direction of the movement. Physical proximity became paramount, and Schneerson's aides claimed to receive his instructions and convey his wishes. Adin Steinsaltz, who visited Brooklyn during this period, recalled being "taken aback by what I saw: considering the circumstances, the intrigue was not only unseemly, but ugly to witness."[34]

The situation was exacerbated when Schneerson's longest-serving aide, Chaim Mordechai Aizik Hodakov, died in April 1993. According to the terms of Schneerson's will, Krinsky was the executor of his estate, and with Hodakov's death he also controlled Chabad's main institutions, which did not strike his colleagues as equitable. Things were further complicated by a second will that had been drafted in the summer of 1988, which laid out an organizational scheme that would have deprived Krinsky of much of his power. Only an unsigned copy of the document was found, however, rendering its contents legally unenforceable. Rumors swirled as to why it had not been signed and whether a signed copy did exist but had been hidden or destroyed.

Schneerson's infirmity left more than a power vacuum. He had alluded to the possibility of his death but had prayed redemption would come first. He had not counted on a prolonged period of incapacitation. What was the meaning of his illness, and how did it fit the eschatological scheme? Many of his followers cited Isaiah 53:4–5, which Schneerson had once applied

to Yosef Yitshak: "But he bore our sickness and endured our suffering . . . he was wounded because of our sins, crushed on account of our iniquities." His affliction, then, was part of the plan.
Whatever residual inhibitions might have held back the
messianic fever were now gone. An organization called the International Campaign to Bring Moshiach escalated the publicity effort, disseminating signs and bumper stickers, publishing
newspaper ads, and plastering billboards. The most fervent Hasidim slept with their clothes ready so they could leave at a moment's notice to greet the Messiah. Whenever Schneerson was
brought out on the balcony, they would sing, "Long live our master, our teacher, and our rebbe, King Messiah forever and ever,"
with Schneerson nodding along. Few seemed to recognize the
tragedy they were witnessing. Here was a man who had been in
complete control of his environment, who had brought a movement to life with his words. Now he was helpless, unable to do
anything but move his head and one arm to the music. A man
who had been celebrated for physical stamina was old and in-
firm, unable to care for himself. How much brain damage he
had suffered, what was going on behind those piercing blue eyes,
was unclear. But video clips from this period are available, and
they are painful to watch.

Despite public assurances that Schneerson was on the mend,
his condition deteriorated. He was hospitalized for gallstone and
cataract surgery, and by the fall of 1993 he was no longer healthy
enough to appear in public. On March 8, 1994, he suffered a
series of seizures and was returned to Beth Israel Medical Center in Manhattan. Two days later he suffered another stroke, then
another a week later. For the next few months, he lay unconscious
in the hospital; since he could no longer be with his Hasidim,
his Hasidim came to him. They packed hallways and waiting
areas, praying for his recovery. Hundreds stayed with him over-
night on the Sabbath.

On Sunday, June 12, 1994, at 12:55 a.m., Schneerson went

into cardiac arrest. He died that night at 1:50 a.m., on the third of Tammuz, 5754. The following afternoon he was buried at the Montefiore Cemetery in Queens, next to Yosef Yitshak, with tens of thousands of mourners in attendance. The Messiah, whom he worked so hard to bring, had not come.

Epilogue

THE OLD SYNAGOGUE in Mykolaiv still stands. Like many
older buildings in the city, it is not well preserved. Exposed stone
walls are crumbling, paint and plaster are peeling. On the eastern side, where the Torah scrolls were kept, the outer wall is
adorned with Soviet-era engravings: a woman hoists a sheaf of
wheat on her shoulder; a scientist haloed by an atomic diagram
looks through a microscope; men and women play some kind
of sport, tossing balls in the air. Graffiti provides a splash of blue
to a rusting iron gate.

Inside, sunshine pours through holes in the partly collapsed
roof. The walls are water damaged; debris is everywhere. Going
up to the balcony, where women once prayed, means taking your
life in your hands. Miraculously, a golden, wheel-shaped chandelier still hangs from the domed ceiling, and the gothic second-
story windows are mostly intact. Some day a wealthy donor might
want to restore the place, but for now it's unusable.

Next door, on the other side of a small courtyard, is the Jewish community center. There is no swimming pool or basketball court, but there is a bright, well-kept synagogue and a modern office space. A large display shows pictures of the city's Jewish community: a couple under a chuppah; a Torah scroll dedication; banquets; picnics; Purim plays; candid shots of kids goofing around. In the main corridor hangs a large portrait of the Lubavitcher rebbe wrapped in tallit and tefillin, holding a small Torah scroll. Naturally, the center is run by Chabad.

I arrived in Mykolaiv on a hot spring day in June, traveling from Odesa on a small, unairconditioned bus. Along the way holiday-goers got off at roadside stops, heading to resorts by the Black Sea. Although most Ukrainian cities are relatively modern and cosmopolitan, going to the countryside feels like stepping back in time. Fields of wheat and barley are dotted with pink and yellow cottages, cows stare lazily over wooden fences, and chickens peck in dirt yards. Though the road was littered with American and Japanese cars, it was easy to imagine what traveling the same route by cart or wagon must have been like.

Since my visit, a lot has changed. On February 26, 2022, two days after Russia launched its full-scale invasion of Ukraine, Russian troops entered the city, taking up positions along the main streets. Ukrainian troops drove them out, but the city continued to come under missile and drone attack. The Regional State Administration Building, the Central City Stadium, a cancer hospital, and three universities were hit by missiles. In April the city lost its water supply from the Dnieper River; afterward, potable water had to be trucked in. Hundreds of thousands of residents evacuated.

But in 2017, when I got off the bus next to Kashtanovy Square, I found a peaceful city of around half a million people awash in late-spring greenery. The small downtown was filled with boutiques, sidewalk cafes, pizza and sushi restaurants, bank branches, and the post office. After checking into the Alexandrovskiy Hotel, I went for a stroll past the Museum of Shipbuilding and the Fleet, a monument to imperial vice admiral Stepan Osipovich Makarov, and the golden-domed Church of St. Nicholas. Along the Ingul River municipal and regional government buildings overlooked grand squares filled with fountains, flower beds, and World War II memorials. The river itself showed signs of heavy industry along with civilian marinas and pleasure craft.

The next day after breakfast, I set out to find what I had come to see: Schneerson's birthplace and the setting of his earliest years. Outside the commercial areas the city was quiet and residential, with a mix of small apartment buildings and single-family bungalows. Behind ramshackle walls, knee-high grasses and red garden roses ran wild in yards. Cracked pavement competed with cobblestones, and a profusion of telephone and power lines ran overhead. Everywhere I looked there was a tangled mixture of old and new: modern concrete buildings beside crumbling ruins of unknown antiquity, graffiti-covered garages next to Soviet edifices with impressive stone facades. From the hotel I walked east along Nikolska Street, past a large sign advertising a zombie-themed escape room, and then south on Moskovska, toward Schneerson's first address.

The house where Schneerson was born is no longer there. In its place stands a low-slung white stucco building with a corrugated red metal roof. Over a brown wooden door hung a large sign advertising notary services in Ukrainian blue and yellow. A blue Lada that might have dated from Soviet days was parked in the gravel driveway.

Although the building showed no sign of Schneerson's residence, a large granite monument in the shape of an open book stood on the boulevard. On the inside pages, inscriptions in English, Russian, and Ukrainian designated the spot as "the place of birth and upbringing" of "the leader of the Jewish people, the Lubavitcher Rabbi, Menachem Mendel Schneerson." The same inscription was engraved in Hebrew on the front cover. The spine read "Zikaron Netsah" (In Eternal Memory), with the logo for Kehot, the Chabad publishing house, at the bottom.

That afternoon I visited the Jewish community center to talk to Rabbi Shalom Gottlieb, the Chabad emissary to Myko-laiv. A middle-aged man with a neat silver beard, he was dressed in the usual Chabad outfit: black suit and shoes, a conservative gray-striped tie, and a neatly pressed white shirt. Gottlieb grew up in Israel and got his first introduction to Ukraine when he spent a summer in Kyiv as a student emissary, not long after Ukrainian independence. After getting married in 1993, he and his wife, Dina, began searching for a permanent posting. Dina preferred to stay in Israel. He would have liked somewhere in the United States or Canada. But after receiving word from 770 that they should go somewhere in the diaspora and finding that spots in North America were hard to come by, they turned their sights on Eastern Europe.

In the mid-1990s plenty of places in the former Soviet Union still had sizable Jewish communities and no Chabad presence. At first, Gottlieb said, they considered Chelyabinsk, a Russian city of more than a million people near the Kazakhstani border, but were dissuaded by the city's remote location. Instead, they came to Mykolaiv, a smaller city but conveniently located be-tween the larger centers of Odesa and Kherson.

When they arrived, the city had around fifteen thousand Jews, Gottlieb estimates. Now that number is fewer, with many having emigrated to Israel, the United States, or Germany. There was no organized community then, although student emissar-ies had laid some of the groundwork. At the beginning, they were still using the Old Shul for prayers. It had been turned into a sports facility during the Soviet era but was returned to the Jew-ish community by the new Ukrainian government. Gottlieb's first two priorities were to open a soup kitchen and to create a program for children, which was held once a week on Sundays. Eventually the Jewish community opened a kindergarten, which grew into an elementary school with 130 students.

The fact that Mykolaiv was Schneerson's birthplace was not a factor in Gottlieb's decision to go there, he said, but it gives him some gratification. His father, who wrote a biography of Schneerson's father, was especially pleased. When Gottlieb first arrived, he met a few older Jews who still remembered Schneerson's family going back to his grandfather, Meyer Shlomo Yanovsky. The local government, with whom Gottlieb said he has an excellent relationship, also takes pride in having Schneerson as a native son—enough pride, at least, to have renamed a street after him.

Gottlieb is less concerned with the city's past, however, than he is with its present. Unlike Chabad emissaries in wealthier countries, he finds himself providing social services as much as doing religious outreach. "The things we're busy with are the practical things of everyday life—the things that people come to us for and the things we can give them, whether material, spiritual, physical," he told me. "This is what we do every day. You're interested in the old Mykolaiv, but I live in Mykolaiv now."

The next day Gottlieb took me to see the school he started, Ohr Menachem. Classes were out for the summer, but they had been replaced by a day camp, and children scampered past as we entered. Gottlieb guided me through classrooms, playrooms, a kitchen, and a cafeteria. A Holocaust exhibit was mounted on the stairway wall. On another wall there was a mural of Schneerson as a child, modeled on the picture taken in a local photo studio when he was just under three years old.

The school, Gottlieb emphasized, served more than educational needs. For many of its students it provided food, clothes, and a safe environment. Despite his warm relationship with the government, he did not take public funding, preferring to retain autonomy instead. (Among other things, this allowed him to reject students with Jewish fathers but not Jewish mothers.) Instead, he receives funds from the Ohr Avner Foundation, which supports Chabad work in the former Soviet Union, although he must fundraise a portion of the budget himself. After he finished showing me around, he gave me instructions for taking the overnight train to Dnipro, where I was heading the next day, and had his driver return me to my hotel.

When Schneerson died in 1994, Chabad was thrown into crisis. He had promised his followers that they were the generation of redemption, and most of them believed he was the Messiah. How could either thing be true if he was dead? For the devout, however, death presented no real difficulty. Schneerson had taught that Yosef Yitshak was the Messiah of his generation even after death and that he would be among the select few brought back before everyone else. If Schneerson could say it of Yosef Yitshak, it could be true of him as well. To others, Schneerson never died at all but was merely concealed until he emerged to take up his messianic role. At his funeral, Hasidim were seen dancing and singing in the belief that his death was not real but only a test, and if they passed the test, he would return.

Three decades after his death the movement remains split by messianic questions, although the contours of the dispute are ambiguous. For a large part of the movement, Schneerson remains the Messiah, and they advertise their belief as loudly as possible. Their signature flag—a blue crown on a yellow background with the word *moshiach* underneath in red Hebrew letters—adorns Chabad homes and institutions around the world. Many Lubavitchers wear it as a pin, like politicians wear an American flag. The *yehi* (long live) slogan adorns everything from bumper stickers to yarmulkes to a large banner in the main synagogue at 770, and it has been incorporated into the liturgy chanted after every prayer. To the most extreme Chabad fringe, Schneerson has become apotheosized and is referred to in prayers as "our creator."[1]

The institutional core of the movement, which includes most of the emissaries, is more restrained. Although these Hasidim would be reluctant to say that Schneerson is not, or could not be, the Messiah, they do not believe that the subject is worthy of speculation. They will also acknowledge that Schneerson did, in fact, die. For these Lubavitchers, bringing the Messiah means encouraging Jewish practice and spreading Hasidic teachings, just as it always did. Insisting on Schneerson's messianic status is irrelevant to those efforts and only serves to alienate outsiders. To many of them it also detracts from the memory of Schneerson as a real person, turning him into a theological icon devoid of humanity.

Occasionally, tensions between the two camps have broken out into the open, as in a long-running series of lawsuits over rights to the synagogue at 770. But institutional leaders have prioritized cohesion over ideological purity, and the movement has avoided an outright schism. In Mykolaiv, I noticed that the monument outside Schneerson's birthplace acknowledged his death and did not refer to him as the Messiah. Gottlieb himself was not sporting any ultra-messianist paraphernalia.

Whatever Chabad's internal disputes, the group has grown enormously in the decades since Schneerson's death—far more, in fact, than when he was alive. There is no official count of the Chabad population but, as with other Orthodox groups, the logic of high birth rates has meant exponential growth. Including all the people Chabad has touched in some way—parents who send their kids to preschools or summer camps, students who have gone to a prayer service or Sabbath dinner, anyone who has attended a menorah lighting or Hanukkah party—would likely add up to a number in the millions. According to an official estimate, there are now 5,000 emissary families operating more than 3,500 institutions in at least 100 countries and territories.[2] By the time these words are published, there will likely be more. Being an emissary in Chabad has become a prestigious position— there are not that many places left for them to go.

At the same time, Schneerson's absence leaves a stark void. As Max Weber theorized, the death of a charismatic leader does not necessarily mean his charisma dies with him. Rather, the founder's personal charisma can be transferred to successors, family members, and the position he occupied. Still, these are not the same thing. And with Schneerson, that process has been frustrated by the lack of a successor. No matter how successful Chabad has been, every portrait hung in a home or an institution is a reminder that he is gone.

Under Schneerson's leadership, Chabad had a future-facing dynamism. That feeling is still prevalent, but it has become tinged by nostalgia. The number of people who knew Schneerson personally diminishes with each passing year. Without a living leader as an arbiter and authority, the movement has stagnated ideologically. Even pictures and recordings bear the mark of time. In an age of high-definition media, VHS recordings are a reminder of Schneerson's pastness. The visual and cultural touchstones of his leadership have taken on a mid-century cast: recognizably modern, but modern in an old-fashioned way. Lubavitchers can turn to Schneerson's writings, talks, and letters for guidance, and may claim to be connected to him despite his physical death. But communing at a gravesite isn't the same as having a rebbe still living in his body.

On my last day in Mykolaiv, while taking a final stroll around town, I thought about what I was doing there. I had come to get a sense of the place where Schneerson was born and spent his childhood. Although the city had evolved in the hundred-plus years since he lived there, much was still unchanged. Many of the old buildings were intact; the street layout was virtually identical; the riotous greenery that festooned the entire city was almost certainly the same. I could now picture the exact route Schneerson would have taken from his home to visit his grandparents or go to synagogue. He knew these streets. After my meeting with Gottlieb, his assistant took me to see the basement of the building opposite, where Schneerson hid with his mother from a pogrom. Aside from the addition of more recent junk, it looked exactly like the dank underground space it would have been then. If I had come to immerse myself in Schneerson's earliest physical surroundings, I had succeeded.

But what would Schneerson have made of all this? His last trip to Europe was shortly after the Second World War, when he went to Paris to reunite with his mother. He never went back to Ukraine or any of the other places he had lived. Would he have felt any nostalgia after seeing how they had changed or stayed the same? Later, while visiting Dnipro—formerly Dnepropetrovsk, and before that, Ekaterinoslav—I saw the apartment block where he played with his cousins, the building where he first went to school, the synagogue where his father had his pulpit. What would he have felt seeing all of that? Sadness? Longing? Anger? Regret? What would it have meant to him?

Human as he was, I am sure he would have felt something— a twinge of memory, sorrow for his father and brothers, some gust from the heady days of his youth. But Schneerson was not a nostalgic person. He rarely spoke about his life, and then only briefly. Instead, he focused on the present and the future, on what must be done before the Messiah arrived. He was concerned less with what was lost than with what needed to be built. What Gottlieb seemed to know, and what took me some time to realize, was that if Schneerson had been here, he would have been relatively uninterested in the ruin of the Old Synagogue or in the plot of land where he was born. But he would have been overjoyed to see the elementary school and its pupils, the rebirth of Jewish life in a place where it had almost died out completely.

That revival is Schneerson's legacy. By his own standard of success—bringing the Messiah—he failed. By any other measure he succeeded enormously. Whatever problems Chabad might have, there is no denying that he took a small and beleaguered Hasidic group and made it into a worldwide force that has touched every corner of the Jewish world. Even the most outspoken critics of Chabad are often moved to acknowledge the positive role its emissaries play in providing social services, education, disaster relief, prison outreach, and more. Whatever Gottlieb's motivations might be and whatever problematic turns his beliefs might take, it is hard to deny that he was doing good work.

For most Hasidim, the fever of the early 1990s has waned considerably. If Chabad messianism was once seen as an extremist hysteria that threatened to repeat the mistakes of past messianic fantasies, the movement in its post-rebbe phase has had to reconcile itself once again with conventional Jewish thinking. Chabad Hasidim still talk about the Messiah more than most, and their work is still guided by messianic aspirations. But redemption has again retreated from an imminent event to a dream perpetually awaiting fulfillment. Schneerson may yet be the Messiah, and he may come tomorrow. But in the meantime, the work goes on.

Prologue

1. Barbara E. Galli, *Franz Rosenzweig and Jehuda Halevi: Translating, Translations, and Translators* (Montreal: McGill-Queen's University Press, 1995), 259, cited in Elliot R. Wolfson, *Open Secret: Postmessianic Messianism and the Mystical Revision of Menahem Mendel Schneerson* (New York: Columbia University Press, 2009), 266.

2. Simon Dubnow, "The Beginnings: The Baal Shem Tov (Besht) and the Center in Podolia," in *Essential Papers on Hasidism: Origins to Present,* ed. Gershon David Hundert (New York: New York University Press, 1991), 26.

Chapter 1. The Prodigy of Ekaterinoslav

1. For a history of Jews in Ukraine, see Paul Robert Magocsi and Yohanan Petrovsky-Shtern, *Jews and Ukrainians: A Millennium of Co-existence* (Toronto: University of Toronto Press, 2016).

2. Chaim Dalfin, *The Seven Chabad-Lubavitch Rebbes* (Northvale, NJ: Aronson, 1998), 10.

3. V. I. Lenin, *Collected Works* (Moscow: Foreign Languages Publishing House, 1962), 8:573.

4. Chana Schneerson, *Reshimat Zikhronot* (New York: Kehot Publication Society, 2012), 33:8.

5. For a history of the Jews of Ekaterinoslav see Zvi Harkavy and Yaakov Goldburt, eds., *Sefer Yekaterinoslav-Dnepropetrovsk* (Jerusalem: Yekaterinoslav-Dnepropetrovsk Society, 1973).

6. Nurit Bertski, "HaRabi—Zikhronot Yalduto," *Maariv*, March 25, 1977.

7. Boruch Oberlander and Elkanah Shmotkin, *Early Years* (New York: Kehot Publication Society, 2016), 114.

8. Oberlander and Shmotkin, *Early Years*, 69.

9. Aharon Friedenthal, "Memoir of a Refugee," *Haynt in bilder*, no. 6 (529), June 14, 1961, 19, cited in Oberlander and Shmotkin, *Early Years*, 93.

Chapter 2. All Is God

1. Ya'akov Yosef of Polnoye, *Ben Porat Yosef* (Korets, 1781), fol. 100a–b.

2. For a comprehensive history of the Hasidic movement see David Biale, David Assaf, Benjamin Brown, Uriel Gellman, Samuel Heilman, Moshe Rosman, Gadi Sagiv, and Marcin Wodziński, eds., *Hasidism: A New History* (Princeton, NJ: Princeton University Press, 2017).

3. For authoritative accounts of the Ba'al Shem Tov's life see Moshe Rosman, *Founder of Hasidism: A Quest for the Historical Ba'al Shem Tov* (Oxford: Littman Library of Jewish Civilization, 2013); and Immanuel Etkes, *The Besht: Magician, Mystic, and Leader*, trans. Saadya Sternberg (Waltham, MA: Brandeis University Press, 2005).

4. Simon Dubnow, "The Beginnings: The Baal Shem Tov (Besht) and the Center in Podolia," in *Essential Papers on Hasidism: Origins to Present*, ed. Gershon David Hundert (New York: New York University Press, 1991), 30.

5. Isaiah 6:3; *Tikkunei Zohar*, tikkun 57, 91b; tikkun 70, 122b.

6. Saint Augustine, *Confessions*, trans. Henry Chadwick (New York: Oxford University Press, 1991), 43.

7. John Scottus Eriugena, *Periphyseon* [III.678c], trans. Inglis Patric Sheldon-Williams and John Joseph O'Meara (Washington, DC: Editions Bellarmin and Dumbarton Oaks, 1987), 305.

8. b. Hagigah 14b.

9. Proverbs 3:6.

10. Martin Buber, "My Way to Hasidism," in *Essential Papers*, ed. Hundert, 500.

11. For thorough explanations of Chabad theology see Rachel Elior, *The Paradoxical Ascent to God: The Kabbalistic Theosophy of Habad Hasidism*, trans. Jeffrey M. Green (Albany: SUNY Press, 1992); and Naftali Loewenthal, *Communicating the Infinite: The Emergence of the Habad School* (Chicago: University of Chicago Press, 1990).

12. Shneur Zalman of Lyady, *Likkutei Amarim Tanya* (New York: Kehot Publication Society, 1956), 219.

13. Shneur Zalman of Lyady, *Torah Or* (New York: Kehot Publication Society, 1991), 1:44, cited in Elior, *The Paradoxical Ascent to God*, 64.

14. Ezekiel 1:14.

15. Ya'akov Yosef of Polnoye, *Toledot Ya'akov Yosef* (Korets: 1780), cited in Dubnow, "The Beginnings," 72.

16. Elimelekh of Lizhensk, *Noam Elimelekh*, cited in Aaron Wertheim, "Traditions and Customs in Hasidism," in *Essential Papers*, ed. Hundert, 373-74.

17. Shneur Zalman of Lyady, *Likkutei Amarim Tanya*, 55.

18. Mordecai L. Wilensky, "Hasidic-Mitnaggedic Polemics in the Jewish Communities of Eastern Europe: The Hostile Phase," in *Essential Papers*, ed. Hundert, 247.

19. Gershom Scholem, *Major Trends in Jewish Mysticism* (Jerusalem: Schocken Publishing House, 1941), 214.

20. Shneur Zalman of Lyady, *Likkutei Torah* (New York: Kehot Publication Society, 2002), Balak 73a, cited in Elior, *The Paradoxical Ascent to God*, 81.

21. *Midrash Tanhuma*, Naso 16.

22. Scholem, *Major Trends*, 76.

23. Aharon ha-Levi of Staroselye, *Avodat Ha-Levi, Derushim le-Rosh Hodesh*, fol. 87a, cited in Elior, *The Paradoxical Ascent to God*, 201.

24. *Midrash Tehillim*, 45:3, cited in Gershom Scholem, *The Messianic Idea in Judaism* (New York: Schocken Books, 1971), 11.

Chapter 3. In the Court of Lubavitch

1. Mordechai Menashe Laufer, *Yemei Melech* (Kfar Chabad: Kehot Publication Society, 1991), 1:149. See also Shaul Shimon Deutsch, *Larger than Life: The Life and Times of the Lubavitcher Rebbe Rabbi Menachem Mendel Schneerson* (New York: Chabad Historical Productions, 1997), 1:97.

2. Ada Rapoport-Albert, *Hasidic Studies: Essays in History and Gender* (Oxford: Littman Library of Jewish Civilization, 2018), 436.

3. The sermon is published in Yosef Yitshak Schneersohn, *Likkutei Dibburim* (New York: Kehot Publication Society, 1984), 4:1578.

4. For a comprehensive account of Chabad activities in the early Soviet Union see David E. Fishman, "Preserving Tradition in the Land of Revolution: The Religious Leadership of Soviet Jewry, 1917–1930," in *The Uses of Tradition: Jewish Continuity in the Modern Era*, ed. Jack Wertheimer (New York: Jewish Theological Seminary of America, 1992), 85–118.

5. Yosef Yitshak Schneersohn, *Igrot Kodesh* (New York: Kehot Publication Society, 1982–2014), 1:486.

6. Ibid., 15:31.

7. Yeshayahu Sher, *Kfar Chabad*, no. 939 (15 Shevat, 5761), 76, cited in Boruch Oberlander and Elkanah Shmotkin, *Early Years* (New York: Kehot Publication Society, 2016), 175–76.

8. *Kfar Chabad*, no. 491, 48, cited in Oberlander and Shmotkin, *Early Years*, 193.

9. Yosef Yitshak Schneersohn, *Sefer Ha-Sihot 5680–5687* (New York: Kehot Publication Society, 1992), 160.

10. Yosef Yitshak Schneersohn, *Likkutei Dibburim* (New York: Kehot Publication Society, 2014), 6:161–67.

11. Alter B. Metzger, *The Heroic Struggle: The Arrest and Lib-

eration of Rabbi Yosef Y. Schneersohn of Lubavitch in Soviet Russia (New York: Kehot Publication Society, 1999), 53.

12. See Menachem Mendel Schneerson, *Likkutei Sihot* (New York: Kehot Publication Society, 1966–2001), 21:435; and Schneerson, *Torat Menachem Hitva'aduyot* (New York: Lahak Hanochos, 1992–2023), 2:96, among other places.

13. Chana Schneerson, *Reshimat Zikhronot* (New York: Kehot Publication Society, 2012), 34:5.

14. *Di yidishe heym*, no. 22 (Kislev 5725), cited in Oberlander and Shmotkin, *Early Years*, 212.

15. Oberlander and Shmotkin, *Early Years*, 215.

Chapter 4. University Days

1. David E. Fishman, "Preserving Tradition in the Land of Revolution: The Religious Leadership of Soviet Jewry, 1917–1930," in *The Uses of Tradition: Jewish Continuity in the Modern Era*, ed. Jack Wertheimer (New York: Jewish Theological Seminary of America, 1992), 99.

2. Boruch Oberlander and Elkanah Shmotkin, *Early Years* (New York: Kehot Publication Society, 2016), 274.

3. Ibid., 288.

4. Ibid., 291.

5. Menachem Mendel Schneerson, *Torat Menachem Reshimat HaYoman* (New York: Kehot Publication Society, 2006), 443.

6. Oberlander and Shmotkin, *Early Years*, 296.

7. Ibid., 304.

8. Levi Yitshak Schneerson, *Likkutei Levi Yitshak—Igrot Kodesh* (New York: Kehot Publication Society, 1985), 387.

9. Oberlander and Shmotkin, *Early Years*, 385.

10. "Di impozante lubavitsher khupe-simkhe in der lubavitsher yeshive," *Der moment*, November 29, 1928, 5.

11. Oberlander and Shmotkin, *Early Years*, 403.

12. Ibid., 383.

13. Shaul Shimon Deutsch, *Larger than Life: The Life and Times of the Lubavitcher Rebbe Rabbi Menachem Mendel Schneerson* (New York: Chabad Historical Productions, 1997), 2:74.

14. Yosef Yitshak Schneersohn, *Igrot Kodesh* (New York: Kehot Publication Society, 1982–2014), 15:78.

15. Ibid., 171–72.

16. Ibid., 5:368, 401.

17. Shneur Zalman of Lyady, *Likkutei Amarim Tanya* (New York: Kehot Publication Society, 1956), 26.

18. Menachem Mendel Schneerson, *Reshimot* (New York: Kehot Publication Society, 2005–11), 3:72–73.

19. Ibid., 12:339–40.

20. Menachem Mendel Schneerson, *Torat Menachem Hitva'aduyot* (New York: Lahak Hanochos, 1992–2023), 5:173–74.

21. Deutsch, *Larger than Life*, 2:134.

22. Levi Yitshak Schneerson, *Likkutei Levi Yitshak—Igrot Kodesh*, 443–44.

23. Chaim Rapoport, *The Afterlife of Scholarship* (Charleston, SC: Oporto Press, 2011), 59.

24. Chaim Miller, *Turning Judaism Outward: A Biography of the Rebbe Menachem Mendel Schneerson* (New York: Kol Menachem, 2014), 106.

25. Samuel Heilman and Menachem Friedman, *The Rebbe: The Life and Afterlife of Menachem Mendel Schneerson* (Princeton, NJ: Princeton University Press, 2010), 120.

26. Yosef Yitshak Scheersohn, *Igrot Kodesh*, 15:212.

27. Miller, *Turning Judaism Outward*, 115.

28. Shalom Ber Levin, ed., *Kovets Chaf Menachem Av Shishim Shana* (New York: Kehot Publication Society, 2004), 56.

29. Ibid., 64.

30. Heilman and Friedman, *The Rebbe*, 125.

31. Levin, *Kovets Chaf Menachem Av*, 54.

Chapter 5. A Home in America

1. Rachel Altein and Eliezer Zaklikofsky, *Out of the Inferno: The Efforts That Led to the Rescue of Rabbi Yosef Yitzchak Schneersohn of Lubavitch from War-Torn Europe in 1939–40* (New York: Kehot Publication Society, 2002), 303.

2. For a comprehensive account of the rescue effort see Bryan

Rigg, *The Rabbi Saved by Hitler's Soldiers: Rebbe Joseph Isaac Schneersohn and His Astonishing Rescue* (Lawrence: University Press of Kansas, 2016).

3. Chaim Miller, *Turning Judaism Outward: A Biography of the Rebbe Menachem Mendel Schneerson* (New York: Kol Menachem, 2014), 461.

4. Rigg, *The Rabbi Saved by Hitler's Soldiers*, 168–69.

5. Shaul Magid, "When Will the Wedding Take Place?" in *One God, Many Worlds: Teachings of a Renewed Hasidism*, ed. Netanel Miles-Yepez (Boulder, CO: Albion-Andalus Books), 95–97.

6. See Menachem Mendel Schneerson, *Igrot Kodesh* (New York: Kehot Publication Society, 1987–2009), 22:410; and Schneerson, *Likkutei Sihot* (New York: Kehot Publication Society, 1966–2001), 6:364, among other places.

7. John Milton, *Paradise Lost*, line 26.

8. For the full text of these proclamations see Steven T. Katz, Shlomo Biderman, and Gershon Greenberg, eds., *Wrestling with God: Jewish Theological Responses During and After the Holocaust* (New York: Oxford University Press, 2007), 171–90.

9. Yosef Yitshak Schneersohn, "Tsveyter kol koyre fun'm lubavitsher rebn," *Hakeri'ah VeHaKedusha* 1, no. 10 (July 1941): 10.

10. Ibid., 10–11.

11. Menachem Mendel Schneerson, *Sefer HaSihot 5751* (New York: Kehot Publication Society 1992), 1:233.

12. Menachem Mendel Schneerson, "Why Did G-d Allow the Holocaust?" [January 28, 1984], Chabad.org, https://www.chabad.org/therebbe/letters/default_cdo/aid/2188391/jewish/Why-Did-G-d-Allow-the-Holocaust.htm.

13. Schneerson, *Igrot Kodesh*, 23:373.

Chapter 6. Becoming the Rebbe

1. Jerome R. Mintz, *Hasidic People: A Place in the New World* (Cambridge, MA: Harvard University Press, 1992), 283.

2. A facsimile of the letter is in Chaim Rapoport, *The Afterlife of Scholarship* (Charleston, SC: Oporto Press, 2011), 210.

3. For a scholarly account of the succession process, see

Avrum M. Ehrlich, *Leadership in the HaBaD Movement: A Critical Evaluation of HaBaD Leadership, History, and Succession* (Lanham, MD: Jason Aronson, 2000).

4. Yoel Kahn, letter of 17 Tammuz, 5750 (July 2, 1950), https://www.mafteiach.app/yomanim/by_year/5710.

5. Yoel Kahn, letter of 3 Adar, 5710 (February 20, 1950), ibid.

6. Yoel Kahn, letter of 4 Nisan, 5710 (March 22, 1950), ibid.

7. Ehrlich, *Leadership in the HaBaD Movement*, 366.

8. Interview with Yehuda Krinsky, November 14, 2017.

9. Chaim Miller, *Turning Judaism Outward: A Biography of the Rebbe Menachem Mendel Schneerson* (New York: Kol Menachem, 2014), 179.

10. *Zohar*, 3:71b. See Shneur Zalman of Lyady, *Likkutei Amarim Tanya* (New York: Kehot Publication Society, 1956), 146.

11. Yosef Yitzchak Kaminetzky, *Dates in the History of ChaBaD: Persons and Events in the History of ChaBaD* (Kfar Chabad: Kehot Publication Society, 1994), 153, cited in Samuel Heilman and Menachem Friedman, *The Rebbe: The Life and Afterlife of Menachem Mendel Schneerson* (Princeton, NJ: Princeton University Press, 2010), 59.

12. *Hamodia*, 19 Elul, 5710 (September 1, 1950), a facsimile in Yosef Yitzchak Greenberg and Eliezer Zaklikofsky, *Yemei Breishit: Historical Biography, 1950–1951* (New York: Kehot Publication Society, 1993), 238.

13. Yosef Yitshak Schneersohn, *Igrot Kodesh* (New York: Kehot Publication Society, 1982–2014), 3:155.

14. Greenberg and Zaklikofsky, *Yemei Breishit*, 84.

15. Plato, *The Republic*, trans. Desmond Lee (New York: Penguin Books, 2007), 29.

16. Yoel Kahn, letter of 4 Av, 5710 (June 18, 1950), https://www.mafteiach.app/yomanim/by_year/5710.

17. Greenberg and Zaklikofsky, *Yemei Breishit*, 344–46.

18. Ibid., 376.

19. Menachem Mendel Schneerson, *Torat Menachem Hitva'aduyot 5711* (New York: Lahak Hanochos, 1995), 1:208–11.

20. Greenberg and Zaklikofsky, *Yemei Breishit*, 381.

21. Song of Songs 5:1.

22. Yosef Yitshak Schneersohn, *Sefer HaMa'amarim 5710* (New York: Kehot Publication Society, 1986), 111.

23. Menachem Mendel Schneerson, *Torat Menachem Sefer HaMa'amarim Melukat* (New York: Vaad Hanachos Lahak, 2002), 2:263–64.

24. Ibid., 265.

25. Ibid.

26. Ibid., 271.

27. Schneerson, *Torat Menachem Hitva'aduyot 5711*, 1:212–16.

28. Daniel 7:13; Zechariah 9:9.

29. b. Sanhedrin 98a.

30. b. Sanhedrin 99a; Berakhot 34b.

31. b. Sanhedrin 98b–99a.

32. Maimonides, *Mishneh Torah Hilkhot Melakhim*, 11:3.

33. Ibid., 11:4.

34. Ibid., 11:5.

35. Ibid., 12:5.

36. See Gershom Scholem, *Major Trends in Jewish Mysticism* (Jerusalem: Schocken Publishing House, 1941), 180.

37. *Midrash Tehillim* 146:7, cited in Gershom Scholem, *The Messianic Idea in Judaism* (New York: Schocken Books, 1971), 55.

38. Scholem, *Major Trends*, 292.

39. Gershom Scholem, "Shabbetai Zevi," in *Encyclopedia Judaica*, 2nd ed., ed. Fred Skolnik and Michael Berenbaum (Detroit, MI: Macmillan Reference USA, 2007), 18:348.

40. Aviezer Ravitzky, *Messianism, Zionism, and Jewish Religious Radicalism*, trans. Michael Swirsky and Jonathan Chipman (Chicago: University of Chicago Press, 1996), 199.

41. Ibid.

42. Ibid.

43. Shalom Dov Ber Schneersohn, *Torat Shalom: Sefer HaSihot* (New York: Kehot Publication Society, 1957), 74.

44. Schneerson, *Igrot Kodesh*, 12:414.

45. Leon Festinger, Henry Riecken, and Stanley Schachter, *When Prophecy Fails* (Minneapolis: University of Minnesota Press, 1956), 28.

46. Shneur Zalman of Lyady, *Likkutei Amarim Tanya*, 92.

47. Israel Shenker, "Lubavitch Rabbi Marks His 70th Year with Call for 'Kindness,'" *New York Times*, March 27, 1972.

Chapter 7. New Beginnings

1. Menachem Mendel Schneerson, *Hayom Yom* (New York: Kehot Publication Society, 1957), 11.

2. Chaim Miller, *Turning Judaism Outward: A Biography of the Rebbe Menachem Mendel Schneerson* (New York: Kol Menachem, 2014), 92.

3. Harvey Swados, "He Could Melt a Blizzard," *New York Times*, June 14, 1994.

4. Joseph Telushkin, *Rebbe: The Life and Teachings of Menachem M. Schneerson, the Most Influential Rabbi in Modern History* (New York: Harper Wave, 2014), 578.

5. Sue Fishkoff, *The Rebbe's Army: Inside the World of Chabad-Lubavitch* (New York: Schocken Books, 2003), 74.

6. Elie Wiesel, "Greatness," April 7, 1992, Chabad.org, http://www.chabad.org/therebbe/article_cdo/aid/143509/jewish/Greatness.htm.

7. Adin Steinsaltz, *My Rebbe* (Jerusalem: Maggid Books, 2014), 119.

8. Ibid., xi.

9. Quoted in Fishkoff, *The Rebbe's Army*, 69.

10. Ibid., 70.

11. Zalmon Jaffe, *My Encounter with the Rebbe* (New York: PCL, 2002), 1:23, cited in Miller, *Turning Judaism Outward*, 217.

12. Edward Hoffman, *Despite All Odds: The Story of Lubavitch* (New York: Simon and Schuster, 1991), 118.

13. Swados, "He Could Melt a Blizzard."

14. Herbert Weiner, *Nine-and-a-Half Mystics* (New York: Holt, Reinhart and Winston, 1969), 159.

15. See, for example, Menachem Mendel Schneerson, *Torat*

Menachem Hitva'aduyot 5745 (New York: Lahak Hanochos, 1986), 3:1483.

16. Israel Shenker, "Lubavitch Rabbi Marks His 70th Year with Call for 'Kindness,'" *New York Times*, March 27, 1972.

17. Isaac Bashevis Singer, "Simkhes toyre in brooklyn yiddishen tsenter un bay di lubavitsher khsidim," *Forverts*, October 29, 1960.

18. See Menachem Mendel Schneerson, *Likkutei Sihot* (New York: Kehot Publication Society, 1966–2001), 3:218, among many other places.

19. Jonathan Sacks, *Torah Studies: Discourses by the Lubavitcher Rebbe, Rabbi Menachem M. Schneerson* (Brooklyn, NY: Kehot Publication Society, 2001), vii–ix.

20. Weiner, *Nine-and-a-Half Mystics*, 153.

21. Steinsaltz, *My Rebbe*, 164.

22. Baila Olidort, "An Interview with the Rebbe's Doctor—Dr. Ira Weiss," Lubavitch.com, March 10, 2013, https://www.lubavitch.com/an-interview-with-the-rebbes-doctor-dr-ira-weiss/.

Chapter 8. Breaking Out

1. Salomon Maimon, "On a Secret Society, and Therefore a Long Chapter," in *Essential Papers on Hasidism: Origins to Present*, ed. Gershon David Hundert (New York: New York University Press, 1991), 15.

2. Max Weber, *The Theory of Social and Economic Organization*, ed. Talcot Parsons, trans. Alexander Morell Henderson and Talcott Parsons (Ann Arbor, MI: University of Michigan Press, 1947), 21.

3. Sue Fishkoff, *The Rebbe's Army: Inside the World of Chabad-Lubavitch* (New York: Schocken Books, 2003), 79.

4. Adin Steinsaltz, *My Rebbe* (Jerusalem: Maggid Books, 2014), 119.

5. See Elliot R. Wolfson, *Open Secret: Postmessianic Messianism and the Mystical Revision of Menahem Mendel Schneerson* (New York: Columbia University Press, 2009), 305n19.

6. Menachem Mendel Schneerson, *Torat Menachem Hitva'aduyot 5719* (New York: Vaad Hanochos B'Lahak, 2002), 1:189.

NOTES TO PAGES 137–152

7. See Menachem Mendel Schneerson, *Likkutei Sihot* (New York: Kehot Publication Society, 1966–2001), 4:1068–69.

8. See Wolfson, *Open Secret*, 186, 368n112.

9. b. Sanhedrin 97b.

10. Schneerson, *Torat Menachem Hitva'aduyot 5742*, 1:48.

11. Menachem Mendel Schneerson, *Torat Menachem Sefer Ma'amarim Melukat* (New York: Vaad Hanachos B'Lahak, 2002), 3:40.

12. Schneerson, *Torat Menachem Hitva'aduyot 5742*, 1:56.

13. Genesis 28:14.

14. Schneerson, *Torat Menachem Hitva'aduyot 5718* (New York: Vaad Hanachos B'Lahak, 2002), 3:133.

15. Ascher Penn, *Yidishkeyt in amerike* (New York, 1958), 1:69.

16. Herbert Weiner, *Nine-and-a-Half Mystics* (New York: Holt, Reinhart and Winston, 1969), 177.

17. Schneerson, *Likkutei Sihot*, 23:220.

18. Shneur Zalman of Lyady, *Likkutei Amarim Tanya* (New York: Kehot Publication Society, 1956), 81.

19. Ibid., 82.

20. Schneerson, *Likkutei Sihot*, 16:320.

21. Schneerson, *Likkutei Sihot*, 23:252.

22. Fishkoff, *The Rebbe's Army*, 112.

23. Chaim Miller, *Turning Judaism Outward: A Biography of the Rebbe Menachem Mendel Schneerson* (New York: Kol Menachem, 2014), 233.

24. Jerome R. Mintz, *Hasidic People: A Place in the New World* (Cambridge, MA: Harvard University Press, 1992), 288.

25. Simon Jacobson, ed., *Portrait of a Chassid: The Life and Legacy of Rabbi Zvi Hirsch Gansbourg* (New York: GJCF, 2008), 105, cited in Miller, *Turning Judaism Outward*, 201.

26. Yosef Yitshak Schneersohn, *Igrot Kodesh* (New York: Kehot Publication Society, 1982–2014), 17:52.

Chapter 9. Expanding Influence

1. Israel Shenker, "Lubavitch Rabbi Marks His 70th Year with Call for 'Kindness,'" *New York Times*, March 27, 1972.

2. Menachem Mendel Schneerson, "The Age of the Universe," Chabad.org, [December 25, 1961], https://www.chabad.org/library/article_cdo/aid/435111/jewish/The-Age-of-the-Universe.htm.

3. Ibid.

4. Menachem Mendel Schneerson, "Theories of Evolution," Chabad.org, [December 25, 1961], https://www.chabad.org/library/article_cdo/aid/112083/jewish/Theories-of-Evolution.htm.

5. Nissan Mindel, ed., *The Letter and the Spirit* (New York: Nissan Mindel, 1998–2014), 2:291–92.

6. Joseph Ginsburg and Herman Branover, eds., *Mind over Matter: Teachings of the Lubavitcher Rebbe on Science, Technology and Medicine*, trans. Arnie Gotfryd (Jerusalem: Shamir, 2003).

7. Schneerson, "The Age of the Universe."

8. Isaiah 11:9.

9. For a thorough treatment of Schneerson's social and political views, see Philip Wexler, *Social Vision: The Lubavitcher Rebbe's Transformative Paradigm for the World* (New York: Herder and Herder, 2019).

10. Menachem Mendel Schneerson, *Torat Menachem Hitva'aduyot* (New York: Lahak Hanochos, 1992–2023), 1:195–96.

11. Schneerson, *Sihot Kodesh 5741* (New York, 1986), 3:106.

12. Schneerson, *Sihot Kodesh 5735* (New York, 1986), 1:328–30.

13. Menachem Mendel Schneerson, "Morality and the Holocaust," Chabad.org, [January 30, 1964], https://www.chabad.org/therebbe/letters/default_cdo/aid/1899565/jewish/Morality-and-the-Holocaust.htm.

14. Ascher Penn, *Yidishkeyt in amerike* (New York, 1958), 1:65–66.

15. Schneerson, *Sihot Kodesh 5735*, 1:328–30.

16. Jonathan Edwards, "Some Thoughts Concerning the Present Revival of Religion in America (1742)," in C. C. Goen, ed., *The Works of Jonathan Edwards* (New Haven: Yale University Press, 1972), 4:353, cited in Shaul Magid, "America Is No Different," in *Fundamentalism: Perspectives on a Contested History*, ed. Simon A. Wood and David Harrington Watt (Charleston: University of South Carolina Press, 2014), 79.

17. Edward Hoffman, *Despite All Odds: The Story of Lubavitch* (New York: Simon and Schuster, 1991), 138.

18. Schneerson, *Sihot Kodesh 5735*, 1:330.

19. John Wicklein, "Warning to Jews Issued by Jesuits," *New York Times*, August 27, 1962.

20. Menachem Mendel Schneerson, "Prayer in Public Schools and Separation of Church and State," [April 8, 1964], Chabad.org, https://www.chabad.org/therebbe/letters/default_cdo/aid/2051611 /jewish/Prayer-in-Public-Schools-and-Separation-of-Church -and-State.htm. Accessed May 8, 2023.

21. Menachem Mendel Schneerson, "12th Day of Tammuz, 5744 (1984)," Chabad.org, https://www.chabad.org/therebbe/ar ticle_cdo/aid/2514929/jewish/12th-Day-of-Tammuz-5744–1984 .htm. Accessed May 8, 2023.

22. See Shneur Zalman of Lyady, *Likkutei Amarim Tanya* (New York: Kehot Publication Society, 1956), 11.

23. Maimonides, *Mishneh Torah Hilkhot Melakhim*, 8:10–10:12.

24. Menachem Mendel Schneerson, *Reshimot* (New York: Kehot Publication Society, 2005–11), 159:12–14.

25. "Proclamation 4921—National Day of Reflection," [April 3, 1982], The American Presidency Project, https://www.presidency .ucsb.edu/documents/proclamation-4921-national-day-reflection. Accessed May 8, 2023.

26. "Proclamation 5956—Education Day, U.S.A., 1989 and 1990," [April 14, 1989], The American Presidency Project, https:// www.presidency.ucsb.edu/documents/proclamation-5956-education -day-usa-1989-and-1990. Accessed May 8, 2023.

27. "H.J. Res. 104—To designate March 26, 1991, as 'Educa- tion Day, U.S.A.,'" January 31, 1991, Congress.gov, https://www .congress.gov/bill/102nd-congress/house-joint-resolution/104 /text/enr. Accessed May 8, 2023.

28. Jonathan Sarna and David Dalin, eds., *Religion and State in the American Jewish Experience* (Notre Dame, IN: University of Notre Dame Press, 1997), 291–92.

29. Ibid., 293–94.

30. "Court Opinions on Religious Displays," *New York Times,* July 4, 1989.

31. See Nathaniel Popper, "Menorahs Light Path for Nativity Displays," *Haaretz,* December 26, 2005.

32. See Sue Fishkoff, *The Rebbe's Army: Inside the World of Chabad-Lubavitch* (New York: Schocken Books, 2003), 293.

33. See Joe Berkofsky, "Supreme Court Allows Menorah," *Jewish Telegraphic Agency,* December 3, 2002.

34. See Herbert Weiner, *Nine-and-a-Half Mystics* (New York: Holt, Reinhart and Winston, 1969), 176.

35. See Shaul Magid, "America Is No Different," in *Fundamentalism: Perspectives on a Contested History,* ed. Simon A. Wood and David Harrington Watt (Charleston: University of South Carolina Press, 2014).

36. Hoffman, *Despite All Odds,* 89–90.

37. The letter is in Yosef Yitzhak Schneersohn, *Sefer Ha-Ma'amarim 5710* (New York: Kehot Publication Society, 1986), 128.

38. Menachem Mendel Schneerson, *Torat Menachem Hitva'aduyot 5713* (New York: Lahak Hanochos, 1997), 1:116.

39. b. Sotah 11b. See Schneerson, *Torat Menachem Hitva'aduyot 5718,* 3:172, and *Torat Menachem Hitva'aduyot 5752* (New York: Lahak Hanochos, 1994), 2:183–84 and 260–66, among many other places.

40. Menachem Mendel Schneerson, *Torat Menachem Hitva'aduyot 5745* (New York: Lahak Hanochos, 1990), 1:129.

41. Naftali Loewenthal, "Women, and the Dialectic of Spirituality in Hasidism," in *Within Hasidic Circles: Studies in Hasidism in Memory of Mordecai Wilensky,* ed. Immanuel Etkes, David Assaf, Israel Bartal, and Elchanan Reiner (Jerusalem: The Bialik Institute, 1999), 53.

42. Ada Rapoport-Albert, *Hasidic Studies: Essays in History and Gender* (Oxford: Littman Library of Jewish Civilization, 2018), 456.

43. J. J. Goldberg, "Chilean Dictator Signs . . . ," *Jewish Week,* January 15, 1988, cited in Jerome R. Mintz, *Hasidic People: A Place*

in the New World (Cambridge, MA: Harvard University Press, 1992), 397.

Chapter 10. A Heart in the East

1. Deuteronomy 11:11–12.

2. Geula Cohen, "BeArba Einayim im HaRabi MiLubavitch," *Maariv*, December 18, 1964, cited in Adin Steinsaltz, *My Rebbe* (Jerusalem: Maggid Books, 2014), 147.

3. *Yalkut Shimoni*, 2:remez 503.

4. Yosef Yitshak Schneersohn, *Igrot Kodesh* (New York: Kehot Publication Society, 1982–2014), 1:485.

5. Cant. R. 2:7; b. Ketubot 111a.

6. Shalom Dov Ber Schneersohn, letter published in Shlomo Zalman Landau and Yosef Rabinowitz, eds., *Or la-Yesharim* (Warsaw, 1900), 57.

7. Abraham Isaac Kook, *Orot ha-kodesh* (Jerusalem: Mosad Harav Kook, 1964), 3:194, cited in Aviezer Ravitzky, *Messianism, Zionism, and Jewish Religious Radicalism*, trans. Michael Swirsky and Jonathan Chipman (Chicago: University of Chicago Press, 1996), 5.

8. Ravitzky, *Messianism*, 102.

9. Ibid., 69.

10. Yosef Yitshak Schneersohn, *Likkutei Dibburim* (New York: Kehot Publication Society, 1984), 4:1384.

11. Steven T. Katz, Shlomo Biderman, and Gershon Greenberg, eds., *Wrestling with God: Jewish Theological Responses During and After the Holocaust* (New York: Oxford University Press, 2007), 187.

12. Quoted in Shalom Dov Wolpo, ed., *Da'at Torah b-inyanei ha-matzav be-eretz ha-kodesh* (Kiryat Gat, 1982), 30, cited in Ravitzky, *Messianism*, 147.

13. Ascher Penn, *Yidishkeyt in amerike* (New York, 1958), 65.

14. Wolpo, *Da'at Torah*, 23–34, cited in Ravitzky, *Messianism*, 158–59.

15. Ibid.

16. Schneerson, *Igrot Kodesh*, 24:332.

17. Ibid., 333.

18. Menachem Mendel Schneerson, *Sihot Kodesh 5727* (New York, 1985), 2:111–13.

19. Shalom Dov Wolpo, *Shemen Sason*, 3:220, cited in Chaim Miller, *Turning Judaism Outward: A Biography of the Rebbe Menachem Mendel Schneerson* (New York: Kol Menachem, 2014), 269.

20. Miller, *Turning Judaism Outward*, 269.

21. Schneerson, *Sihot Kodesh 5727*, 2:298.

22. Nissan Mindel, ed., *The Letter and the Spirit* (New York: Nissan Mindel, 1998–2014), 282.

23. Menachem Mendel Schneerson, *Sihot Kodesh 5736* (New York, 1986), 2:625–26.

24. Yoel Teitelbaum, *Divrei Yoel* (New York: Jerusalem Publishers, 1980), 7:415, cited in Miller, *Turning Judaism Outward*, 415.

25. Herbert Weiner, *Nine-and-a-Half Mystics* (New York: Holt, Reinhart and Winston, 1969), 159.

26. Schneerson, *Igrot Kodesh*, 18:209–10.

27. Miller, *Turning Judaism Outward*, 275.

28. Miller, *Turning Judaism Outward*, 495. See also Schneerson, *Igrot Kodesh*, 11:28.

29. "Rebbe's Influence Blamed for Labor's Failure to Form Governing Coalition," *Jewish Telegraphic Agency*, April 13, 1990.

30. Avrum M. Ehrlich, *The Messiah of Brooklyn: Understanding Lubavitch Hasidism Past and Present* (Jersey City, NJ: Ktav Publishing House, 2004), 110.

Chapter 11. Larger than Life

1. Chana Schneerson, *Reshimat Zikhronot* (New York: Kehot Publication Society, 2012), 34:4.

2. For a history of Chabad broadcasting see Mordechai Lightstone, "How 1970s Chassidic Hackers Created a Worldwide Broadcast Network," Chabad.org, September 6, 2016, https://www.chabad.org/news/article_cdo/aid/3422879/jewish/How-1970s-Chassidic-Hackers-Created-a-Worldwide-Broadcast-Network.htm.

3. For a history and analysis of Chabad iconography see Maya Balakirsky Katz, *The Visual Culture of Chabad* (New York: Cambridge University Press, 2010).

4. See Jeffrey Shandler, *Jews, God, and Videotape: Religion and Media in America* (New York: New York University Press, 2009), 249–50.

5. Peah, 1:1.

6. Shneur Zalman of Lyady, *Likkutei Amarim Tanya* (New York: Kehot Publication Society, 1956), 114.

7. Chaim Miller, *Turning Judaism Outward: A Biography of the Rebbe Menachem Mendel Schneerson* (New York: Kol Menachem, 2014), 365.

8. Moshe Bogomilsky, *Hei Teves Didan Notzach: The Victory of the Seforim* (New York, 2012), 7.

9. David Margolick, "Suit on Books Gives Look at Hasidim," *New York Times*, December 18, 1985.

10. Jerome R. Mintz, *Hasidic People: A Place in the New World* (Cambridge, MA: Harvard University Press, 1992), 290.

11. Ibid., 290–91.

12. Ibid.

13. Ibid., 295.

14. Edward Hoffman, *Despite All Odds: The Story of Lubavitch* (New York: Simon and Schuster, 1991), 189.

15. Ibid., 190.

16. Shalom Dov Wolpo, "Two Stories and a Conclusion," *Kfar Chabad*, 4 Cheshvan 5750, cited in Samuel Heilman and Menachem Friedman, *The Rebbe: The Life and Afterlife of Menachem Mendel Schneerson* (Princeton, NJ: Princeton University Press, 2010), 63.

17. Joseph Telushkin, *Rebbe: The Life and Teachings of Menachem M. Schneerson, the Most Influential Rabbi in Modern History* (New York: Harper Wave, 2014), 197–98.

18. Herbert Weiner, *Nine-and-a-Half Mystics* (New York: Holt, Reinhart and Winston, 1969), 144.

19. Miller, *Turning Judaism Outward*, 162.

20. Zev Segal, "When the Rebbe Saved Ariel Sharon from a Hijacking." Chabad.org, https://www.chabad.org/therebbe/article_cdo/aid/3197335/jewish/When-the-Rebbe-Saved-Ariel-Sharon-from-a-Hijacking.htm. Accessed May 8, 2023.

21. Yosef Yitshak Schneersohn, *Igrot Kodesh* (New York: Kehot Publication Society, 1982–2014), 29:19.

22. Yehudah Avner, *The Prime Ministers: An Intimate Narrative of Israeli Leadership* (New Milford, CT: Toby Press, 2010), 445, cited in Miller, *Turning Judaism Outward*, 254.

23. Weiner, *Nine-and-a-Half Mystics*, 175.

24. Schneerson, *Igrot Kodesh*, 12:226.

25. Mordechai Menashe Laufer, *Yemei Melech* (Kfar Chabad: Kehot Publication Society, 1991), 3, cited in Avrum M. Ehrlich, *Leadership in the HaBaD Movement: A Critical Evaluation of HaBaD Leadership, History, and Succession* (Lanham, MD: Jason Aronson, 2000), 98.

26. Menachem Mendel Schneerson, *Likkutei Sihot* (New York: Kehot Publication Society, 1966–2001), 2:510–11.

27. Mintz, *Hasidic People*, 355.

28. Jon Kalish, "Interview with Rabbi Yehuda Krinsky: Is There a Messiah in Crown Heights?" *New York Newsday*, June 1, 1988.

29. Telushkin, *Rebbe*, 423–24.

30. Ibid., 426.

31. Israel Shenker, "Lubavitch Rabbi Marks His 70th Year with Call for 'Kindness,'" *New York Times*, March 27, 1972.

Chapter 12. End of Days

1. Chaim Miller, *Turning Judaism Outward: A Biography of the Rebbe Menachem Mendel Schneerson* (New York: Kol Menachem, 2014), 382.

2. Israel Shenker, "Lubavitch Rabbi Marks His 70th Year with Call for 'Kindness,'" *New York Times*, March 27, 1972.

3. Mordechai Menashe Laufer, *Yemei Melech* (Kfar Chabad: Kehot Publication Society, 1991), 1268.

4. Baila Olidort, "An Interview with the Rebbe's Doctor—Dr. Ira Weiss," Lubavitch.com, March 10, 2013, https://www.lubavitch .com/an-interview-with-the-rebbes-doctor-dr-ira-weiss/.

5. Menachem Mendel Schneerson, *Sihot Kodesh 5729* (New York, 1985), 2:65–66.

6. Menachem Mendel Schneerson, *Kuntres B'Inyan Mikdash Me'at Zeh Beit Rabeinu SheB'Bovel* (New York: Kehot Publication Society, 1992), 11.

7. Ibid, 10.

8. b. Megillah 29a.

9. Edward S. Shapiro, *Crown Heights: Blacks, Jews, and the 1991 Brooklyn Riot* (Waltham, MA: Brandeis University Press, 2006), xi.

10. David Gonzalez, "As Racial Storm Rages, Hasidic Leader Is Aloof," *New York Times*, August 26, 1991.

11. "The Rebbe's Words to Mayor David Dinkins," Chabad.org, [1991], https://www.chabad.org/therebbe/article_cdo/aid/1599198/jewish/The-Rebbes-Words-to-Mayor-David-Dinkins.htm. Accessed May 8, 2023.

12. Gonzalez, "As Racial Storm Rages, Hasidic Leader Is Aloof."

13. Aviezer Ravitzky, *Messianism, Zionism, and Jewish Religious Radicalism*, trans. Michael Swirsky and Jonathan Chipman (Chicago: University of Chicago Press, 1996), 185.

14. Sue Fishkoff, *The Rebbe's Army: Inside the World of Chabad-Lubavitch* (New York: Schocken Books, 2003), 119.

15. Steve Lipman, "The Messiah Issue," *Jewish Week*, June 17, 1988, cited in Jerome R. Mintz, *Hasidic People: A Place in the New World* (Cambridge, MA: Harvard University Press, 1992), 355.

16. b. Sanhedrin 97b.

17. Gershom Scholem, *Major Trends in Jewish Mysticism* (Jerusalem: Schocken Publishing House, 1941), 88.

18. b. Sanhedrin 97b.

19. *Jewish Week*, August 30–September 5, 1991, cited in Shapiro, *Crown Heights*, 141–42.

20. "Schneerson: 'Have No Fear, Gulf Crisis Heralds the Messiah,'" *Jerusalem Post*, August 20, 1990, cited in Mintz, *Hasidic People*, 358.

21. *Yalkut Shimoni* 2:remez 499.

22. Isaiah 2:4.

23. Yosef Yitshak Schneerson, *Sefer HaSihot 5688–5691* (New York: Kehot Publication Society, 1995), 42.

24. Menachem Mendel Schneerson, *Torat Menachem Hitva'aduyot*

5751 (New York: Lahak Hanochos, 1993), 3:118–19. For an uncensored recording of the talk, see 27 Nissan 5751 - Sicha, Chabad.org, April 15, 1991, https://www.chabad.org/therebbe/article_cdo/aid /555021/jewish/27-Nissan-5751-Sicha.htm. Accessed May 8, 2023.

25. Menachem Mendal Schneerson, *Sefer HaSihot 5751* (New York: Kehot Publication Society, 1992–93), 1:330

26. Ibid., 2:490, 496.

27. Ibid., 690.

28. Menachem Mendel Schneerson, *Sefer HaSihot 5752* (New York: Kehot Publication Society, 1993), 1:26.

29. Schneerson, *Sefer HaSihot 5751*, 2:729.

30. Schneerson, *Sefer HaSihot 5752*, 2:376.

31. Joseph Telushkin, *Rebbe: The Life and Teachings of Menachem M. Schneerson, the Most Influential Rabbi in Modern History* (New York: Harper Wave, 2014), 428.

32. A video of this interaction can be seen at https://www.you tube.com/watch?v=GBBOCZWjp7Q&ab_channel=Moshiach Videos.

33. Yitzchok Frankfurter, "Where Heaven and Earth Touched," *Mishpacha*, September 30, 2009.

34. Adin Steinsaltz, *My Rebbe* (Jerusalem: Maggid Books, 2014), 201.

Epilogue

1. For more on Chabad theology after Schneerson's passing see David Berger, *The Rebbe, the Messiah, and the Scandal of Orthodox Indifference* (Oxford: Littman Library of Jewish Civilization, 2001).

2. "About Chabad-Lubavitch," Chabad.org, https://www .chabad.org/library/article_cdo/aid/36226/jewish/Overview.htm. Accessed May 31, 2024.

ACKNOWLEDGMENTS

I HAVE received the invaluable assistance of many people over the long years of this book's gestation. First and foremost, my heartfelt gratitude goes to Steven Zipperstein for entrusting me with this project and for his immense patience during the time it took to complete. I would like to extend special thanks to Zalman Shmotkin for facilitating portions of my research and for the many hours we spent in study and discussion. Thank you for hearing me out, even when we disagreed.

Thank you to Mordechai Lightstone, my first *Tanya havrusa*, and to Esther-Malke Leysorek Goodman, my friend and Yiddish teacher of many years. To understand Schneerson you must understand his language, and it is largely thanks to Esther that I could do so. My gratitude to Nick Russell for always letting me bend his ear about Hasidism and for that 6:00 a.m. photo shoot in Crown Heights. And to Eileen Reynolds, whose library books I probably still have checked out. I would like to thank Chana Pollack and Chaya Naparstck for their assistance in obtaining photos and the talented editorial and production staff at Yale University Press for bringing this book to completion.

My appreciation goes to the many people who generously shared their time, wisdom, assistance, and expertise: Avrohom Altein, Zelig Brez, Shulem Deen, Shalom Gottlieb, Louise Hager, Shmully Hecht, Sholem Hecht, Toby Hecht, Shmuel Kaminetsky, Yehuda Krinsky, Shaul Magid, Elizabeth Moorhouse-Stein, Baila Olidort, Dovid Olidort, Bentzion Rader (z"l), Hinda Rader, James Adam Redfield, Bryan Rigg, Charlie Roth (z"l), Eli Rubin, Yanki Tauber, Yehuda Teichtal, Boruch Jean Thaler, Faivish Vogel, Elliot Wolfson, and Julia Yatsenko.

Lastly, my undying love and gratitude to my parents, Harry and Nancy Glinter, without whom nothing I do would be possible.

INDEX

Italic page numbers indicate illustrations.

Man Ray: The Artist and His Shadows, by Arthur Lubow
Sidney Reilly: Master Spy, by Benny Morris
Admiral Hyman Rickover: Engineer of Power, by Marc Wortman
Jerome Robbins: A Life in Dance, by Wendy Lesser
Julius Rosenwald: Repairing the World, by Hasia R. Diner
Mark Rothko: Toward the Light in the Chapel,
      by Annie Cohen-Solal
Ruth: A Migrant's Tale, by Ilana Pardes
Menachem Mendel Schneerson: Becoming the Messiah,
      by Ezra Glinter
Gershom Scholem: Master of the Kabbalah, by David Biale
Bugsy Siegel: The Dark Side of the American Dream,
      by Michael Shnayerson
Solomon: The Lure of Wisdom, by Steven Weitzman
Steven Spielberg: A Life in Films, by Molly Haskell
Spinoza: Freedom's Messiah, by Ian Buruma
Alfred Stieglitz: Taking Pictures, Making Painters, by Phyllis Rose
Barbra Streisand: Redefining Beauty, Femininity, and Power,
      by Neal Gabler
Henrietta Szold: Hadassah and the Zionist Dream,
      by Francine Klagsbrun
Leon Trotsky: A Revolutionary's Life, by Joshua Rubenstein
Warner Bros: The Making of an American Movie Studio,
      by David Thomson
Elie Wiesel: Confronting the Silence, by Joseph Berger

FORTHCOMING TITLES INCLUDE:

Abraham, by Anthony Julius
Hannah Arendt, by Masha Gessen
The Ba'al Shem Tov, by Ariel Mayse
Walter Benjamin, by Peter Gordon